Adventures of Huckleberry Finn
by Mark Twain
(S.L. Clemens)

Collection CNED-Didier Concours
Capes / Agrégation d'Anglais

Paul Auster as the Wizard of Odds: Moon Palace
    Marc Chénetier

William Blake: Songs of Innocence and Experience, The Marriage of Heaven and Hell, The Book of Urizen
    François Piquet

Charles Dickens: David Copperfield
    Michael Hollington

John Stuart Mill: On Liberty
    Maurice Chrétien, Philippe Jaudel, Françoise Barret-Ducrocq et Daniel Becquemont

Harold Pinter: The Caretaker
    Ann Lecercle

Ann Radcliffe: The Mysteries of Udolpho
    Maurice Lévy

William Shakespeare: Hamlet
    Pierre Iselin

Mark Twain: Huckleberry Finn
    Joseph Urbas

La Politique indienne des États-Unis
    Philippe Jacquin

La Société anglaise 1939-45
    Monica Charlot

Manuel de linguistique
    Pierre Cotte

Manuel d'anglais oral pour les Concours + CD audio
    Marc Fryd et Jean-Louis Duchet

© Didier Érudition - CNED, 1996
ISBN 2-86460-300-4

Joseph URBAS

Adventures of Huckleberry Finn
by Mark Twain
(S.L. Clemens)

Didier Érudition
CNED, 1996

Table of Contents

Introduction

"Oh, shucks, Huck Finn, if I was as ignorant as you, I'd keep still—that's what *I'd* do." (190)

Since Tom Sawyer pronounced these words, censors of all descriptions and creeds—from the Concord Public Library Committee in 1885 (BSC 285) to the Mark Twain Intermediate School in Fairfax, Virginia, nearly a century later (Cox 1985, 388, Nadeau 141)—have followed suit and tried to silence Huck Finn. The controversy centers no longer on morality but race. But as Twain's biographer Justin Kaplan puts it, "The constituencies denouncing a profoundly antiracist novel for its alleged racism have only changed places with the old, the two having in common a literal-mindedness unable to deal with satire and constitutive irony" (HF-CE x).[1]

Fortunately, Huck Finn cannot be silenced. For one thing, he flatly refuses to keep still, as the novel itself and the various sequels attest. For another, he has too many friends. *Huckleberry Finn* is "unique in being held in the highest esteem by critics and at the same time prodigiously popular in the United States and throughout the world" (Blair 1960, Preface vii). For once, as the author himself might have said, public opinion is right; and for once, critics agree. Writers too, among them T.S. Eliot, Ernest Hemingway, H.L. Mencken, Gertrude Stein, F. Scott Fitzgerald, Sherwood Anderson, William Faulkner, Willa Cather, Langston Hughes, Ralph Ellison, J.D. Salinger, and Saul Bellow. In Hemingway's famous pronouncement: "All modern American literature comes from one book by Mark Twain called *Huckleberry Finn*" (Hemingway 22). By all accounts, *Huck Finn* is a cornerstone of the American cultural tradition. "When one takes up the

---

1. – Kaplan may be alluding to the townspeople's reaction to the "quips and fancies" in Puddn'head Wilson's Calendar: "But irony was not for those people: their mental vision was not focussed for it. They read those playful trifles in the solidest earnest..." (PW 25).

question of the legacy of Mark Twain and more particularly that of *Huckleberry Finn*, one takes up a question of American literary and cultural history" (Quirk 106). *Huck Finn* is not only a central work in the national canon; it is also the linchpin of Twain's *œuvre*. As one critic observes, "*Huckleberry Finn* stands not only chronologically but critically at the center of Mark Twain's career"; "any study of Mark Twain is irrevocably anchored to it. Without it, Mark Twain would be in the position of Nathaniel Hawthorne without *The Scarlet Letter*, Herman Melville without *Moby Dick*, or Henry Thoreau without *Walden*" (Cox 1966, 156).

Classics are subversive. And *Huck Finn* is no exception. It is indeed, in James M. Cox's phrase, "a hard book to take" (1985). Would't it be so much better if it were different? If it were less equivocal, less offensive, not quite so "rough, coarse and inelegant" (BSC 285)? If, say, a real plot were added, the ending changed, Jim made less of a "minstrel darky," or the word "nigger" removed? It cannot be done. All attempts to "improve" the book (Smith 1995, 121; Gerber 11) have been abysmal failures. Twain was always skeptical about reforms and conversions. *Huck Finn* cannot be reformed. It is as impossible to domesticate as the Mississippi River itself. Hard though it may be, it has to be taken as it stands, warts and all.

Manuscript, Composition

If *Huck Finn* is one of those books that can still create a stir, over a century after its publication, it is not only because the reading public is sensitive to the issue of racism:

> In early 1991 the news broke. The announcement of the discovery of the long-lost first half of the manuscript commanded great public attention. *The New York Times* front page featured a photograph of the first leaf, showing Twain's wonderfully clear handwriting and some of his self-editing, with an article about the manuscript. *Huckleberry Finn* continues to be news and new! (HF-CE xiv)

Although all the evidence is not yet in, it is clear that this exciting discovery has already modified some of the standard views of the composition of the novel. Before going into the details, let us quote Justin Kaplan's description of the writing of *Huckleberry Finn* to get an overall feel of the process:

> What had begun in a rush of creative energy in 1876 ("I am tearing along on a new book") turned into an eight-year cycle of plot and motivation problems for Mark Twain, doubts about whether he should "pigeon-hole or burn the MS," dead stops and "booming" resumptions, and finally a decision to tie off the story by bringing back Tom Sawyer and, thereby, some critics say, reducing Jim to a mere prop: all in all a grinding cycle that is a book-length story in itself... (HF-CE ix).

The prevailing scholarly consensus in favor of a three-stage compositional process—roughly: **1876**: chapters 1-16; **1879-1880 to 1883**: chapters 19-21; **1883-1884**: the remaining chapters[2]— would appear to hold, with a few modifications. To indicate some of the findings:

> 1) The first phase ended, not with chapter 16 and the partial destruction of the raft, but in chapter 18, with the conversation between Huck and Buck Grangerford about feuds (Quirk 4-5, HF-CE xi).[3]

> 2) The duke's Shakespeare soliloquy was in all probability not a late (1883) addition. It was apparently "planned as an integral part of the incident as it had originally been written, probably in 1879 or 1880" (Quirk 5).

---

2. – "During this initial stage of composition... between mid-June and 11 September 1876, Mark Twain wrote most of chapters 1-16 (with the exception of the text from paragraph 12 of chapter 12 to the end of chapter 14), after which he evidently halted. When he returned to his manuscript, Mark Twain wrote the final three paragraphs of chapter 16, and portions of chapters 17 and 18, temporarily halting again. Evidence suggests he completed a draft of chapters 17 and 18 in 1879-80, and sketched out some of the material that would appear in chapters 19-21, halting yet again. He may have returned to his work briefly in 1881 or 1882. Certainly by the spring of 1883, he had completed chapter 21. During his final burst of composition in the late spring and summer of 1883, he revised what he had already written, reordering some of the material in chapters 19-21; he wrote chapters 22-43; and he inserted the episode from paragraph 12 of chapter 12 to the end of chapter 14" (HF-WMT xxiv-xxv; cf. also xxvi-xlv and Blair 1960, 198-203).

3. – Consequently, note 6 on page 78 of the Norton Critical Edition should be disregarded.

3) Contrary to previous claims, the first half of the manuscript did have chapter divisions: "Though he evidently plotted his narrative according to episodes or adventures, Twain's chapter divisions in the manuscript do not correspond to those in the printed book" (Quirk 5; cf. also Doyno xvi).

4) Certain revisions show Twain striving for accuracy of tone. The memorable first sentence of the novel, for example, began as "You will not know about me...," was changed to "You do not know...," before Twain finally hit upon the precise combination: "You don't know about me..." (HF-CE x, 365).

5) Other revisions tend either: *a)* to preserve Huck's pre-sexual innocence, for instance by cutting the description of Huck's first kiss—"she [Sophia Grangerford] grabbed me and kissed me right on the mouth" (HF-CE 378-379, 411; brackets added) was finally altered to "she grabbed me and give me a squeeze" (91)—and by hedging on some of the details concerning the floating brothel in chapter 9 (HF-CE 376-377); or *b)* to place less emphasis on the theme of death, with the exclusion of the "cadaver episode" (originally placed in chapter 9, during the storm) in which Jim recounts his hair-raising adventures among the dead in a medical school dissecting room (HF-CE 62-65, 372-376, 405).

As Doyno concludes: "The manuscript sheets of *Adventures of Huckleberry Finn*—with their larger and smaller variations from the first-edition text—suggest, especially in the first half, that Twain started the project as an even darker, more satirical, and more provocative work that the first published edition turned out to be" (HF-CE xvii). In any case, the book that Twain imagined as a sequel to *Tom Sawyer* and that he had been "fooling over"[4] for seven years was to turn out to be his masterpiece.

---

4. – Twain's phrase in a letter dated July 21, 1883 (quoted in Blair 1960, 199-200; HF-WMT xxx).

Chapter 1

Space

Space has a stubborn way of sticking to Americans, penetrating all the way in, accompanying them. It is the exterior fact. The basic exterior act is a BRIDGE. Take them in order as they came: caravel, prarie schooner, national road, railway, plane. Now in the Pacific THE CARRIER. Trajectory. We must go over space, or we wither.

Charles Olson[5]

The River

The face of the water, in time, became a wonderful book—a book that was a dead language to the uneducated passenger, but which told its mind to me without reserve, delivering its most cherished secrets as clearly as if it uttered them with a voice. And it was not a book to be read once and thrown aside, for it had a new story to tell every day. Throughout the long twelve hundred miles there was never a page that was void of interest, never one that you could leave unread without loss, never one that you would want to skip, thinking you could find higher enjoyment in some other thing. There never was so wonderful a book written by man; never one whose interest was so absorbing, so unflagging, so sparklingly renewed with every re-perusal. (LM 94)

The book referred to here is, of course, the Mississippi River, the Father of Waters (NJ2 501), the mile-wide "monster" (RI 184) dwarfing all its European rivals (LM 39), and the ultimate source of the greatness of *Huckleberry Finn*, as Twain's fellow Missourian T.S. Eliot rightly saw (BSC 334). It is the all-informing presence flowing through the work, its familiar deity, as it will later be the "strong brown god" of

---

5. – *Call Me Ishmael* (San Francisco: City Lights Books, 1947) 114.

Eliot's *Four Quartets*. It is a source of food, freedom, regeneration, but also death.

But if there is an undeniably mythic, trans-historical dimension to the river in *Huckleberry Finn*, it is also very much the Mississippi of a distinct age. Much as "Old Times on the Mississippi,"[6] *Huck Finn* describes a period before railway competition and structural improvements like lighting permanently altered the face of the river, stripping the profession of steamboating of all its "romance" (LM 204-205). Those were the "flush times" of life on the river: "Mississippi steamboating was born about 1812; at the end of thirty years, it had grown to mighty proportions; and in less than thirty more, it was dead! A strangely short life for so majestic a creature" (LM 173). Samuel Clemens was a river pilot from 1857 to1861, when the Civil War shut down commercial traffic for the duration.

Life on the Mississippi is the best of all possible introductions to *Huckleberry Finn* (if not to Twain's work as a whole).[7] It affords us the fullest view of the untameable, "lawless stream" (LM 205) that defines the world of the novel; it provides the best insight into the peculiar character of those waters.

The river is full of "freaks" (LM 211). It is the "crookedest river in the world" (LM 39). Small wonder, then, that Huck, like his creator, should have such a difficult time telling a "straight story" when caught (LM 62; RP 240). The river is "fickle," its features in a state of perpetual change. Landmarks *change their places* once a month" (LM 115). The Mississippi "changes its channel so constantly that the pilots used to always find it necessary to run down to Cairo to take a fresh look, when their boats were to lie in port a week" (LM 79). It is a river whose "alluvial banks cave and change

---

6. – That is to say, chapters 4-17 of *Life on the Mississippi*, which are followed by Twain's travelogue account of his return to the river in 1882, which falls within the period of the compostion of *Huck Finn*.

7. – James M. Cox calls it "in many ways his most characteristic performance, containing as it does the whole range of his world, his style, and his literary structure" (LM 9).

constantly, whose snags are always hunting up new quarters, whose sand-bars are never at rest, whose channels are forever dodging and shirking" (LM 97). Reefs move, viciously pursuing boats that seek desperately to avoid them (LM 93). Even the river's overall length is variable: "In the space of one hundred and seventy-six years the Lower Mississippi has shortened itself two hundred and forty-two miles" (LM 146). In this period the mouth of the Missouri River was moving closer to St. Louis ("the wear and tear of the banks" had moved it down eight miles since the author's youth, LM 370). As for the "rises," which occur twice a year (one in December, one in June,), they give birth to a "new world" altogether (LM 104-105).

Even within a twenty-four-hour period the river changes, its shape altering virtually overnight (LM 85). Nor does it remain constant across the varieties of nightlight. A pitch-dark river, which makes all shore lines *seem* straight, does not have the same shape as a starlit one (LM 86); on gray nights, it has "no shape at all" (LM 86, 88). Its contours shift according to the different shades of moonlight (LM 86). At times, floating objects that one might expect to be invisible at night are in fact the easiest ones to spot; black logs stand out clearly whereas white ones are impossible to see (LM 101). The river's appearance also depends on whether one is going upstream or downstream: "Nothing ever had the same shape when I was coming down-stream that it had borne when I went up" (LM 89).

Its waters are a language to be "mastered" (LM 95) by the aspiring steamboat pilot. It exhibits the esthetic excellence—all the elusiveness, all the originality, all the ambiguities, and all the conventions—of a literary masterpiece. The metaphor should be taken seriously, down to the details: it is a text with italicized passages, capital letters, and exclamation points (LM 94). It is not only readable but, as Twain boasts in the very first sentence of *Life on the Mississippi*, "well worth reading about." A marvel, truly, "in all ways remarkable" (LM 39). Like his creator, Huck, though yet a "cub," has already learned to become a fine reader:

> ... by-and-by you could see a streak on the water which you know

> by the look of the streak that there's a snag there in a swift
> current which breaks on it and makes that streak look that way...
> (96)

The river is a work of art that teaches the astute observer—
and a "cub" pilot like Clemens had to become one—some
elementary principles of perception. The role of distance, for
one thing: "the surface of the water, like an oil-painting, is
more expressive and intelligible when inspected from a little
distance than very close at hand" (LM 109).[8] For another, the
difference between reflection and reality:

> By and by, when the fog began to clear off, I noticed that
> the reflection of a tree in the smooth water of an overflowed
> bank, six hundred yards away, was stronger and blacker than the
> ghostly tree itself. The faint spectral trees, dimly glimpsed through
> the shredding fog, were very pretty things to see. (LM 355)

In a word, piloting is a school of perception. One learns how
to develop it, and especially how to know its limits and its
treachery. "Have I got to learn the shape of the river according
to all these five hundred thousand different ways?" young Sam
Clemens asks his chief. Horace Bixby thunders back:

> "*No!* you only learn *the* shape of the river; and you learn
> it with such absolute certainty that you can always steer by the
> shape that's *in your head*, and never mind the one that's before

---

8. – The truth of this lesson in perspective was to be confirmed by Twain's experience
out West: "And I will remark here, in passing, that all scenery in California requires
distance to give it its highest charm" (RI 385; cf. also 387, 390). And in the Old World:
" Imagination labors best in distant fields" (IA 420; cf. also 250 on Naples: "But do
not go within the walls and look at it in detail. That takes away some of the romance
of the thing"; or 359 on Damascus, which needs "distance to soften it"). Distance
cannot poeticize all places and things, however, no matter how exalted our
preconceptions. Palestine is perhaps the supreme example: "distance works no
enchantment here" (485). Memory—temporal distance—acts as a romanticizing filter
as well, as Twain concludes in *The Innocents Abroad*: "We shall remember St. Peter's:
not as one sees it when he walks the streets of Rome and fancies all her domes are
just alike, but as he sees it leagues away, when every meaner edifice has faded out of
sight and that one dome looms superbly up in the flush of sunset, fully of dignity and
grace, strongly outlined as a mountain" (522). This is true of recollections of youth, as
Twain knew full well (IA 467).

your eyes." (LM 86)

No choice but to hit the books, to try to grasp that most elusive of all entities:

> I went to work now to learn the shape of the river; and of all the eluding and ungraspable objects that ever I tried to get mind or hands on, that was the chief. (LM 88)

As a token of its importance for Twain, the problematic of perception continues for Huck in one of the unfinished sequels to *Huckleberry Finn, Huck Finn and Tom Sawyer among the Indians.* There he learns how to read the Great Plains:

> Away off, miles and miles, was one tree standing by itself, and away off the other way was another, and here and yonder another and another scattered around; and the air was so clear you would think they was close by, but it warn't so, most of them was miles away. (HFTSAI 42).

Each landscape confirms the original lessons in its own particular way.

The shape-shifting Mississippi yields an abundance of characters: "When I find a well-drawn character in fiction or biography, I generally take a warm personal interest in him, for the reason that I have known him before—met him on the river" (LM 152).[9] Appropriately, it has its own floating theaters. As in chapter 21 of *Huckleberry Finn*, in the "flush times" before the Civil War, pilots like Sam Clemens would

---

9. – One of the tenets of Twain's realism is that genius draws its imaginative power from the outside: "If Shakspeare [sic] had been born and bred on a barren and unvisited rock in the ocean his mighty intellect would have had no *outside material* to work with, and could have invented none; and *no outside influences*, teachings, mouldings, persuasions, inspirations, of a valuable sort, and could have invented none... and so, Shakspeare would have produced nothing" ("What Is Man?" 1906, TSSE2 736; brackets added); "If you attempt to ‹ build › create & build a wholly imaginary incident, adventure or situation, you will go astray, & the artificiality of the thing will be detectable. But if you found on a *fact* in your personal experience, it is an acorn, a root, & every created adornment that grows up out of it & spreads its foliage & blossoms to the sun will seem realities, not inventions. You will not be likely to go astray; your compass of fact is there to keep you on the right course" (1887, NJ3 343).

occasionally see "a random scow, bearing a humble Hamlet and Co. on an itinerant dramatic trip" (LM 203). The river god creates men in its own image. This fact needs to be kept in mind when we consider the protean characters that haunt these waters, actors and confidence-men like the duke and the king—and Huck.

And what is true of the characters may well be true of the overall form of the novel, with its episodic structure, its peculiar (and peculiarly dissatisifying) ending. Perhaps Eliot was right after all:

> The River cannot tolerate any design, to a story which is its story, that might interfere with its dominance. Things must merely happen, here and there, to the people who live along its shores or who commit themselves to its current. And it is impossible for Huck as for the River to have a beginning or end—a *career*. (BSC 335).

Restricted Area

It is hardly an accident that Mark Twain chose to assert the spatiality of *Adventures of Huckleberry Finn* even before allowing Huck his first words to the reader:

> NOTICE
> Persons attempting to find a motive in this narrative will be prosecuted; persons attempting to find a moral in it will be banished; persons attempting to find a plot in it will be shot.
> BY ORDER OF THE AUTHOR
> Per G.G., CHIEF OF ORDNANCE. (2)

The wording is akin to that of a "NO TRESPASSING" sign. The text itself is thus marked off from the outset, at its very entrance point, as an area under close authorial surveillance, wherein certain traditional activities (plot—and moral—hunting, for example, or attributing special intentions to the author) are declared strictly off-limits. [10] The "Explanatory"

_____

10. – For Fishkin the Notice is Twain's "surface denial that the book is anything more than an amusing, innocuous adventure story of a raft trip on the Mississippi"; it is his way of preserving "the option of denying all subversive intentions in *Huckleberry Finn*.... Indeed, many readers took him at his word, and read *Huckleberry Finn* as a 'boy's book,' a companion volume to its predecessor, *Tom Sawyer*" (1993, 68, 63).

note, with its mention of various local dialects ("Missouri negro dialect," "backwoods South-Western," "ordinary 'Pike-County,'" *ibid.*), plots the coordinates of the linguistic zone the reader is on the verge of entering. The Notice and the Note are necessary precisely because we are about to cross over onto unfamilar, potentially hazardous[11] literary ground—wild country at the outer edge of civilized territory and recognizable language ("the *extremest* form of the backwoods Southwestern dialect"; emphasis added), where only the author's "trustworthy guidance and support of personal familiarity"[12] will keep us from losing our bearings altogether.

Here, as elsewhere in *Huckleberry Finn*, the reader must not be misled by Twain's irony and humor. To read the work properly the spatial metaphor should be taken with the utmost seriousness.

Trouble and Ease, Bad Places and Good

Trouble in *Huckleberry Finn* is pre-eminently a question of spatial relations, of being "up a stump" (137, 175), "in a fix" (176), "cornered" (58), in a "tight" or "close place" (148).

---

11. – "After the Civil War the title 'Chief of Ordnance' would include the individuals who were in charge of a wide range of ammunitions, including underground mines, which were a widely feared additional weapon used by both sides during the war. Contemporary commentators were furious about the devastating effects of unexpected underground explosions" (*HF-CE* 382). In this connection we might also observe, with James M. Cox in his introduction to *Life on the Mississippi*, that "mark twain" (a call made by the "leadsmen" of a steamboat—i.e., the men whose job it is to sound the river in shallow water—when they mark a depth of two fathoms) "signals dangerous passage" (LM 19). The Notice could also be read as an oblique reference to the potentially explosive truths to be found in the narrative by anyone foolhardy enough to go looking for them (Huck will later compare telling the truth to "setting down on a kag of powder and touching it off just to see where you'll go to," 148). For Quirk, the Notice and Explanatory note contradict one another, the second insisting on "a certain cultural diversity," the first demanding that "we yield also to the unequivocal." In a word, "We are to listen to its voices and resist (on pain of prosecution, banishment, or execution) even so slight a temptation to interpret this series of adventures as purposive or instructive or even useful. *Huckleberry Finn* thy tongue is diversity, thy authority is the long arm of the law, G.G., Chief of Ordnance" (147).
12. – See Appendix.

Huck's vision of safety, on the other hand, implies putting as much distance as possible between himself and the source of danger, as for example when the raft is rammed by a steamboat in chapter 16: "I dived—and I aimed to find the bottom, too, for a thirty-foot wheel had got to go over me, and I wanted it to have plenty of room" (78-79). Huck makes the point nicely when he describes the plans he and Jim have made: "We would sell the raft and get on a steamboat and go way up the Ohio amongst the free States, and then be out of trouble" (67). The slave-hunters who are led to believe that Huck is carrying smallpox tell him to "put twenty miles between us, that's a good boy" (76), revealing by the same token that humor is often a question of exaggerated proportion or distances. One can never be *too* safe. After the Grangerford-Shepherdson massacre, Huck confesses: "I never felt easy till the raft was two mile below there and out in the middle of the Mississippi" (95).

Safety is thus a geographical concept; being out of trouble means being in a safe *place*: "out of the woods" (138), for example. Or simply being *elsewhere*, say, to avoid Aunt Sally's rage at the Phelps farm: "I wished I was in Jeruslem or somewheres" (199). This quotation illustrates what we might call the spatial dialectic of adventure which governs the characteristic movement of *Huckleberry Finn* as a whole. Adventure in Tom Sawyer's sense of the word is synonymous with the danger and exoticism of faraway places (the "Castle Deef, in the harbor of Marseilles," 192), which, once encountered or reproduced in homegrown American form, arouse in Huck a longing to be elsewhere. Describing his close call with the robbers on the *Walter Scott*, Huck says, "But before they got in, I was up in the upper berth, cornered, and sorry I come." (58). Likewise, at the door of Mrs. Judith Loftus's shanty, he experiences a similar feeling: "I was getting afraid I had come; people might know my voice and find me out" (48). To give a final example: cooped up at the Widow Douglas's, where he is being "sivilized" by Miss Watson, Huck is in another sort of tight spot ("all cramped up," 7), one that makes him long for faraway places:

> Then she told me all about the bad place, and I said I wished I was there. She got mad, then, but I didn't mean no harm. All I

wanted was to go somewheres; all I wanted was a change, I warn't particular. She said it was wicked to say what I said; said she wouldn't say it for the whole world; *she* was going to live so as to go to the good place. Well, I couldn't see no advantage in going where she was going, so I made up my mind I wouldn't try for it. (8)

The paradox of this novel is that *home*, on the other hand, is not so much a place as a person (the same could be said for the river, as many critics have observed); its representative is Jim:

> When I waked up, just at day-break, he was setting there with his head down betwixt his knees, moaning and mourning to himself. I didn't take notice, nor let on. I knowed what it was about. He was thinking about his wife and his children, away up yonder, and he was low and homesick; because he hadn't ever been away from home before in his life; and I do believe he cared just as much for his people as white folks do for their'n. It don't seem natural, but I reckon it's so. (125)

And home stands for the very antithesis of adventure: "I told Jim all about what happened inside the wreck, and at the ferry-boat; and I said these kinds of things was adventures; but he said he didn't want no more adventures" (64). It is significant that at the beginning of the novel, in a scene that takes place on the night of the inaugural escapade that sees the founding of Tom Sawyer's Gang (chapter 2), and that foreshadows the basic configuration of relations in the novel, Twain insists on placing Huck *between* Jim and Tom, between domesticity ("the kitchen door") and adventure ("robbery and murder" as "highwaymen," 13):

> We scrouched down and laid still. Miss Watson's big nigger, named Jim, was setting in the kitchen door; we could see him pretty clear, because there was a light behind him. He got up and stretched his neck out about a minute, listening. Then he says,
> 'Who dah?"
> He listened some more; then he come tip-toeing down and stood right between us; we could a touched him, nearly. (10)

> So he set down on the the ground betwixt me and Tom. He leaned his back up against a tree, and stretched his legs out till one of them most touched one of mine. (*ibid.*)

We would argue that, as the foregoing passage shows, the moral opposition between Tom and Jim is perhaps more accurately seen in spatial terms. This is one of the profoundly subversive features of *Huckleberry Finn*, for it places the novel quite literally *beyond* good and evil. Right and wrong are not a moral but spatial categories. They are not forces to be defended or combated, principles to be embraced or rejected for doctrinal reasons, but rather simply places to seek or avoid, places that are "comfortable" or "tight," "easy" or "smothery." The supreme irony of all this is that, in one respect, Miss Watson is absolutely right when she lectures Huck about the "good" and the "bad *place*" (8; italics added). At the same time, the prevailing spatial logic of *Huckleberry Finn* makes the expression redundant. Huck's moral code might be termed spatial hedonism.

To understand the full implications of this code we need to analyze the famous passage in chapter 31 that represents Huck's fully considered response to Miss Watson's lecture. It is here of course that Huck decides to go to hell ("the bad place") rather than betray Jim, who is being held captive at the Phelps farm. The physical setting is important here and yet is often ignored in critical commentary:

> I went to the raft, and set down in the wigwam to think. But I couldn't come to nothing. I thought till I wore my head sore, but I couldn't see no way out of the trouble. (168)

Huck writes the letter to Miss Watson that would deliver Jim back into slavery and sets to thinking again: "But somehow I couldn't seem to strike no places to harden me against him, but only the other kind" (169). Here too the justifying moral principle Huck is searching for is imagined in spatial terms ("places"); and the word "hardening" recalls his earlier failed attempt to betray Jim in chapter 16 ("I tried, for a second or two, to brace up and out with it, but I warn't man enough— hadn't the spunk of a rabbit," p. 75; cf. also 182). Lost in his reminiscences of their companionship on the downriver trip, Huck is jolted back to the present by the sight of the letter:

> ... and then I happened to look around, and see that paper.
>> It was a close place. I took it up, and held it in my hand. I was a trembling, because I'd got to decide, forever, betwixt two

things, and I knowed it. I studied a minute, sort of holding my
breath, and then says to myself:
  "All right, then, I'll *go* to hell"—and tore it up. (169)

The term "close place" needs to be seen both literally (Huck
is *inside* the wigwam, in a "hot" climate, 172) and figuratively
(as a moral double-bind). But getting out of this tight space
means deliberately choosing the stark alternative of
damnation—unlike in chapter 1, where, as we have seen, Huck
chooses hell simply "to go somewheres" ("all I wanted was a
change, I warn't particular," p. 8). In this moral geography
where all landmarks appear to be convertible, the values have
been reversed once again, however. Huck makes a *positive*
choice; the very act of choosing redeems the chosen
alternative. The implacable logic of Huck's hedonism, which
the whole novel confirms, automatically converts this bad place
into a good one (or at least one that is preferable to where he
is). Huck relishes the prospect of "wickedness" in what sounds
like a backwoods parody of Satan's "Evil be thou my good"
speech in Book IV of *Paradise Lost*:

> It was awful thoughts, and awful words, but they was said.
> And I let them stay said; and never thought no more about
> reforming. I shoved the whole thing out of my head; and said I
> would take up wickedness again, which was in my line, being
> brung up to it, and the other warn't. And for a starter, I would go
> to work and steal Jim out of slavery again; and if I could think up
> anything worse, I would do that, too; because as long as I was in,
> and in for good, I might as well go the whole hog. (170)

There is of course no doubt in the reader's mind that the right
choice has been made here. Huck is indeed in *for good*.
  Consistent with the spatialization of morality in Huck's
world, lying and truth-telling are no longer acts to be
universally condemned or praised, embraced or shunned in an
everlasting and universally applicable opposition:

> "Honey, I thought you said it was Sarah when you first
> come in?"
> "Oh, yes'm, I did. Sarah Mary Williams. Sarah's my first
> name. Some calls me Sarah, some calls me Mary."
> "Oh, that's the way out of it?"

"Yes'm." (51)

They are, as Judith Loftus nicely puts it here, simply "ways out," escape routes, emergency exits. Whether these are crooked or straight is beside the point, though in practice—the world being what it is—lying is the usually the swiftest and the surest path. Nevertheless, when it is time to choose, Huck does come in for occasional surprises:

> I see I had spoke too sudden, and said too much, and was in a close place. I asked her to let me think a minute; and she set there, very impatient and excited, and handsome, but looking kind of happy and eased-up, like a person that's had a tooth pulled out. So I went to studying it out. I says to myself, I reckon a body that ups and tells the truth when he is in a tight place, is taking considerable many resks, though I ain't had no experience, and can't say for certain; but it looks so to me, anyway, and yet here's a case where I'm blest if it don't look to me like the truth is better, and actuly *safer*, than a lie. I must lay it by in my mind, and think it over some time or other, it's so kind of strange and unregular. I never see nothing like it. Well, I says to myself at last, I'm agoing to chance it; I'll up and tell the truth this time, though it does seem most like setting down on a kag of powder and touching it off just to see where you'll go to. (148)

Note that the potentially explosive consequences of truth-telling are imagined in specifically spatial terms. When you tell the truth, there is no telling where you might end up ("where you'll go to"). The second "unregular" situation, the second "place" where truth seems to assure egress is at the Phelps farm:

> Well, I see I was up a stump—and up it good. Providence had stood by me this fur, all right, but I was hard and tight aground, now. I see it warn't a bit of use to try to go ahead—I'd *got* to throw up my hand. So I says to myself, here's another place where I got to resk the truth (175-176).

Here, obligation ("*got* to") is not a function of pre-established, abstract rules. There are no axioms in Huck's world. Neither is it a matter of following authority. Pragmatism dictates the choice. (With Tom it is the contrary, as we shall see; Huck is right to say, "as for me I think different," 17). But circumstances change: in this last instance Huck is "saved" from truth by the arrival of Uncle Silas.

Conscience: "A do' dat open innerds"

When Huck's conscience bothers him, the consequences in spatial terms are felt immediately, as in chapter 16: "It got to troubling me so I couldn't rest; I couldn't stay still in one place" (73). But the conscience itself is also spatialized in Huck's imagination. This is most obvious in chapter 33, where he feels guilty about the duke and the king, who have just been tarred and feathered and ridden out of Pikesville on a rail:

> So we poked along back home, and I warn't feeling so brash as I was before, but kind of ornery, and humble, and to blame, somehow—though *I* hadn't done nothing. But that's always the way; it don't make no difference whether you do right or wrong, a person's conscience ain't got no sense, and just goes for him *anyway*. If I had a yaller dog that didn't know no more than a person's conscience does, I would pison him. It takes up more room than all the rest of a person's insides, and yet ain't no good, nohow. Tom Sawyer he says the same. (182-183)

To distinguish between danger and guilt in *Huckleberry Finn*—in other words, between being physically and morally "uncomfortable"—is to distinguish between being in trouble and being full of it, as in chapter 31:

> So I was full of trouble, full as I could be; and didn't know what to do. At last I had an idea; and I says, I'll go and writer the letter—and *then* see if I can pray. Why, it was astonishing, the way I felt as light as feather, right straight off, and my troubles all gone. (169)

Huck assuages his guilty conscience through a process of externalization, in this case through writing. When he decides to go to hell in the famous passage we have already quoted above, this exteriorizing movement is simply reconfirmed: "I shoved the whole thing out of my head" (170).[13]

---

13. – Originality or creation would appear be another form of externalization for Huck. The drunken trick-rider at the circus "had got up that joke all out of his own head" (120). Similarly, the boys who take the "real beautful" intiation oath to enter Tom Sawyer's Gang want to know if Tom "got it out of his own head" (12; cf. also

But of course, the spatial metaphor, with its attendant notion of reversibility, may be misleading, for the rest of the same passage in fact emphasizes the idea of irreversibility: "It was awful thoughts, and awful words, but they was said. And I let them stay said" (*ibid.*). As a *narrator* Huck is aware that forgetting some things is no easy matter (94, 146), and Jim is arguably instrumental in showing him both the limits of externalization and the unruliness of individual conscience. The key event here is Jim's story about his daughter Elizabeth in chapter 23. In this scene, which was meticulously revised (Doyno 122, Fishkin 1993, 100-101), Twain places great emphasis on the opposition between outside and inside. What triggers off the action is a noise on the bank, which in turn creates an echo in Jim's conscience:

> "What makes me feel so bad dis time, 'uz bekase I hear sumpn over yonder on de bank like a whack, er a slam, while ago, en it mine me er de time I treat my little 'Lizabeth so ornery" (125).

Jim then tells the story of an unintentional act of cruelty to his daughter that still gives rise to guilt feelings:

> "My, but I *wuz* mad, I was agwyne for de chile, but jis' den—it was a do' dat open innerds—jis' den, 'long come de wind en slam it to, behine de chile, ker-*blam!*—en my lan', de chile never move'! My breff mos' hop outer me; en I feel so—so—I doan' know *how* I feel. I crope out, all a-tremblin', en crope aroun' en open de do' easy and slow, en poke my head in behine de chile, sof' en still, en all uv a sudden, I says *pow!* jis' as loud as I could yell. *She never budge!* Oh, Huck, I bust out a-cryin' en grab her up in my arms, en say, 'Oh, de po' little thing! de Lord God Amighty fogive po' ole Jim, kaze he never gwyne to fogive hisself as long's he live!' Oh, she was plumb deef en dumb, Huck, plumb deef en dumb—en I'd ben a'treat'n her so!" (126)

108, 188). The phrase also echoes to be "out of his head"(126). In Tom's case invention certainly does lead to raving, as the wound he receives during the escape gives way to fever and madness. Note that Emmeline Grangerford also writes elegies "out of her own head" (85).

The door may be taken as a metaphor for the conscience. Moreover, Jim's dialect adds a wonderful ambiguity: "innerds" (or "innards") may be read not only as an adverb but as a noun, not only as "inwards" but also as "insides" (viscera, internal bodily organs), a meaning which Huck echoes later in chapter 33 ("It takes up more room than all the rest of a person's insides"). Elizabeth, who is deaf and dumb, is a symbol of the impossibility of either reception or expression, of communication between inner and outer worlds. And quite appropriately she is the one who shows the limits of reversibility, of turning the inside out, of "shoving it out of your head," as Huck would say. Conscience is a door that opens inwards *and stays open*. It is the disobedient other within—the "yaller dog," the obstinate child (*"She never budge!"*), the words that refuse to come, the repeated failure of expression (admirably rendered here by the image of breath, the hesitation, and the double temporality of "feel"): "My breff mos' hop outer me; en I feel so—so—I doan' know how I feel." It is no accident that the glib characters in *Huckleberry Finn* are also utterly devoid of conscience: Tom and the king especially. Jim and Huck, on the other hand, realize the inner burden of conscience and the limits of expression ("I don't know the words to put it in," 32). Paradoxically, the passages where language seems to break down for both of them are in fact among the most powerfully expressive in the novel.

In sum, then, Jim's heart-rending story is all about the limits of expression but also the limits of what one can require of others in the way of obedience. Conscience, which "takes up more room than all the rest of a person's insides," is the name for those limits. To have no conscience means to be able to close the mind off against all incursions of guilt (or to be able to evacuate it completely). It is also the ability to require unconditional obedience, of a dog, a child—or a slave. Tom can do both, which is doubtless why his name comes to mind when Huck condemns the conscience as "no good, nohow" ("Tom Sawyer he says the same"). The passage in chapter 33, which anticipates Huck's submission to Tom's will, also shows Huck as uncharacteristically cruel: "If I had a yaller dog that didn't know no more than a person's conscience does, I would pison him" (183). But Huck is most admirable at those key moments when his conscience overwhelms him, when he is at a loss for words or leaves them to others: "I didn't answer up prompt. I tried to, but the words wouldn't come" (75); "But the words wouldn't come" (168); "Say it, Jim" (216; Doyno 167-168) Recall too that chapter 23 ends, as it should, on *Jim's* words. Huck remains mute.

Close Calls

"We... had many a hair-breadth escape and blood-curdling adventure which will never be recorded in any history," Twain writes in *Roughing It*, parodying the stock formulae of adventure fiction (RI 157). The "close shave" is a staple of the genre, a dramatic rendering of an intimate encounter with Fate. The hair-raising quality of Huck's adventure aboard the *Walter Scott*, for instance, is in large part a question of *proximity* to danger: the robbers are in fact leaning against the berth where Huck is hiding: "Then they stood there, with their hands on the ledge of the berth, and talked. I couldn't see them, but I could tell where they was, by the whisky they'd been having" (58-59). Here too the episode with Jim in chapter 2 prefigures the spatial logic of adventure in the rest of the novel ("we could a touched him, nearly"; "we all there so close together," 10). On the night of his escape from the log-cabin, Huck sees pap at close range: "he went by so close I could a reached out the gun and touched him" (32). The spectacle of the steamboat sounding the river for Huck's body in chapter 8 is a lighter version of the same sort of experience:

> By-and-by she come along, and she drifted in so close that they could a run out a plank and walked ashore. Most everybody was on the boat. Pap, and Judge Thatcher, and Bessie Thatcher, and Jo Harper, and Tom Sawyer, and his old Aunt Polly, and Sid and Mary, and plenty more. Everybody was talking about the murder... (35; "Bessie" is Twain's mistake; the name should be "Becky"; cf. TS and HF-WMT 385n).

Later in the same chapter, the sight of someone else on Jackson's Island gives Huck a good scare:

> By-and-by, was close enough to have a look, and there laid a man on the ground. It most give me the fan-tods. He had a blanket around his head, and his head was nearly in the fire. I set there behind a clump of bushes, in about six foot of him... (37)

The excitement of adventure ("the fan-tods") is thus a function of nearness.[14] Which explains why Huck as a narrator usually takes pains to indicate his relative distance from places, objects or people: "[the king] come a fumbling under the curtain two or three foot from where I was. I stuck tight to the wall, and kept mighty still, though quivery" (142; Bridgman 122).[15] This accounts, furthermore, for the trepidation Huck feels in the fog or when the night is thick ("You can't tell the shape of the river, and you can't see no distance," 78). The raft accident in chapter 16 falls under this heading of course:

> We could hear her pounding along, but we didn't see her good till she was close. She aimed right for us. Often they do that and try to see how close they can come without touching; sometime the wheel bites off a sweep, and then the pilot sticks his head out and laughs, and thinks he's mighty smart. Well, here she comes, and we said she was going to try to shave us; but she didn't seem to be sheering off a bit. (78).

One might argue that the spatial dynamics of adventure is a metaphor for the act of reading itself. Like the reader, Huck is a silent, unperceived perceiver, close yet invisible.

Closeness creates not only a sense of wonder or adventure but also a heightened awareness of the body. Huck

---

14. – The experience of wonder depends to a large degree on a similar feeling of unexpected closeness (but without the element of danger), as when Huck marvels at his sensory acuteness on the river at night: "And how far a body can hear on the water such nights! I heard people talking at the ferry landing. I heard what they said, too, every word of it"; on the same page Huck hears a raftsman "just as plain as if the man was by my side" (33).

15. – Even Huck's approximations serve paradoxically to underscore the precision of his descriptions: "about two yards" (58), "about four or five foot along the middle of the bottom log" (193).

consciously bates his breath when he finds himself in tight spots on the *Walter Scott* (59) and in the wigwam in chapter 31 (169). But once again, the first encounter with Jim in chapter 2 is paradigmatic. In untoward circumstances, the body itself becomes an uncomfortable place—or rather a multitude of such places:

> There was a place on my ankle that got to itching; but I dasn't scratch it; and then my ear begun to itch; and next my back, right between my shoulders. Seemed like I'd die if I couldn't scratch. Well, I've noticed that thing plenty of times since. If you are with the quality, or at a funeral, or trying to go to sleep when you ain't sleepy—if you are anywheres where it won't do for you to scratch, why you will itch all over in upwards of a thousand places. (10)

> He [Jim] leaned his back up against a tree, and stretched his legs out till one of them most touched one of mine. My nose began to itch. It itched till the tears come to my eyes. But I dasn't scratch. Then it begun to itch on the inside. Next I got to itching underneath. It didn't know how I was going to set still. This miserableness went on as much as six or seven minutes; but it seemed a sight longer than that. I was itching in eleven different places now. I reckoned I couldn't stand it more'n a minute longer, but I set my teeth hard and got ready to try. Just then Jim begun to breathe heavy; next he begun to snore—and then I was pretty soon comfortable again. (*ibid.*; brackets added)

We see the same acute restlessness, the same nagging consciousness of his own physical being when Huck has to keep still in the fog: "I got to set still and float, and yet it's mighty fidgety business to have to hold your hands still at such a time" (68); or in Aunt Sally's hot sitting room, crowded with armed men who are "fidgety and uneasy" ("I warn't easy myself," 213).

Much like the speaker of Whitman's "Song of the Open Road," Huck needs "room." He needs to "inhale great draughts of space."

"I been there before"

> I began to get tired of staying in one place so long. (RI 376)
> No land with an unvarying climate can be very beautiful. The tropics are not, for all the sentiment that is wasted on them. They

> seem beautiful at first, but sameness impairs the charm by and by. *Change* is the handmaiden Nature requires to work her miracles with. (RI 386)

> I wanted another change. The vagabond instinct was strong upon me. (RI 421)

There appears to be no stability of place in *Huckleberry Finn*. Geography as Huck perceives it is not fixed but rather dynamic, very much like the river itself. By night Jackson's Island resembles a ferry: "big and dark and solid, like a steamboat without any lights" (33). Houses move:

> Another night, when we was up at the head of the island, just before daylight, here comes a frame house down, on the west side. (44)

And so do towns: Bricksville, for instance:

> On the river front some of the houses was sticking out over the bank, and they was bowed and bent, and about ready to tumble in. The people had moved out of them. The bank was caved away under one corner of some others, and that corner was hanging over. People lived in them yet, but it was dangersome, because sometimes a strip of land as wide as a house caves in at a time. Sometimes a belt of land a quarter of a mile deep will start in and cave along and cave along till it all caves into the river in one summer. Such a town as that has to be always moving back, and back, and back, because the river's always gnawing at it. (114)[16]

Good places may turn into bad ones or *vice versa*. The book itself is paradigmatic in this respect: a troublesome space that Huck is "rotten glad" (229) to have written his way out of, but which turns into the best of good places for the reader. Jackson's Island provides another illustration. It seems to be the perfect home for Huck and Jim in chapter 9:

> "Jim, this is nice," I says. "I wouldn't want to be nowhere else but here." (43-44).

---

16. – In this, Bricksville takes after its model, Napoleon, Arkansas, which had been washed away from its original site when Twain revisited it in 1882 ("used to be where the river now is," NJ2 539).

In the following chapter, however, Huck's attitude towards "our place" (54) changes markedly: "Next morning I said it was getting slow and dull, and I wanted to get stirring up, some way. I said I reckoned I would slip over the river and find out what was going on" (47). And by the end of chapter 11, it represents a threat to their freedom, a trap (53-54). Similarly, the log-cabin where pap keeps Huck locked up undergoes an impressive series of reversals of value, from prison to school-holiday hideaway to prison again:

> He kept me with him all the time, and I never got a chance to run off. We lived in that old cabin, and he always locked the door and put the key under his head, nights.... The widow she found out where I was, by-and-by, and she sent a man over to try to get hold of me, but pap drove him off with the gun, and it warn't long after that till I was used to being where I was, and liked it, all but the cowhide part.
>
> It was kind of lazy and jolly, laying off comfortable all day, smoking and fishing, and no books nor study. Two months or more run along, and my clothes got to be all rags and dirt, and I didn't see how I'd ever got to like it so well at the widow's, where you had to wash, and eat on a plate, and comb up, and go to bed and get up regular, and be forever bothering over a book and have old Miss Watson pecking at you all the time. I didn't want to go back no more. I had stopped cussing, because the widow didn't like it; but now I took to it again because pap hadn't no objections. It was pretty good times up in the woods there, take it all around.
>
> But by-and-by pap got too hand with his hick'ry, and I couldn't stand it. I was all over welts. He got to going away so much, too, and locking me in. Once he locked me in and was gone three days. It was dreadful lonesome. I judged he had got drowned and I wasn't ever going to get out any more. I was scared. I made up my mind I would fix up some way to leave there. (24).

Here again, we must bear in mind the highly subversive nature of Huck's vision of space: it is not a question of right or wrong[17] but whether or not one can "stand it." As the

_____

17. – The spatial dynamics of *Huckleberry Finn* redefine the epistemological as well as the moral sense of right and wrong. The exegetical argument Huck and Jim have over the meaning of the parable of King Solomon reveals this: "But hang it, Jim, you've

"Explanatory" note had warned us, and as this quotation makes clear, language is spatially determined; so Huck's has changed accordingly ("I had stopped cussing, because the widow didn't like it; but now I took to it again because pap hadn't no objections")—and *twice over,* we might add: first on the plot level, as the setting shifts from town to backwoods; and then again on the narrative level, where other rules apply and where consequently all trace of the "cussing" Huck has resumed simply disappears from the page. Narrative space requires another type of language, one that makes concessions to genteel fastidiousness, that avoids words "too strong for print" (RI 26): "this boy's language," as the author notes, "has been toned down and softened, here and there, in deference to the taste of a more modern and fastidious day" (BSC 286).

Radical instability of place, combined with Huck's native restlessness, poses the constant threat of sameness. Geographical uniqueness collapses into undifferentiation. To return to Jackson's Island for a moment: to the boys in *Tom Sawyer* the "unexplored and uninhabited island, far from the haunts of men," stands for adventure, the opposite of routine and "civilization." But gradually the novelty wears off: "They found plenty of things to be delighted with but nothing to be astonished at" (TS 87-90, 95); boredom sets in. In this novel, too, Huck decides at the outset that "Jackson's Island's the place" (32). But difference soon gives way to sameness:

> When it was dark I set by my camp fire smoking, and feeling pretty satisfied; but by-and-by it got sort of lonesome, and so I went and set on the bank and listened to the currents washing along, and counted the stars and drift-logs and rafts that come down, and then went to bed; there ain't no better way to put in time when you are lonesome; you can't stay so, you soon get over it.
>
> And so for three days and nights. No difference—just the same thing. But the next day I went exploring around down through the island. (36)

---

you've clean missed the point—blame it, you've missed it a thousand mile" (66). Significantly, this argument comes right before the chapter in which another point will be missed—a properly geographical one this time: Cairo.

The discovery of another person on the island provides relief and companionship, but as we have already seen it is not long before the place gets "slow and dull" again. The threat of sameness is also revealed in the symmetry of the opening and closing pages of the book, which frame its shifting yet undifferentiated geography:

> The Widow Douglas, she took me for her son, and allowed she would sivilize me; but it was rough living in the house all the time, considering how dismal regular and decent the widow was in all her ways; and so when I couldn't stand it no longer, I lit out. (7)

> But I reckon I got to light out for the Territory ahead of the rest, because Aunt Sally she's going to adopt me and sivilize me and I can't stand it. I been there before. (229)

The last sentence of the novel should be taken quite literally, rather than in the more abstract sense of, say, "I've been through this experience before." The word "there" refers to a *place*.[18] When read in this way, the dominant spatial opposition of North and South, which had appeared as the controlling axis of movement embodied in the river itself, is simply cancelled out.[19] In the last two chapters, St. Petersburg—Huck, Tom, Jim, Aunt Polly—has moved South. All the way to the Phelps farm. (Recall that St. Petersburg had already come to Jackson's Island: "Most everybody was on the boat," 35.) Geographical points thus appear to be interchangeable; Huck has indeed "been there before." Repetition seems inevitable. Huck might as well go West as anywhere. In a sense he is not any more "particular" than he was at the Widow Douglas's ("All I wanted was to go somewheres; all I wanted was a change," p. 8). Or to quote Eliot, "Huck Finn must come from nowhere

---

18. – For Hoffman, it means "the stasis of being a part of society" (342).
19. – One could argue that the little hut where Jim is kept prisoner is emblematic of this undifferentiation: on the "north side" is a "square window-hole, up tolerable high, with just one stout board nailed across it." Huck thinks this is "the ticket," but Tom rejects this escape route because it is "as simple as tit-tat-toe, three-in-a-row, and as easy as playing hooky." The door to the shed is "at the south-end" and "padlocked," but the boys get past it easily (185). Furthermore, it is through this door that Jim ultimately escapes (214-215). Finally, we should recall that the shanty where Huck is imprisoned is *upriver* (24).

and be bound for nowhere"; "He has no beginning and no end" (BSC 335).

If we seem guilty of "stretching" the point here, to borrow Huck's term, consider the radical sameness of the "one-horse" towns (106, 112) along the river, echoed most obviously in their very names: Pokeville, Bricksville, Pikesville,[20] not to mention the loafers that inhabit them (113, 166). Language of course registers slight variations—indeed as if "all these characters were trying to talk alike and not succeeding"; but if the form may alter, the content remains strictly the same:

> "Gimme a chaw'v tobacker, Hank" (113);

> "Say, gimme a chaw tobacker, won't ye?" (167).

Difference points to identity, just as in Emmeline Grangerford's paintings and poetry ("She warn't particular, she could write about anything you choose to give her to write about, just so it was sadful, "86). Climate and vegetation vary as well:

> We dasn't stop again at any town, for days and days; kept right along down the river. We was down south in the warm weather, now, and a mightly long ways from home. We begun to come to the trees with Spanish moss on them, hanging down from the limbs like long gray beards. It was the first I ever see it growing, and it made the woods look solemn and dismal. (165)

Here too, however, the overwhelming impression is one of sameness. Let us compare the following descriptions of Pokeville:

> There was a little one-horse town about three mile down the bend...

---

20. – It is no accident that in fictionalizing the place names, Twain deliberately wipes out the variety of the originals: Walnut Bend, Napoleon, Grand Lake Landing. Similarly, his description in *Life on the Mississippi* of the model home of the "wealthiest and most conspicuous citizen" (chapter 38, "The House Beautiful")—the prototype the Grangerfords' interior—concludes by laying stress on geographical undifferentiation: "That was the residence of the principal citizen, all the way from the suburbs of New Orleans to the edge of St. Louis" (LM 278).

> When we got there, there warn't nobody stirring; streets empty, and perfectly dead and still, like Sunday (106);

and the Phelps farm, near Pikesville:

> When I got there it was all still and Sunday-like, and hot and sunshiny—the hands was gone to the fields; and there was them kind of faint droning of bugs and flies in the air that makes it seem so lonesome and like everybody's dead and gone...

> Phelps's was one of these little one-horse cotton plantations; and they all look alike. (172-173)

The overall tendency, then, is towards undifferentiation of place, or what the geographer David Harvey has called, in a discussion of the peculiar geographical dynamics of modernity, "the collapse of spatial distinctiveness and identity."[21] We would argue that Colonel Sherburn's diatribe against the mob in chapter 22, which is often criticized as an esthetic lapse on Twain's part insofar as the character seems there to be directly voicing the author's views, needs to be seen in this light; for whole burden of the diatribe is to explode the foundation of Southern pride in the myth of regional distinctiveness. Sherburn is in a priviledged position to attack this[22], having a thorough knowledge of the country *as a whole*:

> "Do I know you? I know you clear through. I was born and raised in the South, and I've lived in the North; so I know the average all around. The average man's a coward. In the North he lets anybody walk over him that wants to, and goes home and prays for a humble spirit to bear it. In the South one man, all by himself, has stopped a stage full of men, in the day-time, and robbed the lot. Your newspapers call you a brave people so much that you think you *are* braver than any other people—whereas you are just *as* brave, and no braver." (118)

The South has at best only a minor claim to distinction here, i.e. in the *style* of lynching ("Southern fashion," 119; cf. also

---

21. – *The Condition of Postmodernity: An Enquiry into the Origins of Cultural Change* (London: Blackwell, 1989) 209.
22. – This advantage is rendered spatially as well: Sherburn's harangue is delivered from "the roof of his little front porch" (118).

LM 334). A dubious distinction indeed, but no more so than
the other marks of social or cultural distinction in *Huckleberry
Finn* (or in *Pudd'nhead Wilson*). The best illustration of this is
Huck's own comical attempt at social classification:

> Col. Grangerford was a gentleman, you see. He was a
> gentleman all over; and so was his family. He was well-born, as
> the saying is, and that's worth as much in a man as it is in a horse,
> so the Widow Douglas said, and nobody ever denied that she was
> of the first aristocracy in our town; and pap he always said it, too,
> though he warn't no more quality than a mudcat, himself. (86-87)

The validity of Huck's reasoning is rendered suspect for reader
by the very fact that his own ideas and words are borrowed;
the truth of these distinctions is thus revealed to be a series of
embedded socio-linguistic constructs: sayings on sayings that
form the basis of a social consensus that unites the mudcat and
the aristocrat, pap and the Widow Douglas, horses and men!

It seems that social and geographical distinctions are
ultimately as counterfeit as the titles of the duke and the king.
Cultural standing is borrowed as well (the steamers that ply
the Mississippi are called the *Walter Scott* and the *Lally Rook*).
The Southern pride of the Grangerfords is manifest in their
copy of Henry Clay's speeches, but they also pride themselves
on their tablecloth, which comes "all the way from
Philadelphia"! The supreme irony of this highly confused,
derivative culture is that America's true claim to socio-political
originality has been lost. As Huck says in chapter 23,
"Sometimes I wish we could hear of a country that's out of
kings." He goes on to add, of course:

> What was the use to tell Jim these warn't real kings and
> dukes? It wouldn't a done no good; and besides, it was just as I
> said; you couldn't tell them from the real kind. (125)

But Twain's point is that cultural imitations and spurious
claims to aristocracy do just as much damage, if not more, than
real ones do. Fictions can be dangerous.

In his effort to underscore the tendency to sameness in a
broad critique of social and cultural imposture, and to point to
the universal traits of what he called the "damned human

race," Twain runs the risk that the reader might overlook a number of the subtle shadings of language he took great pains to apply in the novel, such as those indicated above. That is to say, the spatial dynamics of the novel as a whole, which tends towards virtual undifferentiation, creates the need for an additional space outside the narrative itself (the Notice and Explanatory note) which can be used to emphasize a number of subtleties that might be overlooked and to reassert the artist's control over the text. Twain is thus caught up in the same dialectic of sameness and difference as Huck. The liminary texts are there to underscore the aspect of adventure (i.e., danger, in the Notice; and difference, in the Explanatory note) that the narrative both exploits and denies. The prospect of difference ("several forms of speech") must be continually reaffirmed against the threat of undifferentiation ("without it many readers would supose that all these characters were trying to talk alike and not succeeding," 2), whether real or apparent; Huck has to set off for adventure "ahead of the rest" because he has "been there before" (229).

In *Huckleberry Finn* it seems that adventure can only take place within an overall scheme of repetition and return (given the constancy of human nature and the fundamental convertibility of space), which finally robs the experience of its singularity. If one of the novel's explicit aims is to travesty this genre of fiction, then this is Twain's most brilliant and devastating stroke. He was fully cognizant of the highly corrosive effects of repetition (IA 54, RI 130-136, CY 208). Sameness—say, the "dismal" regularity of life at the widow's (7)—stirs up a longing for adventure, which ends up in sameness, and so on *ad infinitum*. The originality of Huck's narrative vision is perhaps the only original thing that is salvaged from this process.

Paradoxically, it is in repetition that we find the unexpected. Pap embodies both, as do the king and the duke.[23]

---

23. – The repetition of the Royal Nonesuch scam is certainly a source of adventure. The king and the duke are also highly unpredictible; they are specialists in unexpected moves (123, 145, 162-163).

Pap is totally unpredictible: "When I lit my candle and went up to my room that night, there set pap, his own self!" (20); "Thinks I, maybe it's pap, though I warn't expecting him.... Well, it *was* pap, sure enough..." (32). Pap is another name for danger that appears "all of a sudden" (28), out of nowhere. At the same time, he is a creature of habit:

> Every time he got money he got drunk; and every time he got drunk he raised Cain around town; and every time he raised Cain he got jailed. He was just suited—this kind of thing was right in his line. (24)

> Then the old man got to cussing, and cussed everything and everybody he could think of, and then cussed them all over again to make sure he hadn't skipped any, and after that he polished off with a kind of a general cuss all round, including a considerable parcel of people which he didn't know the names of, and so called them what's-his-name, when he got to them and went right along with his cussing. (25)

> Whenever his liquor begun to work, he most always went for the govment. (26).

> After supper pap took the jug, and said he had enough whisky there for two drunks and one delirium tremens. That was always his word. (27).

Pap's first departure is probably the most telling example of repetition:

> When he had got out on the shed, he put this head in again, and cussed me for putting on frills and trying to be better than him; and when I reckoned he was gone, he come back and put his head in again, and told me to mind about that school, because he was going to lay for me and lick me if I didn't drop that. (22).

The comic effect is heightened here by the fact that Pap has already scolded Huck for the same reasons at least three times in the preceding page and a half of chapter 5. We should note, however, that one of the distinctive traits of pap's second return here is its *unexpected* quality ("and when I reckoned he was gone"). The knack for reappearing unexpectedly is what Huck inherits from his father (38, 70, 95, 177). Adventure in *Huckleberry Finn* is not so much an outbound trip as a surprise return, an unannounced repeat performance. [24]

Writing, Semiotic Space

> ... but there orter be writing 'bout a big thing like this.
>
> Huck in *Tom Sawyer* 71

For Huck, the way out of tight spots is through a process of dialectical conversion whereby what is closed, tight, or confined is negated through a process of exteriorization. This is epitomized in the act of writing itself. Just as Huck, as a character, often gets into and out of trouble on the plot level by means of writing or story-telling, so he gets out of the "trouble" of making a book by writing his way on through to "THE END" (229).

Writing is emblematic of the larger problem of "sivilization," which stands for everything that confines— clothes, houses, rituals, codes, daily routines, in a word anything that is "dismal regular" (7)—but also, paradoxically, what provides the means of escape. Writing in *Huckleberry Finn* is a fine example of what Vladimir Jankélévitch called the *organe-obstacle*, in that it is both enabling and disabling, both means and obstacle.

This double status of the written word is obvious from the very outset. The inaugural instance of writing as a way out of trouble occurs—significantly—after Huck has learned to "spell, and read, and write just a little" (18). A bootprint in the snow suddenly confirms Huck's worst fears: pap is still alive and has been prowling around the Widow Douglas's house.

---

24. – This corresponds to what Blair calls "motifs with variations" (1960, 347). Doyno agrees that this—and not a plot worked out in advance—is the structuring principle of the novel: "Twain discovered his pliable plot as he went along, writing without a definite final resolution or plan in mind. His real interests were elsewhere—in writing memorable episodes and frequently in doubling the incidents or repeating the basic situation in varied forms. It is, accordingly, a supreme misreading of the novel to read for plot as plot. It is appropriate to the spirit and craftsmanship of the book to read for episodes, for doublings, for Twainings, finding relationships, repetitions, contrasts, and progressions between episodes. It is not that all significant events are repeated, but that the repetition of an event often signals its significance" (102).

Huck's intention is to put himself beyond pap's reach by divesting himself of all his money. Like "sivilization," this fortune is a burden created by a previous work "by Mr. Mark Twain"—*The Adventures of Tom Sawyer*:

> Now the way that the book winds up, is this: Tom and me found the money that the robbers hid in the cave, and it made us rich. We got six thousand dollars apiece—all gold. It was an awful sight of money when it was piled up. Well, Judge Thatcher, he took it and put it out at interest, and it fetched us a dollar a day apiece, all the year round—more than a body could tell what to do with. The Widow Douglas, she took me for her son, and allowed she would sivilize me...(7)

Huckleberry Finn as a whole is, in a sense, Huck's attempt to write himself out of the constraints imposed upon him by the prior existence of the companion volume ("You don't know about me, without you have read a book by the name of 'The Adventures of Tom Sawyer,'" *ibid.*) and thereby accede to a condition of autonomy.[25] Concerning this particular difficulty of the money, Huck turns to Judge Thatcher, who finds a written solution:

> "Oho-o. I think I see. You want to *sell* all your property to me—not give it. That's the correct idea."
> Then he wrote something on a paper and read it over, and says:
> "There—you see it says 'for a consideration.' That means I have bought it of you and paid you for it. Here's a dollar for you. Now, you sign it."
> So I signed it, and left. (19)[26]

---

25. – The recently discovered first half of the manuscript of *Huckleberry Finn* would appear to confirm Twain's desire to give Huck his own voice and thereby to make his character's independence a major concern of the book (cf. on this point Fishkin 1993,116). The facsimile of the first sheet of chapter 1 shows the title, followed by the indication "Reported by Mark Twain" (*HF-CE* 365, 389), which was omitted in the published version of the novel.

26. – The verb "sign" speaks volumes. During his induction into Tom Sawyer's Gang, it is not only Huck's orphan status that creates a contrast between himself and the rest of the boys ("Here's Huck Finn, he hain't got no family—what you going to do 'bout him?"); it is also his illiteracy: "Then they all stuck a pin in their fingers to get blood to sign with, and I made my mark on the paper" (12).

The murder that Huck stages is the most spectacular illustration of his artful manipulation of signs: covering up his own traces ("I hadn't left a track," 31) and revealing others— a smashed-in door, a blood-smeared axe, a whetstone, two trails—that will tell their own tale when properly arranged in the area in and around the cabin (31-32).[27] Here we see yet another example of the radical convertibility of space, for the status of the cabin has changed once again: Huck has transformed it from a site of emprisonment into one of freedom by making it the setting of a convincing murder story (32). At the Grangerfords', when Huck forgets the name he has assumed, writing is the way to extricate himself from this difficulty:

> "Can you spell, Buck?"
> "Yes," he says.
> "I bet you can't spell my name," says I.
> "I bet you what you dare I can," says he.
> "All right," says I, "go ahead."
> "G-o-r-g-e J-a-x-o-n—there now," he says.
> "Well," says I, "you done it, but I didn't think you could.
> It ain't no slouch of a name to spell—right off without studying."
> I set it down, private, because somebody might want *me* to spell it, next, and so I wanted to be handy with it and rattle it off like I was used to it. (82)[28]

The same is true for the king and the duke:

> And so he [the king] went a-mooning on and on, liking to hear himself talk, and every little while he fetched in his funeral orgies again, till the duke he couldn't stand it no more; so he writes on a little scrap of paper, "*obsequies*, you old fool," and folds it up and goes to goo-gooing and reaching it over people's heads to him. (135; brackets mine)

---

27. – For Kearns, Jim is the "master semiotican" (213).
28. – For Quirk this passage strains our sense of plausibility: "One need not be a metafictionist to see the difficulty here. Huck, as narrator, has spelled George Jackson correctly from the beginning, along with any number of other, more difficult names.... Are we to suppose that in the few months since this exchange with Buck occurred that Huck has undergone some orthographically redemptive experience?" (100).

Writing provides alternatives to presence when presence spells trouble; it is a way for Huck to put distance between himself and danger.[29] Certain solutions are simply unimaginable without it: "I'll steal it [the money], and hide it; and by-and-by, when I'm away down the river, I'll write a letter and tell Mary Jane where it's hid" (140; brackets added). When Huck's plan goes awry, writing still appears to be the answer: "Says I, if it could stay where it is, all right; because when we get down the river a hundred mile or two, I could write back to Mary Jane, and she could dig him up again and get it" (143). The awkwardness of telling Mary Jane where the gold has been hidden is avoided in this way as well:

> "Where did you hide it?"
> I didn't want to set her to thinking about her troubles again; and I couldn't seem to get my mouth to tell her what would make her see that corpse laying in the coffin with that bag of money on his stomach. So for a minute I didn't say nothing—then I says:
> "I'd ruther not *tell* you where I put it, Miss Mary Jane, if you don't mind letting me off; but I'll write it for you on a piece of paper, and you can read it along the road to Mr. Lothrop's, if you want to. Do you reckon that'll do?"
> "Oh, yes."
> So I wrote: "I put it in the coffin. It was in there when you was crying there, away in the night. I was behind the door, and I was mighty sorry for you, Miss Mary Jane." (151-152)

Finally, writing serves as a possible means to expose the duke and the king without Huck's direct testimony: "I'll tell you how to find them. Gimme a pencil and a piece of paper. There— *'Royal Nonesuch, Bricksville.'* Put it away, and don't lose it"

---

29. – In chapter 29, a mere three letters ("P—B—W") stand between Huck and the lynch mob: "here was nothing in the world betwixt me and sudden death but just them tatoo-marks. If they didn't find them—" (161). We should note that this written proof of the true identity of Peter Wilks's heirs is demanded after the partial failure of Levi Bell's trick to produce handwritten evidence from the suspects, which only disproves the duke and the king's claim: "'Well, well, well! I thought we was right on the track of a slution, but it's gone to grass, partly. But anyway, *one* thing is proved—*these* two ain't either of 'em Wilkses'—and he wagged his head towards the king and the duke" (159). It seems that in *Huckleberry Finn* the status of writing is always equivocal, never totally authoritative.

(150). In each case writing represents a spatial solution to a problem posed by *time*: on the one hand, forgetfulness; on the other, awkward or hazardous simultaneity. The same is true of the risks involved in running by day with Jim. The duke keeps his promise to "cipher out" the problem in chapter 21, and printing turns out to be the trick:

> Then he showed us another little job he'd printed and hadn't charged for, because it was for us. It had a picture of a runaway nigger, with a bundle on a stick, over his shoulder, and "$200 reward" under it. The reading was all about Jim, and just described him to a dot. It said he run away from St. Jacques' plantation, forty mile below New Orleans, last winter, and likely went north, and whoever would catch him and send him back, he could have the reward and expenses.
>
> "Now," says the duke, "after to-night we can run in the daytime if we want to. Whenever we see anybody coming, we can tie Jim hand and foot with a rope, and lay him in the wigwam and show this handbill and say we captured him up the river, and were too poor to travel on a steamboat, so we got this little raft on credit from our friends and are going down to get the reward. Handcuffs and chains would look still better on Jim, but it wouldn't go well with the story of us being so poor. Too much like jewelry. Ropes are the correct thing—we must preserve the unities, as we say on the boards."
>
> We all said the duke was pretty smart, and there couldn't be no trouble about running daytimes. We judged we could make miles enough that night to get out of the reach of the pow-wow we reckoned the duke's work in the printing office was going to make in that little town—then we could boom right along, if we wanted to. (109)

Note that the handbill[30] creates a virtuous circle of solutions: this written document solves a problem whose solution (i.e., being able to travel night and day) allows them to solve a problem (the "pow-wow" in that "little town") created by printing the document in the first place. But semiotic space, too, is subject to unforeseen reversals in value (145). The handbill has a distinct disadvantage, which is revealed by Jim

---

30. – Twain notes in *Life on the Mississippi* that "An advertisement of this kind warrants the person to take the property, if found" (LM 213). The duke obviously knows the law. Cf. also Doyno 230.

in chapter 24. Overcoming this involves once again the mediation of the written sign:

> Jim he spoke to the duke, and said he hoped it wouldn't take but a few hours, because it got might heavy and tiresome to him when he had to lay all day in the wigwam tied with the rope. You see, when we left him all alone we had to tie him, because if anybody happened on him all by himself and not tied, it wouldn't look much like he was a runaway nigger, you know. So the duke said it *was* kind of hard to have to lay roped all day, and he'd cipher out some way to get around it.
>
> He was uncommon bright, the duke was, and he soon struck it. He dressed Jim up in King Lear's outfit—it was a long curtain-calico gown, and a white horse-hair wig and whiskers; and then he took his theatre-paint and painted Jim's face and hands and ears and neck all over a dead dull solid blue, like a man that's been drowned nine days. Blamed if he warn't the horriblest looking outrage I ever see. Then the duke took and wrote out a sign on a shingle so—
>
> *Sick Arab—but harmless when not out of his head.*
>
> And he nailed that shingle to a lath, and stood the lath up four or five foot in front of the wigwam. Jim was satisfied. He said it was a sight better than laying tied a couple of years every day and trembling all over every time there was a sound. The duke told him to make himself free and easy, and if anybody ever come meddling around, he must hop out of the wigwam, and carry on a little, and fetch a howl or two like a wild beast, and he reckoned they would light out and leave him alone. (126)

So far so good. Events take another turn, however, when the original written solution—the handbill—is used by the king to sell Jim back into slavery (171), as Huck learns from a boy in Pikesville: "I see the handbill myself. It tells all about him, to a dot—paints him like a picture, and tells the plantation he's frum, below Newr*leans*" (167). Twain shows us here that semiotic space is as unstable and as endlessly transformable as any other form of space. The moral value of the runaway-slave handbill, which would seem to be wrong *in its very essence*, is converted from negative to positive to negative again (just as the log-cabin where pap keeps Huck sequestered). What is more, in this particular case, the *perceived* monetary value of the sign has nothing to do with its intrinsic worth, which is nil,

being a counterfeit document as worthless in reality as the
"three-day drafts" (146) exchanged in the sale of Peter Wilks's
slaves (150). At any rate, as we know, the whole process will
be reversed when Tom and Aunt Polly reveal the existence of
another written document: Miss Watson's will (226, 227).

Authorial Dominion: the Realm of Necessity and Closure

In the first section above we saw that the spatiality
Huckleberry Finn is asserted through an inaugural act of
authority: "BY ORDER OF THE AUTHOR" (2). What
appears to define the narrative as a space with clear lines of
demarcation is the strict enforcement of a code of rules—those
forbidding plot- and moral-hunting, for instance.

"Authority" might be defined as an attempt to impose
order on the chaos of space, to "take dominion everywhere" as
the jar does in the "slovenly wilderness" of Wallace Stevens's
poem. Twain is both eager to establish his authority and aware
of the ultimate futility of the attempt, as he was of attempts to
tame the lawless Mississippi:

> The military engineers of the [United States River] Commission
> have taken upon their shoulders the job of making the Mississippi
> over again,—a job transcended in size by only the original job of
> creating it. They are building wing-dams here and there, to deflect
> the current; and dikes to confine it in narrower bounds; and other
> dikes to make it stay there; and for unnumbererd miles along the
> Mississippi, they are felling the timber-front for fifty yards back,
> with the purpose of shaving the bank down to low-water mark
> with the slant house of a house-roof, and ballasting it with stones;
> and in many places they have protected the wasting shores with
> rows of piles. One who knows the Mississippi will promptly aver—
> not aloud, but to himself—that ten thousand River Commissions,
> with the mines of the world at their back, cannot tame that lawless
> stream, cannot curb it or confine it, cannot say to it, Go here, or
> Go there, and make it obey; cannot save a shore which it has
> sentenced; cannot bar its path with an obstruction which it will not
> tear down, dance over, and laugh at. (LM 205; brackets added)

They cannot "bully the Mississippi into right and reasonable
conduct" (*ibid.*); and readers will do as they please with a
book.

In *Huckleberry Finn* the civilized realm is one of confinement. For Huck "sivilization" means being hemmed in by books, authorities, rules, "regular" ways, clothes, and houses. Or, as he says in a marvelously redundant phrase, being "so cramped up and sivilized" (25). Miss Watson's religion is practiced in a closed space: "Then Miss Watson she took me in the closet and prayed" (14; Huck compares feeling good to "church letting out," 132). The scheming of those phony representatives of European civilization, the king and the duke, is carried out within the confines of the Wilks's cellar (133), the king's room (141), or the wigwam (166). In keeping with the end of the companion volume (TS 210-214), Tom is another representative of the civilized world. And as might be expected, the proper application of his rules, like the duke's "unities" (109), also requires confinement of one sort or another, whether physical or doctrinal.[31] Huck makes this clear at the beginning of chapter 1, where he indicates Tom's conditions for admission into the gang: "But Tom Sawyer, he hunted me up and said he was going to start a band of robbers, and I might join *if I would go back to the widow and be respectable*" (7; emphasis added). Appropriately, the swearing-in ceremony takes place in a cave[32]:

> We went along a narrow place and got into a kind of room, all damp and sweaty and cold, and there we stopped. Tom says:
> "Now we'll start this band of robbers and call it Tom Sawyer's Gang. Everybody that wants to join has got to take an oath, and write his name in blood." (12)

And the execution of Tom's grandiose plans for freeing Jim presuppose the cramped setting of the "little hut" (173) where

---

31. – This is true of informal amusement as well: in chapter 2, Tom wants "to tie Jim to the tree for fun" (10).

32. – The cavern where Huck and Jim seek shelter on Jackson's island suggests, paradoxically, not closure but rather openness and comfort. It is capacious ("The cavern was as big as two or three rooms bunched together, and Jim could stand up straight in it,"); they build their fire not inside but at the mouth of the cavern ("on one side of the door the floor stuck out a little bit and was flat and a good place to build a fire on. So we built it there and cooked dinner,"); and they spend their time eating and looking *outwards* at the spectacle of the storm (43-44).

Jim is kept prisoner. In the Phelps farm episode (up to chapter 40), there is indeed an oscillation between two sites of closure: the hut and the house.[33] When Tom and Huck begin digging after drawing up their plans in chapter 35, it inevitably involves being closed in: "As soon as we reckoned everybody was asleep, that night, we went down the lightning-rod, and shut ourselves up in the lean-to, and got out our pile of fox-fire, and went to work" (193).

On the other hand, it is precisely when Tom tries to extend his swashbuckling dominion to open spaces that his plans go awry: in chapter 3, the "ambuscade" of the Sunday-school picnic is foiled by the intervention of a teacher (who "charged in and made us drop everything and cut," 16); and in chapter 40 Tom is shot by the farmers when the escape plans actually lead the boys out of the hut and over and beyond the fence enclosing the farmyard:

> ... and at last he [Tom] nudged us, and we slid out, and stooped down, not breathing, and not making the least noise, and slipped stealthy towards the fence, in Injun file, and got to it, all right, and me and Jim over it; but Tom's britches catched fast on a splinter on the top rail, and then he hear the steps coming, so he had to pull loose, which snapped the splinter and made a noise; and as he dropped in our tracks and started, somebody sings out:
> "Who's that? Answer, or I'll shoot!"
> But we didn't answer; we just unfurled our heels and shoved. Then there was a rush, and a *bang, bang, bang!* and the bullets fairly whizzed around us! (215; brackets added)

Tom's booklearning eventually leads him to two other places of confinement, the wigwam (215) and his sick-room in chapter 42.

As a general rule, the locus of independent thinking in *Huckleberry Finn* is, by contrast, the wilderness. Huck goes to the woods to think things over (14, 15), to test ideas (17), and to escape his father's tyranny ("I used to take to the woods most of the time when he was around," 15), the stifling routine

---

33. – It is perhaps significant of her fundamental goodness that after the escape Aunt Sally tells Huck: "The door ain't going to be locked" (221).

at the Widow's (18) or Aunt Sally's rage (199). The wide river is where Huck and Jim talk freely.

The shifting nature of space in this novel should give us pause, however. The backwoods, as we have seen, can turn into a place of imprisonment; nor is the raft unencumbered by an enclosing structure, namely the wigwam. And with the appearance of the duke and the king the raft is converted from a realm of freedom and equality to one of servitude.[34] This chronic instability should make us skeptical of sharp spatial oppositions in *Huckleberry Finn*. For example, that between the land and the river, which is one of the *topoi* of *Huck Finn* criticism, is never absolute. (Twain never thought in terms of absolute oppositions, cf. Doyno 30) Certain positive terms—as is shown by the permutations of the word "beautiful" (about which more later) may be applied to both. And as we have seen, the very nature of the Mississippi tends to cancel out the opposition: the waters are full of silt, of earth in suspension; the banks are shifting, water-like. This blurring of categories can also be seen in Huck's depiction of the mob, which should be a clear-cut embodiment of the perversity and irrationality of land values. Nevertheless, the controlling metaphor for the lynch mob in front of Colonel Sherburn's house is aquatic: "the crowd begins to roll in like a wave," "the wave sucked back"; the crowd "washed back sudden" (118-119). The crowd at the graveyard in chapter 29 is also likened to water: "When they got there they swarmed into the graveyard and washed over it like an overflow" (161). As it turns out, the comparison is apt in both cases: the crowd is as angry and unpredictible as floodwater; it threatens the innocent (bystanders, 117; Huck, 161) as well as the guilty (Sherburn, the duke and the king).

The widow's world is also one of obligations:

---

34. – The convertibility of space needs to be considered also within the context of property relations. The raft is converted through an act of appropriation performed by the duke and the king. They lay claim first to the wigwam (103), then to the whole raft ("our raft") and finally to Jim along with it ("our nigger", 171). *Huckleberry Finn* reveals just how difficult it is for the individual (Jim, Huck) to defeat others' title claims (the king's, pap's) on the self—how difficult it is, in other words, to enter into a state of autonomy, of true "self-possession."

> Well, then, the old thing commenced again. The widow rung a bell
> for supper, and you had to come to time. When you got to the
> table you couldn't go right to eating, but you had to wait for the
> widow to tuck down her head and grumble a little over the
> victuals, though there warn't really anything the matter with them.
> (7)

Miss Watson's, one of "don'ts":

> Then for an hour it was deadly dull, and I was fidgety. Miss Watson
> would say, "Don't put your feet up there, Huckleberry;" and "don't
> scrunch up like that, Huckleberry—set up straight;" and pretty soon
> she would say, "Don't gap and stretch like that, Huckleberry—why
> don't you try to behave?" (8; missing apostrophes added to first and
> second contractions; cf. HF-WMT 3)

Similarly, Tom's fantasy world is a realm of rules and
necessities, of "got to" and "must":

> Everybody was willing. So Tom got out a sheet of paper
> that he had wrote the oath on, and read it. It swore every boy to
> stick to the band, and never tell any of the secrets; and if anybody
> done anything to any boy in the band, whichever boy was ordered
> to kill that person and his family must do it, and he mustn't sleep
> till he had killed them and hacked a cross in their breasts, which
> was the sign of the band. And nobody that didn't belong to the
> band could use that mark, and if he did he must be sued; and if
> he done it again he must be killed. And if anybody that belonged
> to the band told the secrets, he must have his throat cut, and then
> have his carcass burnt up and the ashes scattered all around, and
> his name blotted off of the list with blood and never mentioned
> again by the gang, but have a curse put on it and be forgot,
> forever. (12)

It transforms collective longing for adventure ("Everybody was
willing") into submission to an all-encompassing ("if anybody
done anything to any boy"), iron necessity. His power derives
from the written word, a mixture of his own and that of
"authorities":

> Everybody said it was a real beautiful oath, and asked Tom
> if he got it out of his own head. He said, some of it, but the rest
> was out of pirate books, and robber books, and every gang that
> was high-toned had it. (12; cf. also 13, 188, 190, 194)

"Style"[35] is synonymous with enclosure within the bounds laid down by the rules of fashion or literary convention. The Grangefords' interior (82), where order is "perfectly exact" (83), the duke's stage directions (110) and Tom Sawyer's books—all partake in the same sphere of cast-iron rules. Tom's explanation in chapter 3 of the power of genies, and of the magicians who control them, is revealing in this respect. What Tom envisions is unconditional, slave-like obedience[36]:

> "Why they rub an old tin lamp or an iron ring, and then the genies coming tearing in, with the thunder and lightning a-ripping around and the smoke a-rolling, and everything they're told to do they up and do it. They don't think nothing of pulling a shot tower up by the roots, and belting a Sunday-school superintendent over the head with it—or any other man."
>
> "Who makes them tear around so?"
>
> "Why, whoever rubs the lamp or the ring. They belong to whoever rubs the lamp or the ring, and they've got to do whatever he says. If he tells them to build a palace forty miles long, out of di'monds, and fill it full of chewing gum, or whatever you want, and fetch an emperor's daughter from China for you to marry, they've got to do it—and they've got to do it before sun-up next morning, too. And more—they've got to waltz that palace around over the country wherever you want it, you understand."
>
> "Well," says I, "I think they are a pack of flatheads for not keeping the palace to themselves 'stead of fooling them away like that. And what's more—if I was one of them I should see a man

---

35. – Genuine hospitality might be termed anti-style in *Huckleberry Finn*. It represents a form of humble, unconditional obligation, as is made clear when Tom introduces himself at the Phelps farm as a stranger named Archibald Nicholas. Aunt Sally says: "you must come in and eat your dinner with us"; "But we won't *let* you walk—it wouldn't be Southern hospitality to do it"; "You *must* stay"; "you mustn't disappoint us" (179-180).

36. – There are striking parallels between Tom and Pap Finn, who is the "boss" of his son (23, 24), whose authority also requires imprisonment (chapters 6 and 7), and who also goes raving mad (28; "he warn't in his right mind," 222). This last point suggests a form of wry equivalence between Pap's "forty-rod" (23) and the heady adventure fiction Tom prefers. We might note incidentally that these two characters also reveal the way in which extremes of stubbornness, whether out of ignorance or moral rectitude and a sense "style," lead to the same impractical refusal of "all the modern conveniences" (191): knives and forks for pap (who "done everything with his clasp-knife," 31) and picks and shovels for Tom ("They always dig out with a case knife," 192).

in Jericho before I would drop my business and come to him for
the rubbing of an old tin lamp."

"How you talk, Huck Finn. Why, you'd *have* to come when
he rubbed it, whether you wanted to or not."

"What, and I as high as a tree and as big as a church? All
right, then; I *would* come; but I lay I'd make that man climb the
highest tree there was in the country."

"Shucks, it ain't no use to talk to you, Huck Finn. You
don't seem to know anything, somehow—a perfect sap-head."
(17)[37]

The foregoing quotation should be contrasted to Jim's story
about his daughter Elizabeth, which, in addition to being a
parable of the awakening of conscience, as we have seen, is all
about the *limits* of obligation and obedience. The contrast is
most telling in the sign of obedience—or the lack thereof—in
both cases: *movement.* Tom's genies "come tearing in" when
beckoned; they build castles on command, "waltz" them
around, fetch wives from China. As for Elizabeth, *"She never
budge!"* (126). Nor would Huck be inclined to move if he were
a genie. What limits the validity of such principles as parental
authority, which in a sense are as much constructs as Tom's
fantasies, is quite simply *reality*—that of Elizabeth's deafness,
for example, which makes Jim's power over her conditional
rather than absolute. Similarly, Tom's claims, like the power of
prayer according to the Widow Douglas (14), fail Huck's
empirical test:

> I thought all this over for two or three days, and then I
> reckoned I would see if there was anything in it. I got an old tin
> lamp and an iron ring and went out in the woods and rubbed and
> rubbed till I sweat like an Injun, calculating to build a palace and
> sell it; but it warn't no use, none of the genies come. So then I
> judged that all that stuff was only just one of Tom Sawyer's lies.
> (17)

---

37. – This disagreement between Huck and Tom on fictional necessity is not
unprecedented. In *Tom Sawyer* their discussion on the duties of the hermit, who,
according to Tom, has "got to sleep on the hardest place he can find, and put
sackcloth and ashes on his head, and stand out in the rain," elicits the same sort of
response from Huck ("Dern'd if I would") and in turn the same sort of expostulation
from Tom ("Why, Huck, you'd *have* to. How'd you get around it? TS 90-91).

Jim's painful realization of the limits of his own power over Elizabeth goes hand in hand with a remarkable sense of intellectual independence. In chapter 14 Jim does not hesitate to shake two pillars of cultural and spiritual authority, one local, the other universal—the Widow Douglas ("the first aristocracy in our town," 87) and the Bible—in order to deny the wisdom of Solomon the Wise ("I doan k'yer what de widder say, he *warn't* no wise man, nuther," 65), and this despite Huck's objections: "Well, but he *was* the wisest man, anyway; because the widow she told me so, her own self" (*ibid*). On this question of authority, Huck finds himself once again between Tom and Jim, even if both finally submit to Tom's authority in the Phelps farm episode.

As regards rule-following, the opposition between Tom and Huck may once again be seen in spatial terms. Simply put, necessity is what cannot be circumvented. There is simply no *getting around* it. The necessity of Jim's having an inscription and a coat of arms is an instance of this:

> But we had to have it; Tom said we'd *got* to; there warn't no case of a state prisoner not scrabbling his inscription to leave behind, and his coat of arms.
> "Look at Lady Jane Grey," he says; "look at Gilford Dudley; look at old Northumberland! Why, Huck, spose it *is* considerable trouble?—what you going to do?—how you going to get around it? Jim's *got* to do his inscription and coat of arms. They all do. (202-203)

When the boys play Robin Hood in *Tom Sawyer*, the narrator observes that there is "no getting around the authorities" when it comes to the rules of swordplay (TS 63). This purely fictional constraint stands in contradistinction to, say, Huck's sense of the "regular," which is purely empirical (148), or to the regime of necessity that the river imposes on the cub pilot, who must be able to remember all the shapes of its ever-changing shoreline. For the cub, this has "got to be learned; there isn't any getting around it" (LM 86). As Clemens's master Horace Bixby says in *Life on the Mississippi*:

> "My, boy, you've got to remember it. You've got to

> remember the exact spot and the exact marks the boat lay in
> when we had the shoalest water, in every one of the five hundred
> shoal places between St. Louis and New Orleans; and you mustn't
> get the shoal soundings and marks of one trip mixed up with the
> shoal soundings and marks of another, either, for they're not often
> twice alike. You must keep them separate." (LM 90)

Though Huck is conscious of the difference (as for example
when theTom Sawyer-like "adventure" aboard the *Walter Scott*
turns out to be a matter of life and death: "We'd *got* to find
that boat now—had to have if for ourselves," 60), his strategy
in the social realm is typically one of studious avoidance, of
dodging, steering clear, giving trouble a wide berth.[38]

Respectable society does not have a monopoly on
closure and obligation in *Huck Finn*. As in Faulkner's
Sanctuary, here the rules of the civilized world have their dark
parody among the lawless, who are without a doubt the most
scrupulous and legalistic of all the characters in the novel.
They have a high sense of duty, like the hog that Huck finds
in church in chapter 18: "If you notice, most folks don't go to
church only when they've got to; but a hog is different" (91).

Huck's first encounter with pap in almost a year occurs
in the closed space of his room ("I had shut the door to," 20).
There pap lays down the law ("And looky here—you drop that
school, you hear?" 21). He wants to show his son who is
"boss" (23, 24). Pap's solution to the threat of losing custody
of the boy he holds imprisoned is to step up security measures:

> He said he would like to see the widow get me. He said he
> would watch out, and if they tried to come any such game on him
> he knowed of a place six or seven mile off, to stow me in, where
> they might hunt till they dropped and they couldn't find me. (25)

Pap is victim of the abusive authority of the "govment" and
the law. He has "got to sleep with the hogs in the tanyard"
(22); the law "jams him into an old trap of a cabin like this,
and lets him go round in clothes that ain't fitten for a hog"

---

38. – Pierre-Yves Petillon calls this the "stratégie de l'esquive," *La grand-route: Espace
et écriture en Amérique* (Paris: Seuil, 1979) 60. Pursued by duns, the narrator of
Roughing It also becomes "very adept at 'slinking'" (RI 405).

(26). As a result he is keen to get his "rights" (23, 26). Accordingly, he hires a lawyer and takes Judge Thatcher to court (23, 25).

The robbers on the *Walter Scott* are also keenly aware of rights and duties. Their scrupulous side is revealed in their dispute with that "mean skunk," the lying and treacherous Jim Turner:

> "Hear him beg! and yit if we hadn't got the best of him and tied him, he'd a killed us both. And what *for*? Jist for noth'n. Jist because we stood on our *rights*—that's what for. But I lay you ain't agoin' to threaten nobody any more, Jim Turner." (58)

The necessity of killing their partner in crime creates an ethical dilemma, however, as Packard realizes:

> "Shooting's good, but there's quieter ways if the thing's *got* to be done. But what *I* say, is this; it ain't good sense to go court'n around after a halter, if you can git at what you're up to in some way that's jist as good and at the same time don't bring you into no resks. Ain't that so?"
>
> "You bet it is. But how you goin' to manage it this time?"
>
> "Well, my idea is this: we'll rustle around and gether up whatever pickins we've overlooked in the staterooms, and shove for shore and hide the truck. Then we'll wait. Now I say it ain't agoin' to be more 'n two hours befo' this wrack breaks up and washes off down the river. See? He'll be drownded, and won't have nobody to blame for but his own self. I reckon that's a considerable sight better'n killin' of him. I'm unfavorable to killin' a man as long as you can git around it; it ain't good sense, it ain't good morals. Ain't I right?" (59)

It comes as no suprise that Tom, who is also chief of a "band of robbers" (12), also has a strict moral code. He often appeals to the sense of "honor" and "duty," of what is "right" and "moral," of what he and Huck *"ought"* to do (188, 194). Huck must finally take a stand with respect to a binding morality such as this . On the one hand, his pragmatism shows him that necessity is so often a function of immediate circumstances, such as in the example we have already seen from the Phelps Farm episode, where Huck thinks he is obligated to tell the truth ("I'd *got* to throw up my hand," 176). On the other, he feels the full force of conventional morality at crucial moments, such as in chapter 16, which echoes a number of the themes of the *Walter Scott* episode:

> I tried to make out to myself that *I* warn't to blame, because *I* didn't run Jim off from his rightful owner; but it warn't no use, conscience up and says, every time, "But you knowed he was running for freedom, and you could a paddled ashore and told somebody." That was so—I couldn't get around that, noway. That was where it pinched. (73)
>
> Well, I just felt sick. But I says, I *got* to do it—I can't get *out* of it. (74)

As we know, Huck refuses the dictates of his corrupt social conscience, here and in chapter 31. In one of the most insightful commentaries ever made on this last chapter, Ralph Ellison identifies what is at stake in ethical terms:

> We have arrived at a key point of the novel and, by an ironic reversal, of American fiction, a pivotal moment announcing a change of direction in the plot, a reversal as well as a recognition scene (like that in which Oedipus discovers his true identity), wherein a new definition of necessity is being formulated. Huck Finn has struggled with the problem posed by the clash between property rights and human rights, between what the community considered to be the proper attitude toward an escaped slave and his knowledge of Jim's humanity, gained through their adventures as fugitives together. He has made his decision on the side of humanity. ("Twentieth-Century Fiction and the Mask of Humanity," Ellison 87)

Huckleberry Finn is all about this act of redefining necessity. It ends up with the expression of an alternative but no less imperious form of necessity—that of freedom:

> I reckon I got to light out for the Territory ahead of the rest... (229)

Just as death is the greatest of all spectacles in *Huckleberry Finn*, so it appears to be the ultimate source of cultural and especially narrative authority, as the German critic Walter Benjamin once observed. Even that consummate trickster, the king, is compelled to admit that there is no contradicting the dead. Peter Wilks's claim that there is "six thousand dollars cash" hidden in the cellar of his house cannot be gainsaid, even if the count is in fact "four hundred and fifteen dollars short":

> "Oh, shucks, yes, we can *spare* it. I don't k'yer noth'n 'bout that— it's the *count* I'm thinking about. We want to be awful square and open and aboveboard, here, you know. We want to lug this h-yer money up stairs and count it before everybody—then ther' ain't noth'n suspicious. But when the dead man says ther's six thous'n dollars, you know, we don't want to—" (133)

In addition, let us recall that in chapter 29 the ultimate proof of the true identity of Peter Wilks's heirs is to be found on the dead man's body (159-161). Consider also the weight of Miss Watson's will. If Jim sets no great store by a "dead" authority like Solomon, neither does Huck by Moses:

> After supper she got out her book and learned me about Moses and the Bulrushers; and I was in a sweat to find out all about him; but by-and-by she let it out that Moses had been dead a considerable long time; so then I didn't care no more about him; because I don't take no stock in dead people.
>
> Here she was a bothering about Moses, which was no kin to her, and no use to anybody, being gone, you see... (7-8)

Both contest the authority of the dead, if not always with consistency. Both are pragmatic, forward-looking. The comic side of the above passage should not obscure the fact that this is indeed a radical break, every bit as radical as the one Emerson called for in the essay *Nature*, published at roughly the same time as the events in *Huckleberry Finn*: "why should we grope among the dry bones of the past, or put the living generation into masquerade out of its faded wardrobe?"[39] Emerson complained that his age was "retrospective." So does Huck Finn: "Sometimes I wish we could hear of a country that's out of kings" (125).

"Easy Water"

---

39. – Ralph Waldo Emerson, *Essays and Lectures*, ed. Joel Porte (New York: Library of America, 1983) 7.

> With windlasses and with assays of bias,
> By indirections find directions out.
>
> *Hamlet*, II.i. 62-63

Movement is full of paradoxes in *Huckleberry Finn*. Huck travels over a thousand miles ("eleven hundred mile," 227) due South, through all manner of adventures—close calls, separations, reunions, changes in identity, deaths, rebirths—only to remark, when all is said and done: "I been there before" (229). As in Einsteinian theory, space appears to be curved in this novel. Moving in a straight line leads back to the same place. The best shortcuts turn out to be long and winding routes. The only way to get to your destination is by missing it, or going in the opposite direction. (Isn't this what happens to Huck and Jim at the end?) The best way to end up in the North is to go South. People you have missed "along the road" are in fact right in front of you. People who are gone or coming back have, in reality, never left:

> I reckoned the poor king was in for a gaudy time of it with the audience; but nothing of the sort; pretty soon he crawls out from under the wigwam, and says:
> "Well, how'd the old thing pan out this time, Duke?"
> He had'nt been up town at all. (123)

> "So then, what you want to come back and ha'nt *me* for?"
> I says:
> "I hain't come back—I hain't been *gone*." (177)

This paradoxical law of movement enables those who have in fact been gone to pretend they have not, as when Huck plays his trick on Jim after their separation in the fog: "Gone away? Why, what in the nation do you mean? *I* hain't been gone anywheres. Where would I got to?" (70).

Slipping out, sliding away, dodging, faking, backtracking, "crawfishing"—these are Huck's characteristic moves. He is all nimbleness and fluidity—"poetry in motion," as sportswriters say. He shuns the straight and narrow. He prefers the bypaths, the circuitous routes. (Is it a mere coincidence that the jacket Buck Grangerford gives Huck is called a "roundabout"?) All of which is understandable: his habitat, after all, is the "crookedest" river in the world. The very nature of the Mississippi—with its channels of powerful, southbound current on the one hand and on the other, hugging the shoreline, the "easy" (LM 73, 91, 127), "slack," (LM 73, 147), or "dead" water (LM 104), which allows a canoe to move in *both* directions, south or north—dictates that the swiftest path from point A to point B is *not* a straight line. Huck's moral vision, his whole approach to life is an interiorization of this basic fact of navigation on the river. As a result, he never heads directly for his true destination, never lands exactly at a town or landing but rather always above or below it:

> "The first light we see, we'll land a hundred yards below it or above it, in a place where it's a good hiding-place for you and the skiff, and then I'll go and fix up some kind of a yarn, and get somebody to go for that gang and get them out of their scrape, so they can be hung when their time comes." (61)

> I landed below where I judged was the Phelps's place, and hid my bundle in the woods, and then filled up the canoe with water, and loaded rocks into her and sunk her where I could find her again when I wanted her, about a quarter of a mile below a little steam sawmill that was on the bank.
>   Then I struck up the road, and when I passed the mill I see a sign on it, "Phelps's Sawmill," and when I come to the farmhouses, two or three hundred yards further along, I kept my eyes peeled, but didn't see nobody around, though it was good daylight, now. But I didn't mind, because I didn't want to see nobody just yet—I only wanted to get the lay of the land. According to my plan, I was going to turn up there from the village, not from below. So I just took a look, and shoved along, straight for town. (170)

Note that here where he lands on shore is not even his starting point; he began at a "woody island that was down the river a piece" (170), where he found a good hiding place for the raft.

Easy water is a narrow margin of freedom and maneuverability running alongside a main current of necessity. To see more clearly how it affects movement in *Huckleberry Finn,* let us recall once again the description of Huck's close encounter with pap after his escape:

> "He dropped below me, with the current, and by-and-by he come

> a-swinging up shore in the easy water, and he went by so close I could a reached out the gun and touched him." (32)

To get to his destination, pap has no choice but to overshoot it and double back. In the same way, for Huck to land near the head of Jackson's Island inevitably means passing it by: "I shot past the head at a ripping rate, the current was so swift, and then I got into the dead water and landed on the side towards the Illinois shore" (33). Here is Huck going to Judith Loftus's shanty, on the Missouri shore, and back again:

> I started up the Illinois shore in the canoe just after dark.
> I started across to the town from a little below the ferry landing, and the drift of the current fetched me in at the bottom of the town. I tied up and started along the bank. (48)

> I went up the bank about fifty yards, and then I doubled on my tracks and slipped back to where my canoe was, a good piece below the house. I jumped in and was off in a hurry. I went up stream far enough to make the head of the island, and then started across. (53)

Note how movement on land mimics navigation on the river: in the first passage, once ashore, Huck skirts the shoreline on foot before heading inland toward the house; the second passage describes one of Huck's typical looping movements. Moreover, all of chapter 11 and the conversation with Judith Loftus is one long circuitous, discursive route back to St. Petersburg. It is Huck's way of returning home without actually going there. It should be stressed that even if Huck wanted to head straight across the river to a safe point on the opposite shore, he could not do so because of the drift of the current; he is condemned to take a roundabout way, for example when he and Jim return to Jackson's Island after rummaging through the floating house:

> And so, take it all around, we made a good haul. When we was ready to shove off, we was a quarter of a mile below the island, and it was pretty broad day; so I made Jim lay down in the canoe and cover up with the quilt, because if he set up, people could tell he was a nigger a good ways off. I paddled over to the Illinois shore and drifted down most a half a mile doing it. I crept up the dead water under the bank, and hadn't no accidents and

didn't see nobody. We got home all safe. (45)

The road to salvation is not straight but rather a crooked, winding path. No wonder Huck finds Bunyan's *Pilgrim's Progress*, in which Christian strives "to enter in at the straight gate" (Luke 13:24), "interesting, but tough" (83)! Huck is so adroit in his maneuvering that he can teach professional swindlers a thing or two about getaways:

> I was about to dig out from there in a hurry, but they was pretty close to me then, and sung out and begged me to save their lives—said they hadn't been doing nothing, and was being chased for it—said there was men and dogs a coming. They wanted to jump right in, but I says—
> "Don't you do it. I don't hear the dogs and horses yet; you've got time to crowd through the brush and get up the crick a little ways; then you take to the water and wade down to me and get in—that'll throw the dogs off the scent."
> They done it, and soon as they was aboard I lit out for our towhead, and in about five or ten minutes we heard the dogs and the men away off, shouting. We heard them come along towards the crick, but couldn't see them; they seemed to stop and fool around a while; then, as we got further and further away all the time, we couldn't hardly hear them at all; by the time we had left a mile of woods behind us and struck the river, everything was quiet, and we paddled over to the tow-head and hid in the cottonwoods and was safe. (98)[40]

Another roundabout way to safety. Finally, we should also remember how skillfully Huck throws the duke off his trail in chapter 31 by doubling back on him (172). The Phelps farm episode appears all the more absurd when we realize, in view of passages such as these, that the consummate escape artist is Huck and not Tom.

Easy water is the ideal maneuvering zone for escape artists and tricksters. In *Huckleberry Finn* tricking often involves scrambling landmarks, leaving false trails, phony starting points and destinations. This is of course what Huck does in chapter 7. In this novel, only simple-minded yokels like

---

40. – A tow-head is a newly formed or "infant" island. Cf. LM 177, 356.

Tim Collins ("that young flathead," as Huck calls him, 133) are truly going where they claim to be going, or coming from their actual point of departure. Huck pretends to be headed for "Goshen" in chapter 11; Tom, for Mr. Archibald Nicholas's house in chapter 33. On the river, easy water facilitates this sort of deception. It allows Huck to send Mr. Loftus and his friend on a wild goose chase by building a fire at his old camp, near the head of the island (33-36), a mile and a half away from the cavern where he and Jim are really staying ("I went up stream far enough to make the head of the island, and then started across," 53). This probably ensures their escape:

> If the men went to the island, I just expect they found the camp fire I built, and watched it all night for Jim to come. Anyways, they stayed away from us, and if my building the fire never fooled them it warn't no fault of mine. I played it as low-down on them as I could. (54)

Huck's commentary suggests that he may feel responsible for putting Jim into danger. After all, it was *his* fire that attracted Judith Loftus's attention: "I was pretty near certain I'd seen smoke over there, about the head of the island, a day or two before that, so I says to myself, like as not that nigger's hiding over there" (50). Jim's camp was near the foot of the island (36, 37).[41]

One the best examples of switching geographical markers in order to cover up one's tracks occurs in chapter 24. Huck and the king start off from "a little willow towhead out in the middle, where there was a village on each side of the river" (126) and then go through a bewildering series of changes of direction, real and imaginary:

> There was a big steamboat laying at the shore away up under the point, about three mile above the town—been there a couple of hours, taking on freight. Says the king:
> "Seein' how I'm dressed, I reckon maybe I better arrive

---

41. – "Our place"—the cavern—may be interpreted as a transitional space between land and the equality of life on the raft: it is *equidistant* from both ends, since it is a mile and a half below the head of the island (54), which is "only three miles long" (43).

down from St. Louis or Cincinnati, or some other big place. Go
for the steamboat, Huckleberry; we'll come down to the village on
her."

      I didn't have to be ordered twice, to go and take a
steamboat ride. I fetched the shore a half a mile above the village,
and then went scooting along the bluff bank in the easy water.
Pretty soon we come to a nice innocent-looking country jake
setting on a log swabbing the sweat off of his face, for it was
powerful warm weather; and he had a couple of carpet-bags by
him.

He asked the king where he was going, and the king told him he'd
come down the river and landed at the other village this morning,
and now he was going up a few mile to see an old friend on a
farm up there. The young fellow says:

      "When I first see you, I says to myself, 'It's Mr. Wilks,
sure, and he come mighty near getting here in time.' But then I
says again, 'No, I reckon it ain't him, or else he wouldn't be
paddling up the river.' You *ain't* him, are you?" (127)

Not surprisingly, one of the key events in the inquest into the
real identity of the duke and the king is the appearance of a
witness, Hines, who can re-establish part of the king's real
itinerary: "Well, then," he asks the king, "how'd you come to
be up at the Pint in the *mornin'*—in a canoe?" (156). The
king's rationale for pretending to have come from a big
northern town ("Seein' how I'm dressed") is adopted by Huck
later on in his circuitous approach to the Phelps farm. Huck
wants to appear to be arriving from the village because he has
put on his "store clothes" (170). Thus even when he comes to
a place for the first time the trickster has in a sense already
"been there before."

      What this passage reveals among other things is that
plausibility is often a matter of direction; identity, of coming
from a particular place. This is clear at the beginning of the
Phelps farm episode when Huck, who is taken for someone
else but does not as yet know the exact identity of the person,
finds himself in the following dilemma: "I didn't rightly know
what to say, because I didn't know whether the boat would be
coming up the river or down" (174). Huck's idea of inventing
an engine explosion to account for the steamboat's delay skirts
the difficulty inherent in the geographically-specific incident of

running aground on a bar. When he discovers he is Tom Sawyer, the geographical landmark falls neatly into place: "And I explained all about how we blowed out a cylinder-head at the mouth of White River and it took us three days to fix it" (177). The dependence of identity on direction is obvious too when Huck convinces the duke and the king that Jim is not a runaway slave:

> They asked us considerable many questions; wanted to know what we covered up the raft that way for, and laid by in the daytime instead of running—was Jim a runaway nigger? Says I—
> "Goodness sakes, would a runaway nigger run *south*?"
> No, they allowed he wouldn't. (102-103)

In order "to account for things some way," in the following paragraph Huck launches into a tortuous tale of family misfortune which brings them in a long discursive loop from Pike County, Missouri, back to their present location.

Of course, directional verisimilitude was a problem for Twain as well, once he decided to have Huck and Jim miss Cairo in the fog. For the continuance of the journey in a southerly direction to be plausible, Twain needed to get rid of their only means of going back[42]—the canoe—which can move upstream in easy water, unlike the raft. This he does in chapter 16:

> We talked it all over. It wouldn't do to take to the shore; we couldn't take the raft up the stream, of course. There warn't no way but to wait for dark, and start back in the canoe and take the chances. So we slept all day amongst the cotton-wood thicket, so as to be fresh for the work, and when we went back to the raft about dark the canoe was gone! (77)

> By-and-by we talked about what we better do, and found there warn't no way but just to go along down with the raft till we got a chance to buy a canoe to go back in. We warn't going to borrow it when there warn't anybody around, the way pap would do, for that might set people after us.
> So we shoved out, after dark, on the raft. (78)

_____

42. – Huck does find a canoe in chapter 19, but it is only instrumental in getting them tangled up almost immediately in another kind of servitude, as Huck happens upon the duke and the king (98).

Unfortunately, Twain apparently got turned around himself in the course of writing chapter 19, in the passage which recounts Huck's first meeting with the duke and the king: "One morning about day-break, I found a canoe..." (98). As the editors of the standard edition of the novel note:

> Mark Twain first wrote "I took the canoe," an error he overlooked until the publisher's proofreader noticed that the canoe had been "lost" in chapter 16... Because the book was in page proof, almost ready to print, Mark Twain was obliged to make an economical correction. He therefore substituted "found a" for "took the." But this solution left a larger problem unresolved: why, when Huck finds a new canoe, does he say nothing about going north with it? Mark Twain's wish to write about the Mississippi he knew had, in 1876, collided with the implausibility of Jim's trying to escape slavery by traveling south. The loss of the canoe had made continuing south temporarily plausible, as Huck and Jim decide to go "along down with the raft" and look for another canoe to buy for their northward journey. Mark Twain's next solution, also temporary, was to have the steamboat crash into the raft, shifting the action ashore. He may have written a portion of chapter 17... [NB: recent evidence points instead to a stopping point in chapter 18, where Huck and Buck talk about feuds, HF-CE xi], but soon put the book aside for three years, the basic problem unsolved. When Mark Twain returned to his manuscript in 1879-80, he made a note about two characters who would eventually provide him with the solution to his dilemma: "The two printers deliver temp. lectures, teach dancing, elocution, feel heads, distribute tracts, preach, fiddle, doctor (quack)." To this note he added parenthetically, "Keep 'em along." Bringing the tramps aboard the raft, where they could *enforce* a southward journey, meant Mark Twain could continue to write about the river he knew, but it also required resurrecting the raft, to which end he wrote another note to himself: "Back a little, CHANGE—raft only *crippled* by steamer.".. Having at last devised a plausible motive and means for sustaining Huck and Jim's southward journey, he had forgotten the ostensible reason they were still drifting south: the lost canoe and the need for a new one. When the proofreader caught the inconsistency, Mark Twain concealed the oversight as best he could be the slight change in wording... (HF-WMT 406-407n, 723; brackets added. Cf. also Blair 1960, 250-259).

Like lying, sentimentalism is discursive equivalent of easy water, an excellent medium for maneuvering. One might argue that in the Wilks episode Huck's utter disgust at the king is due to the incredible ease with which the latter manipulates the townsfolk, "a passel of sapheads" (132): "Well, if ever I struck anything like it, I'm a nigger. It was enough to make a body ashamed of the human race" (131). Tears are indeed "easy water" for the two frauds, who can cry, and make others do likewise, at will:

> And then he [the king] busted into tears, and so did everybody. (108)

> Sudden as winking, the ornery old cretur went all to smash, and fell up against the man, and put his chin on his shoulder, and cried down his back...

> Then he turns around, blubbering, and makes a lot of idiotic signs to the duke on his hands, and blamed if *he* didn't drop a carpet-bag and bust out a-crying. If they warn't the beatenest lot, them two frauds, that I ever struck. (130)

> And when they got there, they bent over and looked in the coffin, and took one sight, and then they bust out a crying so you could a heard them to Orleans, most; and then they put their arms around each other's necks, and hung their chins over each other's shoulders; and then for three minutes, or maybe four, I never see two men leak the way they done. And mind you, everybody was doing the same; and the place was that damp I never see anything like it. Then one of them got one one side of the coffin, and t'other on t'other side, and they kneeled down and rested their foreheads on the coffin, and let on to pray all to themselves. Well, when it come to that, it worked the crowd like you never see anything like it, and so everybody broke down and went to sobbing right out loud—the poor girls, too; and every woman, nearly, went up to the girls, without saying a word, and kissed them, solemn, on the forehead, and then put their hand on their head, and looked up towards the sky, with the tears running down, and then busted out and went off sobbing and swabbing, and give the next woman a show. I never see anything so disgusting. (131-132)

The king and the duke have achieved what Twain called, in connection with the spurious Hunt letter (about which more in our chapter on illusion), a "watery" triumph (LM 366). Huck has perhaps met his match here. He too has often maneuvered in "easy water." We might recall his crocodile tears for the captain of the steamboat in chapter 13:

> I skimmed around for the watchman, a-wondering whereabouts he slept; and by-and-by I found him roosting on the bitts, forward, with his head down between his knees. I give his shoulder two or three little shoves, and begun to cry.
> He stirred up, in a kind of startlish way; but when he see it was only me, he took a good gap and stretch, and then he says:
> "Hello, what's up? Don't cry, bub. What's the trouble?"
> I says:
> "Pap, and mam, and sis, and—"
> Then I broke down. He says:
> "Oh, dang it, now, *don't* take on so, we all has to have our troubles and this'n 'll come out all right. What's the matter with 'em?" (61-62)

And Huck will of course use the "blubbering" tactic on the slavehunters in chapter 16 and finally on the duke, when he bumps into him near Pikesville (171). His sad stories continue in one of Twain's unfinished sequels to *Huckleberry Finn* (HFTSAI 71). On the other hand, one might argue that in the Wilks episode Huck's language—his barbed superlatives and vituperative pairings ("sobbing and swabbing," "tears and flapdoodle," "rot and slush," "soul-butter and hogwash,"132; Bridgman 36), together with his use of *indirect* discourse to envelop and expose the whole fraud—rivals the efficiency of the sentimentalism it denounces, finally undoing it completely.

Paradoxically, even Huck's comparatively limited vocabulary can turn out to be a source of increased maneuverability. Basic verbs such as "to let" function as so many lightweight, nimble vehicles for expressing his ideas, as in the following wonderful phrase concerning Peter Wilks's gold:

> But I better hive it to-night, if I can, because the doctor maybe hasn't let up as much as he lets on he has... (140)

Then, too, the simple negation of the phrasal form "to let on" takes us from the idea of pretending to that of concealing or not showing—often two ways of achieving the same end, one active, the other passive. Or we might instance the swift reversal of meaning that takes place when we move from "to be in a fix" to "to fix up."

    Tale-telling is not the only discursive equivalent of easy water. Descriptive digression achieves the same end: to get at the heart of the matter by going around it. Huck's description of the Grangerfords' parlour is a case in point. Beginning with the pictures on the walls (84), it leads into a two-page digression on Emmeline Grangerford, which branches out from painting to another genre, poetry, with the appearance on the page of her "Ode to Stephen Dowling Bots, Dec'd," before moving on upstairs to a view of Emmeline's room and then back downstairs to the parlor: "Well, as I was saying about the parlor, there was beautiful curtains on the windows..." (86). Paradoxically, the quickest way to the sentimental "soul" of the Grangerford family is through this sort of detour: physically, by way of Emmeline's room; and generically, through the poetry in her scrapbook. "Well" is the verbal marker of return, signalling the looping-back movement towards the parlor. This marker recalls another—"Now"—on the opening page of the novel ("Now the way that the book winds up, is this...," 2), where Huck makes his inaugural return, as it were, to *The Adventures of Tom Sawyer*. *Huckleberry Finn* is in this respect a seemingly never-ending series of returns Huck makes whether he will or no (25, 30). The whole book may be seen as a rather roundabout way out of *Tom Sawyer*. The unfinished sequel *Huck Finn and Tom Sawyer among the Indians* shows that in Twain's imagination Huck was still firmly associated with a dynamic of doubling back or encircling (HFTSAI 48).

    Huck's description and narration of his approach to the Phelps farm follows a similar circling movement. Huck approaches the farm "through the woods" (172). In the description, his eye explores the grounds in a rather orderly movement from front to back, entering first the yard:

> A rail fence round a two-acre yard; a stile, made out of longs sawed off and up-ended, in steps, like barrels of a different length, to climb over the fence with...;

and finally, after a catalogue of everything within this

perimeter, he ends up on the other side:

> ... outside of the fence a garden and a water-melon patch; then the cotton fields begins; and after the fields, the woods"

But when the narration proper resumes, he does not follow the same trajectory; rather, he swings around and enters the back way: "I went around and clumb over the back stile by the ash-hopper, and started for the kitchen" (173). Morever, in the rest of the Phelps farm episode this arc is in a sense retraced, for Huck's final destination is in fact the little hut that he has just passed by ("that hut down by the ash hopper," 183), which is where Jim is being held prisoner.

As with dead water, so with death itself: dead water is the space of maximum maneuverability on the river; similarly, for Huck death is a "certainer way" to shake off the Widow Douglas, pap, and anybody else pursuing him ("I says to myself, I can fix it now so nobody won't think of following me," 30). Death is the ultimate, foolproof escape route, the swiftest, surest path to freedom and safety, as Huck confirms later on after the Grangerford-Shepherdson bloodbath ("they won't find me, and they'll think I've been killed, and floated down the river," 95). It is perhaps no coincidence that Huck and Jim moor the raft in the the sheltering zone of dead water: "soon as night was most gone, we stopped navigating and tied up—nearly always in the dead water under a tow-head" (96). They sleep "like dead people" (64).

Fog: A "No-Space World"

If for Huck the perfect escape route is through his own meticulously staged murder, this is because it takes him, so to speak, beyond the dimension of space altogether.[43] The tracks

---

43. – Vladimir Jankélévitch observes that the moment of death itself is by definition extra-categorial (*"L'instant mortel est hors catégories"*); the concept of space therefore does not apply (*"L'instant mortel récuse toute topographie"*): "...la mort *'a lieu'* quelque part, hic et nunc, et devient sur-le-champ et sur place un mystère trans-spatial"; "Celui qui meurt 'quelque part' émigre ensuite 'nulle part'. La mort est un 'mouvement' qui ne va nulle part comme elle est un 'devenir' qui ne devient rien"; "A partir de ce moment la question *Où ?* reste sans réponse. Car le mort, toute métaphore mise de côté, n'est pas parti en voyage au sens où les voyageurs quittent leur résidence et se déplacent de lieu en lieu dans l'espace... Le mort n'est pas parti fût-ce inconcevablement loin, fût-ce à des milliards de millions d'années-lumière, fût-ce dans

that Huck leaves behind at the shanty (31-32) lead to nowhere, other than to water (the river and the lake) or to the conclusion of his own violent death.[44] In this case, the tell-tale signs of a murder are much to be preferred to none at all. Huck has disappeared *with* traces—ones that severely limit the possibilities for the search party: "They won't ever hunt the river for anything but my dead carcass. They'll soon get tired of that, and won't bother no more about me" (32). Huck plays the trace-filled world of spatial reality off against itself by leaving self-evident signs and false clues behind him of a passage into a realm beyond time and space. Jim's strategy is the reverse. He wants to disappear without a trace:

> "I'd made up my mine 'bout what I's agwyne to do. You see ef I kep' on tryin' to git away afoot, de dogs 'ud track me; ef I stole a skift to cross over, dey'd miss dat skift, you see, en dey'd know 'bout whah I'd lan' on de yuther side en whah to pick up my track. So I says, a raff is what I's arter; it doan' *make* no track." (40)

Even so, in both cases the ideal escape route leads ultimately to a realm of tracelessness, extra-spatiality, disembodiment, a realm where the very idea of "following" is meaningless. As Jim says of his hiding place in the Grangerford episode:

> "Early in de mawnin' some er de niggers come along, gwyne to de fields, en dey tuck me en showed me dis place, whah de dogs can't track me on accounts o' de water... "(92)

---

les parages d'Orion ou dans l'île des Bienheureux: car Près et Loin, et les années-lumière, représentent encore des distances empiriques! Le mort n'est donc pas relativement absent: si en effet il était relativement absent, il serait 'ailleurs', alibi—, entendez: ailleurs qu'ici, non pas ici mais là; ailleurs, mais enfin quelque part; comme, en vertu de la disjonction et collocation des lieux, celui qui est présent ici est absent partout ailleurs, de même et vice versa celui qui est absent d'ici et bien présent là où il se trouve... Non, mourir n'est pas s'absenter en ce sens! Le mort est *absolument absent*, c'est-à-dire ailleurs non pas qu'ici ou là, mais ailleurs que partout; non pas autre part, mais nulle part!" This ultimate "disappearing act," this sudden movement from somewhere to nowhere is a source of profound ambiguity: "En tout cas l'ambiguïté de la mort est une ambiguïté d'escamotage, puisque la mort est le passage de quleque part à nulle part, puisque l'existence locale et l'abandon de tout lieu se succèdent," *La Mort* (Paris: Flammarion, 1977) 244, 245, 246, 247, 253.

44. – Mrs. Judith Loftus's opinion is Huck's first full confirmation of this: for her the question is not whether Huck was killed but "whodunit."

At the center of a narrative that points continually to a fundamental interchangeability of place stands a zone of solid whiteness that is, as it were, beyond space altogether—the fog. The plot hinges on Huck and Jim's passage through this zone, and their subsequent journey in the wrong direction eventuates in a spectacular confirmation of that interchangeability in a negation of the polarity of North and South. Appropriately enough, when Huck finally does get clear of the fog, he finds himself completely turned around: "I was spinning down a big bend stern first" (69). And the loss of landmarks is obvious in the overall movement of the fog episode, during which Huck and Jim travel from "somewheres" (68) to "nowheres" (69). "Huck Finn must come from nowhere and be bound for nowhere" (BSC 335), Eliot asserted. And he was right. The fork in the road—that is, where the Mississippi and the Ohio Rivers meet—has thus been obliterated by circumstance. The moral choice that it emblematizes has given way to a situation where necessity seems to prevail over human will.

The experience of fog calls forth images of death and disembodiment, of voices without bodies, of talking spirits:

> Once there was a thick fog, and the rafts and things that went by was beating tin pans so the steamboats wouldn't run over them. A scow or a raft went by so close we could hear them talking and cussing and laughing—heard them plain; but we could'nt see no sign of them; it made you feel crawly, it was like spirits carrying on that way in the air. Jim said he believed it was spirits; but I says:
> "No, spirits wouldn't say, 'dern the dern fog.'" (97)

Huck's realism notwithstanding, fog is the reign of material indeterminacy and tracelessness ("and things," "a scow or raft," "no sign of them"). It is a realm of death, where fixed visual landmarks are swallowed up in "solid" whiteness (68, 69), where at best Huck may catch "little dim glimpses" (69) of a few spectral forms ("smoky ghosts of big trees," 68). The thickening night gives a hint of what the extra-spatial experience of fog is like; it begins with a severe erosion of the three dimensions, here indicated as form and depth:

> "Well, the night got gray, and ruther thick, which is the next

meanest thing to fog. You can't tell the shape of the river, and you can't see no distance" (78).

Fear is not only aroused in Huck as a result of imminent danger (for example, on board the *Walter Scott*); it is also the feeling that prevails when he loses all sense of orientation, whether as a result of falling asleep or being rapidly engulfed in the sepulchral whiteness of the fog:

> I was pretty tired, and the first thing I knowed, I was asleep. When I woke up I didn't know where I was, for a minute. I set up and looked around, a little scared. Then I remembered. The river looked miles and miles across. The moon was so bright I could a counted the drift logs that went a slipping along, black and still, hundreds of yards out from shore. Everything was dead quiet, and it looked late, and *smelt* late. You know what I mean— I don't know the words to put it in. (32)

> I see the fog closing down, and it made me so sick and scared I couldn't budge for most a half a minute it seemed to me—and then there warn't no raft in sight; you couldn't see twenty yards. I jumped into the canoe and run back to the stern and grabbed the paddle and set her back a stroke. But she didn't come. I was in such a hurry I hadn't untied her. I got up and tried to untie her, but I was so excited my hands shook so I couldn't hardly do anything with them. (68)

In the first example, from chapter 7, not only memory but returning sense impressions (sight, hearing, smell) bring Huck back to reality; in the second, the feeling of panic will be more than momentary. Again, the loss of bearings, the disappearance of spatial co-ordinates and directionality, is the metaphorical equivalent of death:

> I shot out into the solid white fog, and hadn't no more idea which way I was going than a dead man.

> I whooped and listened. Away down there, somewheres, I hears a small whoop, and up comes my spirits. I went tearing after it, listening sharp to hear it again. The next time it come, I see I warn't heading for it but heading away to the right of it. And the next time, I was heading away to the left of it—and not gaining on it much, either, for I was flying around, this way and that and 'tother, but it was going straight ahead all the time.

> I did wish the fool would think to beat a tin pan, and beat

> it all the time, but he never did, and it was the still places between
> the whoops that was making the trouble for me. Well, I fought
> along, and directly I hears the whoop *behind* me. I was tangled
> good, now. That was somebody else's whoop, or else I was turned
> around. (68)

It is symptomatic of the stubborn spatiality of Huck's
imagination that he should, in these trying circumstances
where the normal categories of experience are suspended[45],
express a purely temporal relation in terms of space: *the still
places between the whoops*. The problem for him is the
desperate confusion of spatial and auditory terms; sounds are
places and the places are constantly shifting:

> Well, I warn't long losing the whoops, down amongst the tow-
> heads; and I only tried to chase them a little while, anyway,
> because it was worse than chasing a Jack-o-lantern. You never
> knowed a sound dodge around so, and swap places so quick and
> so much. (69; cf. also HFTSAI 69 for a similar experience in the
> fog).

When Huck finds himself alone in the fog, all of his senses are
distorted: "I couldn't tell nothing about voices in a fog, for
nothing don't look natural nor sound natural in a fog" (68);
but for the most part he is thrown back on his sense of
hearing.

The fog-bound river, where visual landmarks have
disappeared and where sound is virtually the only perceptual
marker, is, like death itself, the equivalent of an extra-spatial
world. Movement itself, which appears to define Huck's being
and identity, has lost all meaning; it has become aimless. In the
fog, Huck's usual strategies of passiveness or circumvention
are unavailing; he cannot even hang fire:

> Thinks I, it won't do to paddle; first I know I'll run into the bank

---

45. – Which provides the perfect occasion for some tall-tale-telling: "I had to claw
away from the bank pretty lively, four or five times, to keep from knocking the islands
out of the river" (69). The remarkable thing about this sentence is its unobstrusiveness
in context. It is as if, the ordinary categories of experience suspended, the tall-tale lost
its extraordinary qualities. In *Life on the Mississippi* a steamboat barely avoids
knocking a tow-head "into the middle of the Gulf of Mexico" (LM 108).

> or a towhead or something; I got to set still and float, and yet it's
> might fidgety business to have to hold your hands still at such a
> time.
>
>   I throwed the paddle down. (68)
>
>   I just give up, then.
>
>   I was good and tired, so I laid down in the canoe and said I
> wouldn't bother no more. (69)

Against his own will this time, Huck has entered a world where
the verb "to follow" has no meaning: "Next, for about a half an
hour, I whoops now and then; at last I hears the answer a long
ways off, and tries to follow it, but I couldn't do it..." (69).

    The impression of extra-spatiality is rendered by Huck's
almost exclusive reliance on hearing, as well as by the
contrasting abundance of temporal markers, Huck's sole grip
on reality:

> half a minute it seemed to me
>
> in about a minute
>
> in another second or two
>
> about fifteen minutes
>
> for about half and hour
>
> at last
>
> by-and-by
>
> they seemed to come up dim out of last week (68-69)

But it is clear from the foregoing list that even these markers
become less and less precise as Huck is gradually overcome by
exhaustion and finally sleep, which brings the process of
perceptual confusion to its height in the conflation of reality
and dream: "First I didn't know where I was; I thought I was
dreaming." The trackless world of the fog, where voluntary
movement has become impossible because all directions are
alike, leads to nowhere but oblivion.[46]

    As the philosopher Peter Strawson has persuasively

---

46. – The philosopher Clément Rosset calls the experience of the Consul in Malcom
Lowry's *Under the Volcano*, who can no longer find his way because there are too
many possible ways, an instance of a radical loss of meaning, akin to a form of
forgetfulness: "De même que l'insignifiance se définit non par le manque mais par la

argued, in a purely auditory universe the category of space would no longer obtain:

> Sounds of course have temporal relations to each other, and may vary in character in certain ways: in loudness, pitch and timbre. But they have no intrinsic spatial characteristics: such expressions as "to the left of," "spatially above," "nearer," "farther," have no intrinsically auditory significance.... Of a purely visual, or a purely tactual-kinaesthetic, concept of space, one might feel that it was impoverished compared with our own, but not that it was an impossibility. A purely auditory concept of space, on other hand, is an impossibility. The fact that, with the variegated types of sense-experience which we in fact have, we can, as we say, "on the strength of hearing alone" assign directions and distances to sounds, and things that emit or cause them, counts against this not at all. For this fact is sufficiently explained by the existence of correlations between the variations of which sound is intrinsically capable and other non-auditory features of our sense experience.... Whatever it is about sounds that makes us say such things as "It sounds as if it comes from somewhere on the left," this would not alone (i.e., if there were no visual, kinaesthetic, tactual phenomena) suffice to generate spatial concepts. I shall take it as not needing further argument that in supposing experience to be purely auditory, we are supposing a No-Space world.[47]

---

prolifération des chemins, de même l'oubli se caractérise non pas par une perte du souvenir mais bien par une omniprésence des souvenirs, par la masse indistincte de tous les souvenirs qui, lors de l'oubli, affluent en rangs si serrés qu'il devient impossible d'y repérer le souvenir recherché, " p. 18. See the section entitled "La confusion des chemins" in *Le Réel, Traité de l'idiotie* (Paris: Minuit, 1977) 14-23.

47. – P.F. Strawson. *Particulars: An Essay in Descriptive Metaphysics.* (London: Methuen, 1959) 65-66. A purely auditory world would be bereft of what Strawson terms the "reindentifiable" spatial particulars that lend stability to our ordinary world: "In the auditory and in the ordinary worlds alike, the possibility of reidentification of particulars depends on the idea of a dimension in which unperceived particulars may be housed, which they may be thought of as occupying. But, for our ordinary world, the word 'housed' is barely a metaphor and the word 'occupying' is not a metaphor at all. For in our ordinary world that 'dimension' is, precisely, three-dimensional space. Now it is the general character of this dimension which, for *any* conceptual scheme, determines the types of particular which can be reidentified without dependence on particulars of other types. So, in our actual scheme, the particulars which can be thus independently reidentified must at least be intrinsically spatial things, occupiers of space; and sound-particulars, not being of this character, are not independently

We would claim that on a metaphorical level the fog that Huck is engulfed in represents a powerful literary approximation of the No-Space world Strawson describes here. Symptomatic of the dematerialization such a world implies, even Huck's relation to his own body appears to be based largely on his sense of hearing:

> In another second or two it was solid white and still again. I set perfectly still, then, listening to my heart thump, and I reckon I didn't draw a breath while it thumped a hundred. (69)

It comes as no surprise, then, that Huck should have an initial feeling of disorientation after waking up, as in chapter 7:

> But I reckon it was more than a cat-nap, for when I waked up the stars was shining bright, the fog was all gone, and I was spinning down a big bend stern first. First I didn't know where I was; I thought I was dreaming; and when things begun to come back to me, they seemed to come up dim out of last week. (69)

"Things begun to come back to me" suggests recollection, of course, but may also be interpreted as signalling the gradual return of material bodies after the passage through a metaphorical No-Space world.

As we know, Jim thinks Huck is dead:

> "Goodness gracious, is dat you, Huck? En you ain' dead?—you ain' drowned—you's back agin? It's too good for true, honey, it's too good for true. Lemme look at you, chile, lemme feel o' you. No you ain' dead! you's back agin, 'live en soun', jis de same ole Huck—de same ole Huck, thanks to goodness!" (70)

---

reidentifiable," *ibid.* 78. Which is why Huck, who is, in the fog, almost solely dependent on his hearing, ends up "'tangled good" (68). We should add that elsewhere in his study Strawson does make a convincing case for reidentifiable auditory particulars by recourse to a pitch of master-sound which provides a stable reference point for establishing the position of discrete sounds within the auditory world. This might be loosely compared to Huck's desire for a *continuous* sound to enable him to get his bearings: "I did wish the fool would think to beat a tin pan, and beat it all the time" (68).

This tactile check ("lemme feel o' you") anticipates Tom's confrontation with the "ghost" of Huck Finn in the Phelps farm episode (178). Identity equals embodiment, which means occupying a particular position in space:

> "Well, then, what makes you talk so wild?"
> "How does I talk wild?"
> "*How?* why, hain't you been talking about my coming back, and all that stuff, as if I'd been gone away?"
> "Huck—Huck Finn, you look me in de eye; look me in de eye. *Hain't* you ben gone away?"
> "Gone away? Why, what in the nation do you mean? *I* hain't been gone anywheres. Where would I go to?"
> "Well, looky here, boss, dey's sumf'n wrong, dey is. Is I *me*, or who *is* I. Is I heah, or whah *is* I? Now dat's what I wants to know?"
> "Well, I think you're here, plain enough, but I think you're a tangle-headed old fool, Jim."
> "I is, is I?" (70)

Here, as in the King Solomon debate in chapter 14, Jim's is the truly philosophical mind: "Is I *me*, or who *is* I. Is I heah, or whah *is* I?"[48] He is right: to be someone means, crucially, to be some*where* in particular. In a sense, when Huck says "I hain't been gone anywheres," he is telling the truth, since, as we have seen, the passage through the fog bank is, metaphorically speaking, a voyage from "somewheres" to "nowheres."

Stories, which involve positioning bodies in space in successive narrative sequences, are the means of re-establishing identity in the rest of the passage (71, 72). The return of material signs ("the leaves and rubbish on the raft, and the smashed oar," 71) also serves to restore the distinction between dream and reality ("but what does *these* things stand for?")

---

48. – This, too, is prefigured in chapter 2, where Jim asks, "Say—who is you? Whar is you?" (10).

Surface, Depth, and Meaning:
Huck's Esthetics of the Beautiful

The description of the Grangerfords' "mighty nice house" in chapter 17, when contrasted with other instances of beauty in *Huckleberry Finn*, shows how perception of space can affect meaning and produce tension within Huck's discourse. Their home is the epitome of "style": "It was a mighty nice family, and a might nice house, too. I hadn't seen no house out in the country before that was so nice and had so much style" (82). The Grangerfords' parlor is a world of veneers and surfaces, of the artificial and the decorative, the ceremonial (87) and the sentimental (84-86). One Twain scholar refers to it punningly as a nice example of "interior desecration" (Blair 1960, 207). The controlling adjectives are "nice" (which appears 6 times), "big" (5), "beautiful" (4), "lovely" (2), "painted" or "whitewashed" (7). Huck's vision is naive, his eye obviously bedazzled by appearances, by the surface beauty of this interior. Nevertheless, his perception of *depth* creates an ironic tension that effectively subverts the value of the whole description:

> Well, there was a big outlandish parrot on each side of the clock, made out of something like chalk, and painted up gaudy. By one of the parrots was a cat made of crockery, and a crockery dog by the other; and when you pressed down on them they squeaked, but didn't open their mouths nor look different nor interested. They squeaked through underneath. There was a couple of big wild-turkey-wing fans spread out behind those things. On a table in the middle of the room was a kind of a lovely crockery basket that had apples and oranges and peaches and grapes piled up in it which was much redder and yellower and prettier than real ones is, but they warn't real because you could see where pieces had got chipped off and showed the white chalk or whatever it was, underneath.
>
> This table had a cover made out of beautiful oil-cloth, with a red and blue spread-eagle painted on it, and a painted border all around. It come all the way from Philadelphia, they said. There was some books too, piled up perfectly exact, on each corner of the table. (83)

Not withstanding the profusion of surfaces and coverings, Huck's keen eye allows the reader a glimpse of "whatever it was, underneath." His emphasis on what the decorations are "made out of" produces the same effect of depth that belies surface. There is nothing living, nothing "natural" here; nothing is made of what it should be made of (not even the basket!), nor responds the way Huck expects: "when you pressed down on them they squeaked, but didn't open their mouths nor look different nor interested. They squeaked through underneath." The whole house is in an incongruous piece of town-style living set in the country: "It didn't have an iron latch on the front door, nor a wooden one with a buckskin string, but a brass knob to turn, the same as houses in a town" (82). The arrangement of everything has the sterility of the "perfectly exact." Like his home, the Colonel himself[49] is a sort of human veneer ("the qualities of an etching," Bridgman 125), all purity and thinness, a parody of aristocratic fine breeding and stormy Romantic sentiment:

> Col. Grangerford was very tall and very slim, and had a darkish-paly complexion, not a sign of red in it anywhere; he was clean-shaved every morning, all over his thin face, and he had the thinnest kind of lips, and the thinnest kind of nostrils, and a high nose, and heavy eyebrows, and the blackest kind of eyes, sunk so deep back that they seemed like they was looking out of caverns at you, as you may say. His forehead was high, and his hair was black and straight, and hung to his shoulders. His hands was long and thin, and every day of his life he put on a clean shirt and a full suit from head to foot made out of linen so white it hurt your eyes to look at it; and on Sundays he wore a blue tail-coat with brass buttons on it. He carried a mahogany cane with a silver head to it. There warn't no frivolishness about him, not a bit, and he warn't ever loud. He was as kind as he could be—you could feel that, you know, and so you had confidence. (87)

---

49. – The proliferation of spurious military titles was, for Twain, symptomatic of the dreaded "Walter Scott disease": "It was Sir Walter that made every gentleman in the South a Major or a Colonel, or a General or a Judge, before the war; and it was he, also, that made these gentlemen value these bogus decorations. For it was he that created rank and caste down there, and also reverence for rank and caste, and pride and pleasure in them " (LM 328). Twain was strongly opposed to the use of "Honorable" by members of the House of Representatives, as this 1878 notebook entry reveals: "Our adoration of titles. 'Hon'—procured in legislature 30 yrs ago. No congressman is entitled to a title" (NJ2 57).

We would argue furthermore that in the Grangerford chapters narration is to description as depth is to surface. Where Huck's penetration fails him, the narrative itself— beginning with the greeting at gunpoint and ending with the massacre in chapter 18—affords an in-depth view of the Grangerford family in action that heightens the irony of certain descriptive details: the table cloth that comes "all the way from Philadelphia" ("the city of brotherly love"!), a book entitled "Friendship's Offering" (83), not to mention Colonel's kindly demeanour.

We might also say that the novel as a whole affords an even fuller perspective on the question of beauty, further undermining the validity of the term as applied to the Grangerfords' home. It is hardly a coincidence that this idea recurs in chapter 19, immediately after Huck and Jim escape from the massacre: "Two or three days and nights went by; I reckon I might say they swum by, they slid along so quiet and smooth and lovely" (96). In this chapter, Huck's description of the life on the raft gives an entirely different meaning to the same words:

> Sometimes we'd have that whole river all to ourselves for the longest time. Yonder was the banks and the islands, across the water; and maybe a spark—which was a candle in a cabin window—and sometimes on the water you could see a spark or two—on a raft or a scow, you know; and maybe you could hear a fiddle or a song coming over from one of them crafts. It's lovely to live on a raft. We had the sky, up there, all speckled with stars, and we used to lay on our back and look up at them... (97)

> Once or twice of a night we would see a steamboat slipping along in the dark, and now and then she would belch a whole world of sparks up out of her chimbleys, and they would rain down in the river and look awful pretty... (98)

Huck's account of the circus in chapter 22, which also follows bloodshed (with the killing of Boggs in chapter 21), reinforces this semantic shift:

> It was a real bully circus. It was the splendidest sight that ever was, when they all come riding in, two and two, a gentleman and lady, side by side, the men just in their drawers and under-

> shirts, and no shoes nor stirrups, and resting their hands on their
> thighs, easy and comfortable—there must a' been twenty of
> them—and every lady with a lovely complexion, and perfectly
> beautiful, and looking just like a gang of real sure-enough queens,
> and dressed in clothes that cost millions of dollars, and just
> littered with diamonds. It was a powerful fine sight; I never see
> anything so lovely. And then, one by one they got up and stood,
> and went a-weaving around the ring so gentle and wavy and
> graceful, the men looking ever so tall and airy and straight, with
> their heads bobbing and skimming along, away up there under the
> tent-roof, and every lady's rose-leafy dress flapping soft and silky
> around her hips, and she looking like the most loveliest parasol.
> (119)

In addition to "beautiful" and "lovely," other terms applied to
the Grangerfords themselves ("gentleman," "tall," "straight,"
87) undergo alterations in value. Here a later example of naive
vision ("in clothes that cost milllions of dollars, and just
littered with diamonds") serves to correct an earlier one. A
change in spatial relations (with the introduction of depth and
distance) thus effects a change in meaning. But this
readjustment of meaning was in fact already latent in Huck's
description of the Grangerford girls:

> Then there was Miss Charlotte, she was twenty-five, and
> tall and pround and grand, but as good as she could be, when she
> warn't stirred up; but when she was, she had a look that would
> make you wilt in your tracks. She was beautiful.
> So was her sister, Miss Sophia, but it was a different kind.
> She was gentle and sweet, like a dove, and she was only twenty.
> (87-88)

The appropriately named Sophia (the only family member to
escape the bloodbath, 94) is indeed a beauty who differs *in
kind* from her sister.

A change in the position of a word within the narrative
and textual space produces a shift in meaning.[50] Signifiers are
not fixed but free-floating. As a result, reading *Huckleberry*

---

50. – As Doyno observes, "'Adventures' appears as a word with favorable
connotations at the beginning of the novel, but the word and the title gradually
acquire negative connotations" (29).

Finn with *in*sight, seeing beyond Huck's limited vantage point, resembles a process of triangulation. More than one coordinate is needed to calculate the true value of words.

Chapter 2

Time

The day before we left Hannibal, a curious thing fell under
my notice,—the surprising spread which longitudinal time
undergoes there. I learned it from one of the most unostentatious
of men,—the colored coachman of a friend of mine, who lives
three miles from town. He was to call for me at the Park Hotel at
7.30 p.m., and drive me out. But he missed it considerably,—did
not arrive till ten. He excused himself by saying:—

"De time is mos' an hour en a half slower in de country en
what it is in de town; you'll be in plenty time, boss. Sometimes we
shoves out early for church, Sunday, en fetches up dah right plum
in de middle er de sermon. Diffunce in de time. A body can't
make no calculations 'bout it."

I had lost two hours and a half; but I learned a fact worth
four. (LM 391)

Delayed Disclosure

In *Huckleberry Finn* there is a significant time-element in
perception, thinking, and feeling, which is another way of
saying that they are *processes*. The elementary form these
assume is that of a delay, or a two-stage process, the first stage
often negative: not noticing, then noticing, for instance. The
sheer number of examples of this sort suggests that we are
dealing with a fundamental fact about the vision reality in the
novel. It is as if, initially at least, error always had the upper
hand, as if an inaugural negation were required to set off a
process leading to a more accurate view of things. To adopt
Hegelian phraseology, we might say that Huck has to do a bit
of "tarrying with the negative." This is time well spent, though;
for the negative is, as we shall see, fundamentally dynamic, a
"moving principle."[51] We should hasten to add that this holds

---

51. – G.W.F. Hegel, *Phenomenology of Spirit*, trans. A.V. Miller (Oxford: Oxford UP,
1977) 19, 21.

for the act of reading as well. For the reader, Huck's naive perspective constantly calls for its own supersession at the same time its partial truth is acknowledged. The narrative draws its power from the perception of differential insight.

There is thus an element of adventure in the very logic of perception itself. A kernel of suspense is built into Huck's experience of the world. Adventure in its most basic form is simply this temporal indeterminacy, this uncertainty with regard to the future, the mystery of what is going to happen next.[52]

There is no doubt about it: Huck is clever. But in a way, he is most interesting, not when the right words or ideas come to him spontaneously, but rather when he makes mistakes or runs aground. Arguably, Tom is often the more discerning of the two boys, a fact Huck recognizes implicitly, as when he describes his friend leading them into the cave in chapter 2: "Tom poked about amongst the passages and pretty soon ducked under a wall where you wouldn't a noticed that there was a hole" (11-12); or explicitly, as in chapter 34, after Tom figures out where Jim is being held: "What a head for just a boy to have!" (183).[53] It goes without saying that Huck demonstrates his superiority over Tom in countless ways, some of which we have already examined; but our point is that it is Huck's slowness, his very limitations that make him an effective bearer of truth, an effective portrayer of the fundamental nature of the world around him, in a way that Tom could never be.

---

52. – This is what Jankélévitch refers to as "l'aventure infinitésimale," "l'aventureuse futurition," or, in other words, the adventure inherent in the very nature of futurity: "Pour retrouver, dans le temps, ce seuil de l'aventure, cette aventure élémentaire, peut-être serait-il bon de rappeler que l'aventure porte la désinence du futur. L'aventure est liée à ce temps du temps qu'on appelle le temps futur et dont le caractère essentiel est d'être indéterminé, parce qu'il est l'empire énigmatique des possibles et dépend de ma liberté; le possible n'est-il pas ce qui peut être ainsi ou autrement, et qui sera ceci ou cela selon mon courage, selon les risques que je consentirai à courir, selon ma bonne ou ma mauvaise chance?"; "l'aventure infinitésimale est liée à l'avènement de l'événement. Distinguons plus précisément *Evenit* et *Advenit*. L'événement n'est qu'une date sur le calendrier; mais l'avènement se devine comme l' 'avent' d'un mystère," *L'aventure, l'ennui et le sérieux* (Paris: Aubier/Montaigne, 1963)10,12.

53. – Twain continued to endow Tom with a keen eye in the unfinished sequel to *Huckleberry Finn*, *Huck Finn and Tom Sawyer among the Indians* (for two telling examples, cf. HFTSAI 47, 77).

Delay stands as temporal equivalent of Huck's roundabout ways. Perception and feeling often lag behind events. Insight is not always immediate (if it is gained at all). Rather, Huck seems to go through an initial phase of blindness or confusion. Things have to be overlooked or misunderstood before they can be properly seen, just as Huck and Jim's destination has in some sense to be missed in order to be reached. As we saw in our discussion of beauty, what we encounter first is what meets the eye. The in-depth view comes afterwards. Discovery and understanding thus take place in stages, the first involving what we might term, with Clément Rosset, the exercise of the "anti-perceptive faculty."[54] This epistemological lag obviously has important consequences for plot and narrative strategy.[55]

Let us look first, however, at perception. A fine example of delayed perception is Huck's discovery of pap's bootprint in the snow in chapter 4:

> I went down the front garden and clumb over the stile, where you go through the high board fence. There was an inch of new snow on the ground, and I seen somebody's tracks. They had come up from the quarry and stood around the stile a while, and then went on around the garden fence. It was funny they hadn't come in, after standing around so. I couldn't make it out. It was very curious, somehow. I was going to follow around, but I stooped down to look at the tracks first. I didn't notice anything at first, but next I did. There was a cross in the left boot-heel made with big nails to keep off the devil.
>
> I was up in a second and shinning down the hill. I looked over my shoulder now and then, but I didn't see nobody. I was at Judge Thatcher's as quick as I could get there. (18)

Huck's eye follows the path of the footprints, which enable him to reconstruct the stranger's movements in a simple

---

54. – Our translation. See his essay entitled "L'inobservance du réel" in *Le Principe de cruauté* (Paris: Minuit, 1988) 59-72; as well as *Le Réel,* 123-133, on what Rosset calls "la représentation tardive du réel."

55. – Similarly, David Wilson's repeated failure to see the true identity of the "mysterious girl" (in fact Tom Driscoll disguised) is a key structural device in *Puddn'head Wilson* (PW 32, 62, 64, 97, 98, 104).

narrative line. Interestingly enough, though, this story does not
afford immediate insight into the meaning of the signs ("I
couldn't make it out"). It does not remove their strangeness
("It was funny"; "It was very curious, somehow"). The value of
narrative as a heuristic tool would seem to be limited. Stories
often mislead.

It is not until Huck takes a closer look and sees the sign
within the sign, as it were, that he realises whose tracks these
are. The reaction is then immediate ("I was up in a second and
shinning down hill"). But the reader must wait until "that
night," until after the break on the following page before he
knows for certain who the stranger is ("So I went to him [Jim]
that night and told him pap was here again, for I found his
tracks in the snow," 19; brackets added). Huck keeps him in
suspense.[56] The reader's understanding thus follows in the
tracks of the character's. Form mimics content.

We might also recall how long it takes Huck to find the
saw that will help him escape from the cabin: "I reckon I had
hunted the place over as much as a hundred times; well, I was
'most all the time at it, because it was about the only way to
put in the time. But this time I found something at last..." (25).
In Huck's defense, we should add that this failure to notice
objects or details happens to other characters as well, even to
the extremely perspicacious lawyer Levi Bell, who overlooks
the similarity between the handwriting of the letters from
Peter Wilks's true heirs. His attention has to be drawn to it: "I
believe it's so—and if it ain't so, there's a heap stronger
resemblance than I'd noticed before" (159).

What is perhaps the key example of perceptual slippage
in the novel occurs as Huck and Tom are returning from their
failed expedition to forewarn the duke and the king. The boys
have been "on the lookout all the time" (182) for hints as to
Jim's whereabouts, but to no avail. Suddenly it dawns on Tom:

---

56. – "Le roman d'aventures organise son suspens de telle sorte qu'aucun événement ne
porte en lui-même de signification immédiate, que la solution (en termes de vie ou de
mort) comme l'explication (en termes de vérité ou d'erreur) en soient toujours différées,"
Jean-Yves Tadié, *Le roman d'aventures* (1982; Paris: Quadrige/PUF, 1996) 8. As Tadié
remarks: "La phénoménologie de la lecture est... au coeur de l'étude du genre" (7).

We stopped talking, and got to thinking. By-and-by Tom says:

"Looky here, Huck, what fools we are, to not think of it before! I bet I know where Jim is."

"No! Where?"

"In that hut down by the ash-hopper. Why, looky here. When we was at dinner, didn't you see a nigger man go in there with some vittles?"

"Yes."

"What did you think the vittles was for?"

"For a dog."

"So'd I. Well, it wasn't for a dog."

"Why?"

"Because part of it was watermelon."

"So it was—I noticed it. Well, it does beat all, that I never thought about a dog not eating watermelon. It shows how a body can see and don't see at the same time." (183)

"By-and-by" foregrounds the time-element once again. Full, intelligent perception—that is, to use Huck's terms, seeing that is not at the same *not* seeing—comes in the fullness of time (in this case following the thinking process).[57] The repetition of "looky here" suggests that this is indeed a lesson on how to be an astute observer.[58] Given this emphasis on the anti-perceptive faculty, it comes as no suprise that Huck should dwell on perceptual quirks in nature, like the sound lag on the river:

Next you'd see a raft sliding by, away off yonder, and maybe a galoot on it chopping, because they're almost always doing it on a raft; you'd see the ax flash, and come down—you don't hear nothing; you see that ax go up again, and by the time it's above the man's head, then you hear the *k'chunk!*—it had took all that time to come over the water. (97)

---

57. – "Le réel précède ainsi, le plus souvent, sa représentation, en sorte que la fonction de la représentation est d'évoquer non pas le réel tel qu'il serait contemporain de la perception, mais de dévoiler un réel qui lui est antérieur, qui existe avec toute la force de la réalité sans avoir cependant été clairement enregistré," Rosset, *Le Réel,* 125-126.

58. – The problematic of perception is present in Twain's work from *The Innocents Abroad* onwards. James M. Cox argues that that work, as its preface suggests, constitutes "a training of the reader to see with his own eyes" (1966, 54). Cf. also this remark from *Life on the Mississippi*: "Partialities often make people see more than really exists" (LM 188). As Tom Sawyer says, "Some people can see, and some can't..." (TSA 51).

Ideas often come belatedly to Huck as well. His delayed reaction during the induction ceremony of Tom Sawyer's Gang is a good illustration: the idea of offering Miss Watson as a surrogate family member and sacrificial victim does occur to Huck, but only after being at first stumped like everyone else: "Well, nobody could think of anything to do—everybody was stumped, and set still. I was most ready to cry; but all at once I thought of a way, and so I offered them Miss Watson—they could kill her" (12). Then, too, there are times when Huck simply changes his mind, finds a better idea. For instance, when he finds the canoe floating down the river in chapter 7:

> Thinks I, the old man will be glad when he sees this—she's worth ten dollars. But when I got to shore pap wasn't in sight yet, and as I was running her into a little creek like a gully, all hung over with vines and willows, I struck another idea; I judged I'd hide her good, and then, stead of taking to the woods when I run off, I'd go down the river about fifty mile and camp in one place for good, and not have such a rough time tramping on foot. (29)

The question is, why does Huck strike upon "another idea" at this precise moment ("as I was running her into a little creek like a gully, all hung over with vines and willows")? Though not "in sight," Pap is a lurking presence here. We might say that it is his shadow that elicits the new idea in Huck. To see this more clearly, let us quote the first full description of pap's face in chapter 5: "His hair was long and tangled and greasy, and hung down, and you could see his eyes shining through like he was behind vines" (20). It is as if the reawakening of self-interested, rebellious thought in Huck required some token of pap, just as the initial, naive idea presupposed pap's physical absence from the scene. The swift reversal of position reminds us, too, of the highly maneuvrable character of the very object he is hiding—the canoe. Mental and physical agility, though at times dormant qualities in Huck, are nonetheless instrumental in the success of his escape down the river.

Huck's ideas are often *second* thoughts, parts of an extemporaneous process, as is evidenced in his preparations of the murder scene in chapter 7, when he retrieves certain things he has already stored in the canoe: "Now I thought of something else. So I went and got the bag of meal and my old saw out of the canoe and fetched them to the house" (31). The narrator's silence as to his purpose here further heightens the effect: the reader participates all the more closely in the improvisation as he has to guess as he reads along what exactly Huck is doing (31-32). Spontaneity and self-correction are of course characteristic of Huck's narrative method as well (see for example his retake on the king's clothing: "home-knit galluses—no, he had only one," 99).

Ideas and intuitions have a short life-span in *Huckleberry Finn*. Conceptual space, if we may use the term, proves to be as reversible as physical space and is as closely (and causally) linked to the "hairbreadth escape," but with a distinct temporal dimension. In this case, the "close shave" due to a bad idea that seemed good at the time is experienced with a retrospective shudder. Two examples come to mind here. The first occurs in chapter 26, where Huck decides to eavesdrop on the duke and the king in order to find out where they have hidden the gold. Huck is groping around in the dark:

> About that time, I hears their footsteps coming, and was going to skip under the bed; I reached for it, but it wasn't where I thought it would be; but I touched the curtain that hid Mary Jane's frocks, so I jumped in behind that and snuggled in amongst the gowns, and stood there perfectly still. (141)

Huck goes "a good deal on instinct" (174), but in this instance, his "natural" reflex was a bad one:

> They come in and shut the door; and the first thing the duke done was to get down and look under the bed. Then I was glad I hadn't found the bed when I wanted it. And yet, you know, it's kind of natural to hide under the bed when you are up to anything private." (*ibid.*)

Paradoxically, the path to safety lies through darkness (though Huck is doubtless helped out by his visual memory of the room, which he visited earlier that day, 137). Our second example appears in chapter 28, on the day of the Grangerford-

Shepherdson massacre, when Huck realizes with hindsight that he might have been killed if he had followed his instinct as to the best hiding place: "There was a wood-rank four foot high, a little ways in front of the tree, and first I was going to hide behind that; but maybe it was luckier I didn't" (93). That is the exact spot where Buck Grangerford will be surprised and wounded by the Sheperdsons. This basic pattern of reversal in value can of course become more complex. The idea of stealing the gold, for instance, shifts from good (140) to bad (143, 145) and back again (when the discovery of the bag at the graveside gives Huck an opportunity to slip away, 161). Huck's decision to send Mary Jane away undergoes a similar series of permutations (151, 161, 162).

    This is another way of saying that Huck can be proved wrong by events whereas Tom cannot. Tom is pedantic and doctrinaire where Huck is flexible and always able to learn from experience. Huck spends a surprising amount of time not understanding—think of the frequency of the expression "I couldn't make it out"—or having his impressions or instincts belied by circumstances. But in the end, these errors redound to his credit. Huck's thinking partakes as much of the character of process as the reality in which he is immersed. To say that "Huckleberry Finn is primarily a record of feeling, not cognition" (Quirk 86) is to overstate the case.

    Delayed understanding has tragic consequences in the Grangerford episode. The characteristic feeling of puzzlement prevails when Huck comes back from church with Sophia Grangerford's Testament:

> Says I to myself something's up—it ain't natural for a girl to be in such a sweat about a Testament, so I give it a shake, and out drops a little piece of paper with *"Half-past two"* wrote on it with a pencil. I ransacked it, but couldn't find anything else. I couldn't make anything out of that, so I put the paper in the book again... (91).

After talking with Sophia, Huck goes off down the river "studying over this thing," is waylaid by another enigma—the "mighty curious" behaviour of his servant, who wants to show him some "water-moccasins" (Jim, in reality, 93)—and presumably thinks no more about it until the following day, when he finally realizes the import of the secret message. Too late to head off the massacre, of course.

Let us remark in passing that here, as elsewhere in *Huckleberry Finn*, guilt ("I reckoned I was to blame, somehow," 95) turns out to be a particular kind of temporal relation. Simply put, it is the result of belatedness. The tarring and feathering of the king and the duke is a case in point. Hoping to warn them away from trouble, Huck and Tom arrive "too late—couldn't do no good." As a result, Huck feels "kind of ornery, and humble, and to blame, somehow—though *I* hadn't done nothing" (182).[59] His heavy-heartedness after the unexpectedly quick sinking of the *Walter Scott* is another instance of this sort of belatedness (64). We should point out that "usefulness" ("too late—couldn't do no good") is an equivocal norm. Huck's inability to serve others is a source of guilt; but the same norm can lead to a hedonistic privileging of present gratification over any dry moral lessons the past might teach us, as Huck's first Bible lesson with the widow shows (7-8). As we have already suggested, this is Huck's radical break with history, and the immediate experience of pleasure is one of the driving forces behind it.

Emotions often arise belatedly as well. When Huck suddenly finds pap seated in his room, he discovers he is misled by his own feelings. Let us recall that the two paragraphs that appear below are separated by a chapter break:

> When I lit my candle and went up to my room that night, there set pap, his own self!

> I had shut the door to. Then I turned around, and there he was. I used to be scared of him all the time, he tanned me so much. I reckoned I was scared now, too; but in a minute I see I

---

59. – Huck has in fact thoroughly learned the Widow Douglas's lesson: "I must help other people, and do everything I could for other people, and look out for them all the time, and never think about myself" (15). Guilt is presumably the "spiritual gift" that Huck receives in return for his efforts!

> was mistaken. That is, after the first jolt, as you may say, when my breath sort of hitched—he being so unexpected; but right away after, I see I warn't scared of him worth bothering about. (20)

This is a remarkable piece of introspection. The exclamation point renders Huck's alarm ("the first jolt") quite nicely,[60] and the suspense of the chapter break enhances the effect. But in order to indicate the precise emotional dynamics Huck has to circle back in time (with the past perfect "I had shut the door to"). He is growing out of his deep-seated fear of his father. The feeling of panic is more attributable to circumstances than anything else. His first words to his father—which are pure insolence ("Maybe I am, maybe I ain't"), as pap perceives ("Don't give me none o' your lip")—confirms this intuition. The very inadequacy of the narrative kernel ("I had shut the door to. Then I turned around, and there he was"), in which fear has all the simplicity of a physical reflex, seems to generate a compensatory pyschological elaboration, an introspective process which is itself a way of overcoming instinctive fear. A thinking cure, later supplemented by a talking and writing cure. What this reveals, among other things, is that feelings require time to develop, to describe—and to indulge, as we can see in the *Walter Scott* episode:

> Well, I catched my breath and most fainted. Shut up on a

---

60. – This is a perfect example of what Rosset calls the surprise-effect of the real when directly encountered *after* a prefiguration *[représentation anticipée]* or prior representation of it, *Le Réel*, 134. This phenomenon—the reverse of the *"représentation tardive"*—also occurs in chapter 29, when Huck thinks he has finally got rid of the duke and the king: "I had to skip around a bit, and jump up and crack my heels a few times, I couldn't help it; but about the third crack, I noticed a sound that I knowed mighty well—and held my breath and listened and waited—and sure enough, when the next flash busted out over the water, here they come!—and just a laying to their oars and making their skiff hum! It was the king and the duke" (162-163). When Huck happens upon Uncle Silas in chapter 41, the situation may be compared to Rosset's "représentation panique" (i.e., when the contact with the real is direct, with neither lag nor anticipation, *ibid.*, 136: "So away I shoved, and turned the corner, and nearly rammed my head into Uncle Silas's stomach!" (217). It is interesting to note that it is always adult male figures who take Huck by surprise, who seem to represent this kind of sudden encounter with brute reality (even if Uncle Silas is, admittedly, harmless: "gentle as mush," TSD 111), whether prefigured or not. Men, in particular pap, the king and the duke, embody the unexpected, as we have seen (18, 20; in the case of the two frauds, this unexpectedness is often expressed through italics, superlatives, and exclamation points: 135, 155, 159, 160, 162, 170).

wreck with such a gang as that! But it warn't no time to be sentimentering. We'd *got* to find that boat, now—had to have it for ourselves. (60)

Then Jim manned the oars, and we took out after our raft. Now was the first time that I begun to worry about the men—I reckon I hadn't had time to before. I begun to think how dreadful it was, even for murderers, to be in such a fix. (61)

Feelings are not always immediate. "Sentimentering" does indeed take time.

Huck's decision in chapter 31 to go to hell rather than betray Jim is the finest example of thinking and feeling as a complex and subtle process, full of false starts, unexpected turns and reversals. It is fitting that Huck's soul-searching, which spans two pages, should give rise to what is surely one of the most syntactically complex sentences in the whole novel[61]:

---

61. – Unsurprisingly, Huck's dizzying passage through the fog provides the occasion for a number of impressive syntactical convolutions (68, 69). His forays into complicated grammatical structure in direct speech, on the other hand, often mean there is trickery afoot. Two examples will suffice: the first occurs in chapter 27, when Huck hoodwinks the duke and the king into believing the servants have stolen the gold: "They tip-toed away; so I seen, easy enough, that they'd shoved in there to do up your majesty's room, or something, sposing you was up; and found you *warn't* up, and so they was hoping to slide out of the way of trouble without waking you up, if they hadn't already waked you up" (147); the second, when Huck accounts for Mary Jane's sudden disappearance to her sisters in chapter 28: "Yes, she said, say she has run over for to ask the Apthorps to be sure and come to the auction and buy this house, because she allowed her uncle Peter would ruther they had it than anybody else; and she's going to stick to them till they say they'll come, and then, if she ain't too tired, she's coming home; and if she is, she'll be home in the morning anyway. She said, don't say nothing about the Proctors, but only about the Apthorps—which'll be perfectly true, because she *is* going there to speak about their buying the house; I know it, because she told me so, herself." After such a barrage of details and dependent clauses, what else could the sisters do but submit ("All right," 154)? This is not to say that *all* instances of Huck's yarn-spinning in direct speech have the same syntactical characteristics or, as a consequence, *precisely* the same aims (beyond the general one of fooling his listeners). Indeed, it often seems that a proliferation of subordinate clauses, as in the passages above, aims at obfuscation, whereas a style in which coordinating conjunctions predominate intends to break down any residual skepticism or indifference in his listener, not so much by complexity as by an inexorable accumulation of "tear-jerking" events (p. 52, 82, 218). The tactical, in other words, is already lurking within the syntactical. See also Huck's description of Uncle Silas's warming-pan (202, § 2) for complex syntax as an expression of confusion and absurdity.

> And at last when it hit me all of a sudden that here was the plain
> hand of Providence slapping me in the face and letting me know
> my wickedness was being watched all the time from up there in
> heaven, whilst I was stealing a poor woman's nigger that hadn't
> ever done me no harm, and now was showing me there's One
> that's always on the lookout, and ain't agoing to allow no such
> miserable doing to go only just so fur and no further, I most
> dropped in my tracks I was so scared. (168)

With this long inverted period, one has once again the impression of a backwoods pastiche of Milton. Here as elsewhere in *Huckleberry Finn*, departures from the comparatively simple conjunctive arrangements typical of Huck's naive style ("and...and...") [62] are always significant. Huck's syntax renders the involuted nature of the inner struggle (note the suggestion of movement in "I most dropped in my tracks," whereas Huck is in reality sitting inside the wigwam), the meanderings of feeling and thought. Huck may pause after writing the letter, but there is certainly no lull in cognitive activity:

> I felt good and all washed clean of sin for the first time I
> had ever felt so in my life, and I knowed I could pray now. But I
> didn't do it straight off, but laid the paper down and set there
> thinking—thinking how good it was all this happened so, and how
> near I come to being lost and going to hell. And went on thinking.
> And got to thinking over our trip down the river... (169)

This delay, like all the other major delays in *Huckleberry Finn*, will be fatal. Huck's lingering in memory eventuates in a complete reversal of his position. The long double detour through writing and then memory and then back to the materiality of the paper will reverse the intended course of action.

In our discussion on "easy water," we argued that the looping pattern of Huck's movements was in effect an interiorization of the flow of the river itself. Similarly,

---

62. – Cf. McKay 1985, 67; Bridgman 31, 36, 124; Fishkin 1993, 18. For a remarkable poetic rendering of the breathless, headlong rhythm of the child's conjunctive style, see the 1923 e.e. cummings poem "In Just-."

perception, thought, and feeling appear to have their own currents, eddies, snags, towheads, islands, and easy water. They are most often characterized by process and delay rather than immediacy.

It is possible to see Huck's use of the conjunction (to say nothing of his use of prepositions) as *already* an expression of process in its elemental form. Let us quote the philosopher Alfred North Whitehead here: "The taint of Aristotelian Logic has thrown the whole emphasis of metaphysical thought upon substantives and adjectives, to the neglect of prepositions and conjunctions." As a result of the absence of such "interconnections between real things," reality becomes static. For Whitehead, by contrast, reality is process:

> ... the very essence of real actuality—that is, of the completely real—is *process*. Thus each actual thing is only to be understood in terms of its becoming and perishing. There is no halt in which the actuality is just its static self, accidentally played upon by the qualifications derived from the shift of circumstances. The converse is the truth.[63]

For Huck, too, reality is an experiential continuum, even when the grammar he employs is comparatively unsophisticated. There is nothing particularly static about this sentence describing the circus, for instance, in which the "ands" proliferate:

> The minute he was on, the horse begun to rip and tear and jump and cavort around, with two circus men hanging onto his bridle trying to hold him, and the drunk man hanging onto his neck, and his heels flying in the air every jump, and the whole crowd of people standing up shouting and laughing till the tears rolled down. (120)

Rather, what is described is a series of overlapping, intermerging actions. And it is not only the verbs that lend dynamism to the passage; the conjunctions and prepositions meld the different elements into a total, fluid process. Yet even

---

63. – *Adventures of Ideas* (New York: Mentor, 1933) 275, 137, 273-274.

where the reality described appears to be static, as in the case of the Grangerfords' parlour or the Phelps farm, Huck's conjunctive style renders, if nothing else, the movement inherent in the very act of perceiving itself, the characteristic drift of his gaze.

In sum, then, we have not only perception of process—of the pulse of life on the river, for example, which gives us some of the most lyrical passages in *Huckleberry Finn*—but perception *as* process. The opening pages of chapter 19 provide several excellent examples of perceptual fluidity, in particular the oft-quoted first paragraph. In each case the rhythms of the prose mimic the flux of experience on (and of) the river. It is as if the river had become both subject and object of perception, the two intermingling in the act of writing itself.

A final word about the variations in tempo in *Huckleberry Finn*. The rhythm of Huck's movements reveals an extraordinary responsiveness to an ever-shifting reality, whether external:

> ... I went poking along over rough ground for a quarter of a mile or more (79);

> I didn't hurry, I couldn't if I'd a wanted to. I took one slow step at a time... (80);

> ... I took out after the raft, hot and heavy (68);

or internal:

> I never tried to do anything, but just poked along low-spirited and on the watch-out (18);

or both:

> I was paddling off, all in a sweat to tell on him; but when he says this, it seemed to kind of take the tuck all out of me. I went along slow then, and I warn't right down certain whether I was glad I started or whether I warn't (74);

> So we would put in the day, lazying around, listening to the stillness. (97)

The most powerful, moving passages (in all senses of the term) achieve a perfect harmony of form and content:

/   /   /   /   /

And how slow and still the time did drag along. (29)

Unstable Identities

It seems that the only way to secure one's identity in *Huckleberry Finn* is to locate the self in a space-time continuum leading up to the present, and that typically assumes the form of a narrative. This is what Huck does at the beginning of his own narrative (in the second paragraph of chapter 1), which nonetheless constantly underscores the risk of discontinuity in the experience of selfhood.

Huck's second death—i.e., his passage through the fog—is paradigmatic in this regard, insofar as the instability of his identity—or rather, the denial of this instability, its displacement—seems to contaminate Jim's as well. We recall from our analysis of chapter 15 the close link in Jim's mind between identity and space: "Is I *me*, or who *is* I? Is I heah, or whah *is* I?" (70). To try to convince Huck (and himself), Jim is forced to fill in the time-gap with a plausible narrative. In a pattern that has by now become familiar to us, to secure the present he must take a detour through the past, reconstructing the missing events, reassuring himself he exists in the present by virtue of his existence in the past:

> "Well, you answer me dis. Didn't you tote out de line in de canoe, fer to make fas' to de tow-head?"
>
> "No, I didn't. What tow-head? I hain't seen no tow-head."
>
> "You hain't seen no tow-head? Looky here—didn't de line pull loose en de raf' go a hummin' down de river, en leave you en de canoe behine in de fog?"
>
> "What fog?"
>
> "Why *de* fog. De fog dat's been aroun' all night. En didn't you whoop, en didn't I whoop, tell we got mix' up in de islands en one un us got los' en 'tother one was jis' as good as los', 'kase he didn' know whah he wuz. En didn't I bust up agin a lot er dem islands en have a turrible time en mos' git drownded? Now ain' dat so, boss—ain't it so? You answer me dat." (70-71)

This   passage   shows   just   how   problematic   narrative

restabilizing of the self can be. As Jim recounts the period
when their shared confusion was at its height, i.e. the passage
through the thickest patch of fog, the last paragraph moves
from "you" and "I" to "one" and "'tother." At that point
they passed into a zone where, with the disappearance of
bodily outlines and the contours of the riverscape, the
boundary lines between selves vanished.[64] Hence the
disappearance of distinguishing personal pronouns. It is no
longer clear to whom particular experiences belong, who was
"los'" and who was "as good as los.'" What is clear, on the
other hand, is that the stability of Jim's identity depends on
Huck's as a stable reference point; but in the fog this
landmark, like all others, simply disappeared, and along with
it the difference between self and other. Their reconciliation
at the end of the chapter simply confirms this
interdependence on a moral level. What is interesting is that,
once again, even *after* the trick has been revealed by the light
of day, the meaning of present reality must be secured by a
detour through the past, through narrative completion:

> "What do dey stan' for? I's gwyne to tell you. When I got
> all wore out wid work, en wid de callin' for you, en went to sleep,
> my heart wuz mos' broke bekase you wuz los', en I didn' k'yer no
> mo' what become er me en de raf'. En when I wake up en fine
> you back agin', all safe en soun', de tears come en I could a got
> down on my knees en kiss' yo' foot I's so thankful. En all you wuz
> thinkin' 'bout wuz how you could make a fool uv ole Jim wid a
> lie. Dat truck dah is trash; en trash is what people is dat puts dirt
> on de head er dey fren's en makes 'em ashamed."
> Then he got up slow, and walked to the wigwam, and went
> in there, without saying anything but that. But that was enough.
> It made me feel so mean I could almost kissed *his* foot to get him
> to take it back. (72)

Jim has in a sense replaced Huck as narrator of past events
(doesn't the reader depend heavily on *Jim's* eyes to see clearly in
the fog?). At the same time he denies Huck's identity as a

---

64. – Strawson acknowledges that in his model of a purely auditory universe the risk
of solipsism cannot be ruled out, in so far as material bodies—our basic reference
points—have disappeared and, along with them, the fundamental criterion for
distinguishing between the "me" and the "not me." See *Particulars* 81-86.

human being (Huck is now "trash"); and interestingly enough, the last sentence underscores the kind of undifferentiation that is the starting point for the building of a self. On a moral level what we are talking about is *reciprocity* (which extends, as Shelley Fisher Fishkin has so admirably shown, to language). This is what forms the solid basis of their friendship, built, paradoxically on the shifting sands of the radically unstable self. Their shared instability and confusion is what makes their admirable friendship possible. Too sharp a distinction between self and other—note that Jim calls Huck "boss" for the first time—rules out the possibliity of a friendship based on mutual recognition.

A "stable" identity is nothing but a plausible, continuous narrative (for many of the sentimental characters, as Huck is well aware, "plausible" means a narrative of continuous misfortune and suffering). The lesson to be drawn from Huck's success in tricking Jim and the case with which the latter persuades himself that it was all a dream is not that Jim is ignorant and gullible—he is no more so than any of the other characters Huck fools—but rather that it does not make much difference whether the grounds for selfhood are real or fictional. In this regard, persuasiveness is not a question of truth but rather of plausibility, of convincing narrative construction. In this, Huck is a true pragmatist, for as William James argued in a 1906 lecture on "Pragmatism's Conception of Truth":

> Truth lives, in fact, for the most part on a credit system.
> Our thoughts and beliefs "pass," so long as nothing challenges
> them, just as bank-notes pass so long as nobody refuses them.[65]

What challenges Huck's tale and Jim's "dream" is "trash" (71).

The proliferation of fictional narratives of the self is not only for reasons of survival in a hostile world; it underscores the basic instability of identity over time shared by most of the characters. Huck stands for the extreme case.

Pap starts "a new life" in chapter 5 before reverting to his old ways (23). Tom Sawyer pretends to be first William

---

65. – Williams James. *Pragmatism and The Meaning of Truth* (Cambridge, Mass: Harvard UP, 1978) 100.

Thompson, from Hicksville, Ohio (180), then his brother, Sid Sawyer (181), and finally reassumes his real identity once again (227-228). Jim is "Miss Watson's Jim" (10, 37), then simply "Jim," before going on to become, in a bewildering succession, a slave from Pike County headed for a farm below New Orleans with his white owner (103), a slave who has run away from St. Jacques' plantation (109), King Lear and a "Sick Arab" rolled into one (126), a runaway slave again (167); any one of a number of "heroes" (188) of European adventure: Iron Mask (190), Dantès (192), "Baron Trenck," "Casanova," "Benvenuto Chelleeny," Henry IV (188); and finally an ex-slave (226). The duke and the king, of course, are experts at assuming false identities (99, 105).

Phoenix-like, Huck goes through a series of figurative deaths and rebirths in the novel. On a conservative estimate— i.e., excluding the passages where Huck wishes he were dead (7, 73, 144, 173) or compares himself to a dead person (64, 68)—there are at least three: after his staged murder in chapter 7, the fog claims Huck's life a second time (70), and the Grangerford-Shepherdson massacre a third ("Laws bless you, chile," says Jim as they sail away from the shore, "I 'uz right down sho' you's dead agin," 95). Recall, too, Huck's, relief at finding out who he is at the Phelps farm: "it was like being born again, I was so glad to find out who I was" (177). Then, too, there is a long list of assumed or imposed identities (examples from the Rafsmen's passage have been reinserted in their proper place in the narrative sequence):

> Huck Finn (7)
> A "poor lost lamb" (*ibid.*)
> The Angel of Death (28)
> Sarah Mary Williams (51)
> George Peters (53)
> The son of victims of the wreck of the *Walter Scott* (61-62)
> Charles William Allbright (RP 240)
> Aleck James Hopkins (*ibid.*)
> The son of small-pox victims (74-75)
> George Jackson (79)
> A Boy from Pike County with his slave (103)
> Reverend Elexander Blodgett's servant "Adolphus" (127)
> Harvey Wilks's "valley" (136)
> A boy threatened at knife-point by a runaway slave (167)

"Tom Sawyer" (176-227)
Huck Finn (227)[66]

What further complicates matters is the layering of different masks. With Mrs. Judith Loftus Huck is playing the role of a person playing a role: he pretends to be a runaway apprentice boy (George Peters) who makes "a clean breast" of it after failing to pass himself off for a girl (Sara Mary Williams). In other words, as Mrs. Loftus says, he is "Sara Mary Williams George Elexander Peters."[67] Likewise, with the king and the duke, Huck is pretending to be a boy from Pike county on his way to his uncle Ben's farm, who in turn plays the part of Harvey Wilks's servant. The same is true of course of the duke and the king, though their real identities remain unknown. And as we shall see, even the dead are disguised in this novel.

The Book of Laughter and Forgetting (to Remember)

Chapter 13 of *Life on the Mississippi* ("A Pilot's Needs") insists on the necessity for a riverboat pilot to have a good memory (LM 118) and shows how difficult it was for Samuel Clemens to overcome the chronic weakness of his own. Like Huck, he forgot things easily and was consequently a poor impostor at times:

> ... although Smith, Jones, and Johnson are easy names to remember when there is no occasion to remember them, it is next to impossible to recollect them when they are wanted. How do criminals manage to keep a brand-new *alias* in mind? This is a great mystery. (LM 167)

---

66. – It is significant that it is a character explicity identified as coming from *Tom Sawyer*—Aunt Polly (7)—who re-establishes Huck's identity publicly (227). This seems to give a rather pessimistic conclusion to Huck's efforts to free himself from the emprisoning space of the companion volume.

67. – It is worth remarking that even Mrs. Loftus, doubtless one of the cleverest characters in the book, is ultimately taken in by a sad story—moreover, one of her own imagining ("You see, you're a runaway 'prentice—that's all. It ain't anything. There ain't any harm in it. You've been treated bad, and you made up your mind to cut," 52)! Thus, in spinning tales of suffering childhood, Huck is simply acting as a mirror wherein a whole society, from the dirt-poor Loftuses to the wealthy Grangerfords, may admire the reflection of its own sentimental self.

Clemens's attempt to travel *incognito* during his return trip to the Mississippi came to grief when a riverboat pilot called him by his real name, thus putting an end to his "fictitious-name business" (LM 183).

In *Huck Finn*, sincerity and deceitfulness are particular forms of memory or forgetfulness. Forgetting, or "disremembering" as Huck colloquially puts it (62), is among the most useful stratagems in the trickster's bag of tricks:

> I found Jim had been trying to get him [the king] to talk French, so he could hear what it was like; but he said he had been in this country so long, and had so much trouble, he'd forgot it. (109; brackets added)

> "What's the name of them people over on t'other side of the river that you all goes to see sometimes?"
> They says:
> "There's several; but it's the Proctors, mainly."
> "That's the name," I says; "I most forgot it. Well, Miss Mary Jane she told me to tell you she's gone over there in a dreadful hurry—one of them's sick."
> "Which one?"
> "I don't know; leastways I kinder forget, but I think it's—"
> "Sakes alive, I hope ain't *Hanner?*"
> "I'm sorry to say it," I says, "but Hanner's the very one."
> (152)

> "Yes, Miss Mary Jane she wanted you to do that. She says, 'Tell them to give Uncle Harvey and William my love and a kiss, and say I've run over the river to see Mr.—Mr.—what *is* the name of that rich family you uncle Peter used to think so much of?—I mean the one that—"
> "Why, you must mean the Apthorps, ain't it?"
> "Of course; bother them kind of names, a body can't ever seem to remember them, half the time, somehow." (154)

But so is a vigilant memory:

> ... I knocked at the door, and made up my mind I wouldn't forget I was a girl. (48)

In *Puddn'head Wilson*, Roxana, much like Huck, realizes at the outset that the success of her scheme to prevent her baby from being sold down the river requires training or "practicing":

> She put her cub in Tommy's elegant cradle and said—
> "You's young Marse *Tom* fum dis out, en I got to practice and git used to 'memberin' to call you dat, honey, or I's gwyne to make a mistake some time en git us bofe into trouble." (PW 14-15; cf. also TSD 147-148)

Imposture frequently boils down to this: efficient remembering or convenient forgetting. Or to put it another way, not forgetting to remember:

> "Well, try to remember it, George. Don't forget and tell me it's Elexander before you go, and then get out by saying it's George Elexander when I catch you." (53)

> They both got powerful mellow, but I noticed the king didn't get mellow enough to forget to remember to not deny about hiding the money bag again. (165)

> "Well, then," I says, "joking or no joking, if you hear anything said about a runaway nigger, don't forget to remember that *you* don't know nothing about him, and *I* don't know nothing about him." (178)

As with the layering of masks, the reader gets easily turned around in the labyrinth of negations of negations, of "not forgetting to remember to not deny."

Among the funniest—and the cruellest—passages in the book are those where the impostor's mask slips, when he is caught (or nearly caught) in the act of forgetting to remember. While travelling under an assumed identity, Huck is liable simply to forget what his name is (51, 82) or what his role (or that of others) implies, which is what happens more than once in conversation with Joanna; the duke and Tom slip up as well:

> "But I thought *you* lived in Sheffield?"
> I see I was up a stump. (137)

> "Why, I thought he'd be in the pulpit?"
> Rot him, I forgot he [i.e., the king] was a preacher. (138; brackets added)

> "Why, Harel—why, Joanna..." (139)

> "But *you* always went to church."

> Well, I was gone up again. I forgot I was the old man's servant. (139)
>
> "A farmer by the name of Silas Ph—" (172)
>
> "What! Why Jim is—" (178)

These last two examples show that the act of withholding, of remembering (or not forgetting) not to say is more than simply a strategy for survival or deception; it is also a recurrent structural device in the plot (as it will be in *Huck Finn and Tom Sawyer among the Indians*, 53). Like many other characters, Huck spends a lot of time keeping things to himself (8, 19, 29-30, 102, 125, 130; Poirier 95). The book as a whole is an extended interplay of volubility and muteness, of concealment and revelation.

In *Huckleberry Finn*, delayed disclosures appear to produce compensatory movements in space (in the case of the delayed disclosure of Jim's freedom, an elongation of narrative space). In a sense, they explain both the excitement of the downriver trip and the tediousness of the Phelps Farm episode.

If memory is clearly a burden (94, 146; CY 200), comedy often resides in the spontaneous or accidental unburdening of the conscience, in self-surrender to the joy of the moment, in self-forgetfulness:

> Then we took the trunk and put it in my wagon, and he drove off his way, and I drove mine. But of course I forgot all about driving slow, on accounts of being glad and full of thinking; so I got home a heap too quick for that length of a trip. The old gentleman was at the door, and he says:
> "Why, this is wonderful. Who ever would a thought it was in that mare to do it. I wish we'd a timed her. And she hain't sweated a hair—not a hair. It's wonderful. Why, I wouldn't take a hundred dollars for that horse now; I wouldn't, honest; and yet I'd a sold her for fifteen before, and thought 'twas all she was worth." (178)

It is obvious too from this example that plausibility is a function of *time* as well as direction (Tom's instructions show he is aware of this relation: "you turn back and fool along slow, so as to get to the house about the time you ought to,"

178). But then again, Uncle Silas is a believer in miracles.

In a famous phrase, Twain described *Huckleberry Finn* as "a book of mine where a sound heart and a deformed conscience come into collision and conscience suffers defeat" (quoted in Doyno 167). We would argue that the "heart" should be seen as a temporal relation, a certain quality of memory, and not as some abstract virtue or benevolent reflex (though Huck is undeniably benevolent). The climactic episode in this conflict is of course chapter 31. There the triumph of the heart depends on Huck's reminiscing ("got to thinking over our trip down the river," 169) [68], which stands in stark contrast to the short memory of the king and the duke, which Huck stresses on the previous page ("after all we'd done for them scoundrels," 168). Without a doubt there is virtue in remembering:

> "Dat *wuz* de smartes' doge! I tell you, chile, I 'speck it save' ole Jim—ole Jim ain't gwyne to forgit you for dat, honey" (76);

as well as vice: the blackguard king has a prodigious memory (111, 130). It is in keeping with the sentimental strain in *Huckleberry Finn* that in the virgin and the child, in Mary Jane (149) as in Huck, forgetting is symptomatic of a truthfulness deeper than any lie. The comparison may seem outrageous. After all, Mary Jane is constitutionally incapable of lying: "I don't want no better book than what your face is," Huck tells her; "A body can set down and read it off like coarse print" (151). Huck, on the other hand, is an inveterate liar, knows a good lie when he sees one, and lives in a world where everyone lies except a few select women ("I never seen anybody but lied, one time or another, without it was Aunt Polly, or the widow, or maybe Mary," 7). Huck's chronic forgetting, however, has more than mere comic value; it needs to be interpreted as a sign of his fundamental goodness. Huck cannot lie when his heart is not in it—whether he likes to admit it or not. Being caught telling an unbelievable lie

---

68. – Richard Poirier, in "*Huckleberry Finn* and the Metaphors of Society," presents an opposing view stressing, among other things, the ease with which Huck forgets Jim (99).

provides the occasion for one of the most hilarious examples of Huck's humorlessness:

> "Set down, my boy, I wouldn't strain myself, if I was you. I reckon you ain't used to lying, it don't seem to come handy; what you want is practice. You do it pretty awkward."
> I didn't care nothing for the compliment, but I was glad to be let off, anyway. (158; cf. Doyno 99)

Then, too, the resolution of the moral crisis in chapter 31 depends on Huck's deep-seated honesty: "You can't pray a lie—I found that out" (169). As might be expected, the parting scene in chapter 28 bonds Huck and Mary Jane in an image of steadfast, mutual loyalty:

> "*Good*-bye—I'm going to do everything just as you've told me; and if I don't ever see you again, I shan't ever forget you, and I'll think of you a many and a many a time, and I'll *pray* for you, too!"—and she was gone.
> Pray for me! I reckoned if she knowed me she'd take a job that was more nearer her size. But I bet she done it, just the same—she was just that kind. She had the grit to pray for Judus if she took the notion—there warn't no backdown to her, I judge. You may say what you want to, but in my opinion she had more sand in her than any girl I ever see; in my opinion she was just full of sand. It sounds like flattery, but it ain't no flattery. And when it comes to beauty—and goodness too—she lays over them all. I hain't ever seen her since that time that I see her go out of that door; no, I hain't ever seen her since, but I reckon I've thought of her a many and a many a million times, and of her saying she would pray for me; and if ever I'd a thought it would do any good for me to pray for *her*, blamed if I wouldn't a done it or bust. (152; first apostrophe in "shan't" removed in accordance with HF-WMT 244)

The same sense of reciprocity that we saw between Huck and Jim governs these lines as well. Huck follows suit, repeating Mary Jane's phrase "a many and a many," and even outdoes her in his refusal to forget.

This sentimentalism needs to be qualified, however. The disturbing and inescapable conclusion of our analysis is that empathy, goodheartedness, and tricksterism have the *same* source, i.e. in the willingness or the courage to step outside the self, to resemble another.[69] There is an undeniable moral quality to remembering and forgetting, which, together with reverence for nature, are the principal manifestations of the heart; at the same time, they are the instruments of guile. Is Huck to be trusted? How can we reconcile, on the one hand, the fundamental unreliability of his memory (46) and his artful use of forgetting (to conceal his ignorance for example, 20; TSC 144) with, on the other hand, his ability to learn "easy enough" the duke's speech from Shakespeare (111) or the king's story of his encounter with Tim Collins ("the king told him everything, just like the young fellow had said it—every last word of it," 130), to say nothing of the difficulty of remembering the events in the novel as a whole? Nor should we neglect the fact that every time Huck says, "Honest, I'll tell you everything, just as it happened" (163), he never keeps his promise. Huck never tells all. The openness that characterizes his relationship with Jim ("I told Jim everything," 165) is in fact, on both sides, only partial (cf. 46, 102, 125; 229). Writing, as we have seen, is a way of overcoming a weak memory, but it is also a tool of imposture. Huck escapes the charge with difficulty. Or should we instead consider the implausibility of the narrative as an illustration of *Huckleberry Finn*'s "magical" realism (Quirk 100)?

Irreversibility and Counterfactuals

In terms of temporality, one of the key events in *Huckleberry Finn* occurs in chapter 30, where, during one of his major escapes, Huck realizes something crucial about the irreversibilty of time:

> When I struck the town, I see there warn't nobody out in

---

69. – "Le courage consiste parfois non pas à être différent des autres, mais très humblement à leur ressembler. Contre les tentations de l'automatisme le courage sera un effort toujours vigilant vers la simplicité, le naturel et l'impartiale honnêteté, quoi qu'il en puisse coûter à notre égoïsme; il électrise la volonté toujours prête à s'installer à l'enseigne de son bon vouloir; il défait les 'genres' que nous nous donnons, même si notre genre (le plus subtil de tous) est de n'en avoir pas," Vladimir Jankélévitch, *Les vertus et l'amour*, vol. 1 (Paris: Flammarion, 1986) 132.

the storm, so I never hunted for no back streets, but humped it straight through the main one; and when I begun to get towards our house I aimed my eye and set it. No light there; the house all dark—which made me feel very sorry and disappointed, I didn't know why. But at last, just as I was sailing by, *flash* comes the light in Mary Jane's window! and my heart swelled up sudden, like to bust; and the same second the house and all was behind me in the dark, and wasn't ever going to be before me no more in this world. She *was* the best girl I ever see, and had the most sand. (162)

Nostalgia[70] is a special time and place, an instant of joy instantaneously swallowed up in the darkness of the past. Commentators have often remarked, and rightly so, on the nostalgia that pervades *Huckleberry Finn*, a novel set "Forty to Fifty Years Ago," before war and modernity transformed life on the Mississippi forever (HF-WMT xxxviii-xxxix). If it were just a question of "sentimental atmosphere," however, it would not even be worth dwelling on. We would submit that nostalgia contributes to the popularity and greatness of the work because of the way in which Twain made the recognition of irreversibility a cornerstone of Huck's moral and intellectual development. And a concomitant of this growth is Huck's ability to imagine counterfactual situations, alternative pasts and presents, in other words his ability to *fictionalize* and futhermore to use those fictions as a yardstick to pass

---

70. – The very specificity of Huck's description of this instant suggests that nostalgia, which supposes a memorial geography of distinct, non-interchangeable places, is in constant tension with the convertibility of space that we have remarked elsewhere. Jankélévitch analyzes this paradoxical nature of nostalgic space: "Et d'abord le paradoxe le plus général est celui d'un espace nostalgique où les lieux ne sont pas interchangeables et indifférents comme ils devraient l'être dans l'espace abstrait et homogène des géomètres. Car la géométrie n'a rien à voir avec la nostalgie... C'est pour les mathématiciens que tout lieu en vaut un autre; et c'est au contraire pour un cœur nostalgique qu'il existe un espace concret diversifié par les sites qualitativement hétérogènes, par le contraste des climats et par toute la variété pittoresque des nations. Aussi peut-on parler d'une espèce de géographie pathétique, d'une topographie mystique dont la seule toponymie, par sa force évocatrice, met déjà en branle le travail de la réminiscence et de l'imagination. La valeur, sur cette mappemonde passionnelle, est inégalement répartie: elle se concentre en certains points privilégiés...," Vladimir Jankélévitch, *L'Irréversible et la nostalgie* (Paris: Flammarion, 1974) 341.

judgement on human actions (his own in particular), to evaluate reality rather than to replace it (as Tom always wishes to do). Simply put, coming into maturity means being able to use a moral grammar of conditionals and might-have-beens. Chapter 31 shows very clearly that moral development goes hand in hand with increased grammatical sophistication (but, unfortunately, so does underhandedness!).

We have already shown the importance of belatedness in the novel and its relationship to guilt. Guilt might be described as a hypersensitivity to time, a painful awareness of its (often tragic) irreversibility, of our powerlessness to change the past. Consider these examples:

> It was fifteen minutes before I could work myself up to go and humble myself to a nigger—but I done it, and warn't ever sorry for it afterwards, neither. I didn't do him no more mean tricks, and I wouldn't done that one if I'd a knowed it would make him feel that way. (72)

> "I wish I'd never seen that snake-skin, Jim—I do wish I'd never laid eyes on it." (77)

> I was mighty down-hearted; so I made up my mind I wouldn't ever go anear that house again, because I reckoned I was to blame, somehow. I judged that that piece of paper meant that Sophia was to meet Harney somewheres at half-past two and run off; and I judged I ought to told her father about that paper and the curious way she acted, and then maybe he would a locked her up and this awful mess wouldn't ever happened. (95)

These examples should not mislead us, though. Counterfactuals are not only expressions of regret and shame. In chapter 16, which anticipates the crisis of chapter 31, what Huck feels is not so much guilt as a sense of moral confusion that will later lead to the defeat of his "deformed conscience":

> Then I thought a minute, and says to myself, hold on,—s'pose you'd a done right and give Jim up; would you felt better than what you do now? No, says I, I'd feel bad—just the same way I do now. Well, then, says I, what's the use you learning to do right, when it's troublesome to do right and ain't no trouble to do wrong, and the wages is just the same? I was stuck. I couldn't answer that. So I reckoned I wouldn't bother no more about it, but after this always do whichever come handiest at the time. (76;

cf. Doyno 141-142)

This sort of imaginative projection into alternative pasts or presents defines Huck's "mature, empathic thought" (Doyno 153), and Jim's as well.[71] Recall the latter's reaction to the misfortunes of the "dolphin" ("Po' little chap," 66) or his refusal to abandon Tom:

> "Well, den, dis is de way it look to me, Huck. Ef it wuz *him* dat 'uz bein' sot free, en one er de boys wuz to git short, would he say, 'Go on en save me, nemmine 'bout a doctor f'r to save dis one?' Is dat like Mars Tom Sawyer? Would he say dat? You *bet* he wouldn't! *Well*, den, is *Jim* gwyne to say it? No, sah— I doan' budge a step out'n dis place, 'dout a *doctor*; not if it's forty year!" (216; closing single quotation mark, missing from Norton edition, added; cf. HF-WMT 340)

A corrolary of Huck's recognition of irreversibility is his rejection of the idea of reform: "It was awful thoughts, and awful words, but they was said. And I let them stay said; and never thought no more about reforming" (170). The weight of habit and training (CY 52, 65, 155, 162) on the one hand and the obduracy of native "disposition" (TSSE2, "What is Man," 766) on the other are recurrent themes in Twain's writings, which are rife with failed, "impossible schemes of reform" (IA 508): from the narrator's "dying" resolution to give up smoking in *Roughing It* (RI 214-219) to Tom's Sawyer's efforts to be a good boy (TS 75) to Tom Driscoll's repeated promises to mend his ways in *Puddn'head Wilson* (PW 73). The "uplifting" examples of conversions—such as the Hunt letter in *Life on the Mississippi* (LM 360-369) or, in this novel, the "reformed pirate" (i.e., the king) in chapter 20 or the repentant cutthroat who leaves the anonymous letter in chapter 39—are in fact frauds. In a word, Twain's writings are full of phony converts and true reprobates and backsliders. The fallacy of reform consists in ignoring the effects of time and "education" (66, 124, 154, 168), pretending as if the past had no influence on

---

71. – For other examples of counterfactual thinking in the novel see: 51, 58, 61, 92, 93, 94, 141, 147, 158, 160, 163, 167, 168, 199, 209, 220-221.

the present, as if its effects could be instantly cancelled out. Huck's moral retreat and Jim's "minstrel darky" behavior in the Phelps farm episode are perhaps intended to make just this point, that the corrupting effects of the "peculiar institution" of slavery are bound to endure, even in those who have seen and lived beyond it. Perhaps the ending of *Huckleberry Finn* is not "inexcusably happy" (Quirk 37) after all, despite the sudden freeing of the two runaways. If the sequels Twain imagined but left unfinished are any indication of his thinking here, these changes do not usher in a new era of millennial hope. Far from it. Though free, Jim lives under constant threat: "there was white men around our little town that was plenty mean enough and ornery enough to steal Jim's papers from him and sell him down the river again" (HFTSAI 34). For Jim, oppression and bondage will assume new guises (wrongful imprisonment for murder, captivity at the hands of Indians). As Huck puts it in *Tom Sawyer's Conspiracy*: "he was a free nigger this last year and more, and that made everybody down on him, of course, and made them forget all about his good character"; "of course he hain't got any friends, becuz he's free" (TSC 188,194).[72]

Finally, we should not omit Huck's closing counterfactual, which seems to call the whole process of writing into question:

> ... and so there ain't nothing more to write about, and I am rotten glad of it, because if I'd a knowed what a trouble it was to make

---

72. – See Doyno's excellent discussion of the Phelps Farm's possible historical subtext in the "convict-lease" system (228-239), which enabled authorities in the South to transform Black freedmen, easily convicted on charges such as "vagrancy," into conscript labor. This system "had been used prior to the Civil War in the North" but "grew to dominate the post-War Southern penal process" (231). Doyno remarks that a "manumitted Black would certainly not enjoy genuine freedom in 1845" (the time-frame of *Huck Finn*), when kidnappings by "slave-hunters" and legal loopholes made re-enslavement the fate of many freedmen ("For example, anyone could contest the freed status of a Black such as Jim by claiming that he was not in Missouri when Miss Watson died," 230). But with post-War abuses of the convict-lease system, neither would Southern Blacks be "genuinely free" in 1885. This lends bitter irony to the idea of "setting a nigger free that was already free before" (228)

a book I wouldn't a tackled it and ain't agoing to no more. (229)

Thus, paradoxically, a book imbued with nostalgia ends up making us thankful that the past *is* irreversible.

Time and Tom Sawyer

> "It's all right, I've got it. Take my trunk in your wagon, and let on it's your'n; and you turn back and fool along slow, so as to get to the house about the time you ought to; and I'll go towards town a piece, and take a fresh start, and get there a quarter or a half an hour after you; and you needn't let on you know me, at first." (178).

The ambition of Tom's schemes in the Phelps farm episode, from this prank to the "evasion" itself, is to secure control not only of space but also time. That Huck should let "driving slow" slip his mind completely seems symptomatic of his contrasting indifference to the niceties of synchronization. Whether in St. Petersburg or in Arkansas, Huck cannot live by the clock; he cannot come and go "to time" (7). "Regular" hours are an anathema to him. The "lovely" time on the raft does not tick away; it is not geared to a pendulum, portioned out in units, or punctuated by bells. Rather, it follows the leisurely flow of the river itself: "Two or three days and nights went by; I reckon I might say they swum by, they slid along so quiet and smooth and lovely" (96). Two *or* three days and nights, what does it matter? The life that Jim and Huck lead stands civilized, shore time on its head:

> After midnight the people on shore went to bed, and then for two or three hours the shores was black—no more sparks in the cabin windows. These sparks was our clock—the first one that showed again meant morning was coming, so we hunted a place to hide and tie up, right away. (98)

The clock is borrowed and inverted. Given this rebellious attitude towards time, it is fitting that Huck's major attempt in the Wilks episode to modulate the rhythm of events to suit his own purposes ("so I could take my own time, if I wanted to") should be a fiasco: "everything was going so different from what I had allowed for " (161).

Tom is the official time-keeper of *Huckleberry Finn*:

> Tom's 'most well, now, and got his bullet around his neck on a watch-guard for a watch, and is always seeing what time it is... (229);

as he will be for the adventures to come:

> And then Tom he talked along, and talked along, and says, le's all three slide out of here, one of these nights, and get an outfit, and go for howling adventures amongst the Injuns, over in the Territory, *for a couple of weeks or two...* (228-229; emphasis added)

For Tom even "howling adventures" in "Ingean Territory"[73] have a time limit. During the escape preparations, he appeals to the "best authorities" to speed things up (with the "nonnamous" letters) or, in most cases, to slow things down.

Like the Widow's, Tom's concept of the "regular" is moral. Like plausibility, duty has a clear temporal dimension: "By rights I reckon we ought to be a couple of years" (192), as do all the values that come into play in the Phelps farm episode. Honor and glory are directly proportional to the time-span of the "evasion":

> Tom was in high spirits. He said it was the best fun he ever had in his life, and the most intellectual; and said if only he could see his way to it we would keep it up all the rest of our lives and leave Jim to our children to get out; for he believed Jim would come to like it better and better the more he got used to it. He said that in that way it could be strung out to as much as eighty year, and would be the best time on record. And he said it would make us

---

73. – "The area known as Indian Territory originally included all the present state of Oklahoma, except the panhandle, and was set aside by the federal government as a home for certain Indian tribes who had been forced to relocate there during the 1820s and 1830s. Never an organized territory, it became a haven for white outlaws" (HF-WMT 422n). Doyno points out that the "idea of 'lighting out for the Territory' would make good sense" for Jim. "In 1846 the Wilmot Poviso, although not passed into law, had suggested a norm that there would be no slavery or involuntary servitude 'except for crime, whereof the party shall first be duly convicted'" (Doyno 230).

> all celebrated that had a hand in it. (196)
>
> "Why, Aunty, it cost us a power of work—weeks of it—hours and hours, every night, whilst you was all asleep" (225).

The result of trying to impose the time-schemes of Romantic fiction on reality is not efficiency but waste, as we shall see in more detail in our next chapter. Tom's motto is: "*Maggiore fretta, minore atto.* Got it out of a book—means, the more haste the less speed" (203). The longer, the more tedious, the more excruciating—the better: "I bet we can find a way that's twice as long. There ain't no hurry; le's keep on looking around"; "Now we're all right. We'll *dig* him out. It'll take about a week!" (185). In one of those internal echoes that are so much a part of the peculiar esthetic of *Huck Finn*, the time-scale of Tom's escape plans corresponds to the life-cycle of a feud:

> "Well," says Buck, "a feud is this way. A man has a quarrel with another man, and kills him; then that other man's brother kills *him*; then the other brothers, on both sides, goes for one another; then the *cousins* chip in—and by-and-by everybody's killed off, and there ain't no more feud. But it's kind of slow, and takes a long time." (89)

The correspondence is hardly surprising, given that the ethos of European romance is behind both of these "jackass ideas," to use Huck's strong language (195). Tom has world enough and time for everything but Huck's irritating questions as to the sense of what they are making or doing. The meaning of Jim's armorial insignia? "We ain't got no time to bother over that" (203).

Tom gives a very apt definition of fiction writing in general and plot construction in particular: "Why, drat it, Huck, it's the stupidest arrangement I ever see. You got to invent *all* the difficulties. Well, we can't help it, we got to do the best we can with the materials we've got" (188). Tom does invent his *own* plot (time-frame included), and—in an eery echo of the warning in the "Notice"—he gets shot for his reckless disregard of authority. Caveat lector!

By-and-by

The adverbial phrase "by-and-by," which appears over sixty times in the novel (Bridgman 32), is arguably the most revealing expression of Huck's vision of time. More than a mere synonym for "soon," "before long," "later on," or "eventually," it expresses something profound about the way Huck perceives and experiences events, about his idea of fate. A terse, vivid rendering of the very idea of sequentiality, "by-and-by" is also part and parcel of the deep narrative logic of *Huckleberry Finn*.

The idea for staging the murder, for example, comes to Huck "by-and-by":

> Well, I didn't see no way for a while, but by-and-by pap raised up a minute, to drink another barrel of water, and he says:
>
> "Another time a man comes a-prowling round here, you roust me out, you hear? That man warn't here for no good. I'd a shot him. Next time, you roust me out, you hear?"
>
> Then he dropped down and went to sleep again—but what he had been saying give me the very idea I wanted. (30)

(But of course, the reader will not know exactly what this idea is until "by-and-by.") Similarly, what draws pap away from the shanty comes in due time: "By-and-by along comes part of a log raft..." (30). On Jackson's island, a loaf of bread seems to drift Huck's way providentially: "But by-and-by along comes another one, and this time I won" (34). The same goes for:

> the raft that helps Jim escape: "I see a light a-comin' roun' de p'int, bymeby" (40);

> the news Huck is seeking from Mrs. Loftus: "I was afeard I had made a mistake coming to her to find out what was going on in the town; but by-and-by she dropped onto pap and the murder..." (49);

> and the answer to the question of Jim's whereabouts on the Phelps farm: "By-and-by Tom says: 'Looky here, Huck, what fools we are, to not think of it before!'" (183).

In *Huckleberry Finn*, things come to those who know how to wait, who let time do its work.

By-and-by smacks of inevitability, of what will necessarily come to pass. By-and-by is not only "soon" but "sooner or later." As Jim says when Huck scoffs at his prediction of bad luck from the snake skin: "Dont you git too peart. It's a-coming," (46). By-and-by, through its very imprecision, seems to hint ominously at the mysterious and inalterable workings of fate. It points to what is looming, what is bound to occur, ultimately, eventually, unavoidably—never mind when, exactly:

> I judged the old man would turn up again, by and by, though I wished he wouldn't. (15)

> "—and by-and-by everybody's killed off, and there ain't no more feud." (89)

Prophecies come true in good time:

> "What you want to want to know when good luck's a-comin' for? want to keep it off?" And he said: "Ef you's got hairy arms en a hairy breas', it's a sign dat you's agwyne to be rich. Well, dey's some use in a sign like dat, 'kase it's so fur ahead. You see, maybe you's got to be po' a long time fust, en so you might git discourage' en kill yo'sef 'f you didn' know by de sign dat you gwyne to be rich bymeby" (41; cf. 228).

It is just a question of time before Huck meets with adventure:

> By-and-by says I, "Hel-*lo*, Jim, looky yonder!" It was a steamboat that had killed herself on a rock (56);

or excitement:

> There was considerable whiskey drinking going on, and I seen three fights. By-and-by somebody sings out—"Here comes old Boggs!—in from the country for his little old monthly drunk—here he comes, boys!" (114);

or human cowardice and stupidity:

> Well, by-and-by somebody said Sherburn ought to be lynched. In about a minute everybody was saying it; so away they went, mad and yelling, and snatching down every clothes-line they come to, to do the hanging with. (117)

It is only a matter of time before Huck will be called to

account: "And by-and-by they had me up to tell what I knowed" (158). Or before reality gives him a rude awakening:

> Now I was feeling pretty comfortable all down one side, and pretty uncomfortable all up the other. Being Tom Sawyer was easy and comfortable; and it stayed easy and comfortable till by-and-by I hear a steamboat coughing along down the river—then I says to myself, spose Tom Sawyer come down on that boat?—and spose he steps in here, any minute, and sings out my name before I can throw him a wink to keep quiet? Well, I couldn't *have* it that way—it wouldn't do at all. I must go up the road and waylay him. (177)

Time is an important factor in the convertibility of lived space. One can get used to almost anything after a while:

> At first I hated the school, but by-and-by I got so I could stand it. Whenever I got uncommon tired I played hookey, and the hiding I got next day done me good and cheered me up. So the longer I went to school the easier it got to be. I was getting sort of used to the widow's ways, too, and they warn't so raspy on me. Living in a house, and sleeping in a bed, pulled on me pretty tight, mostly, but before the cold weather I used to slide out and sleep in the woods, sometimes, and so that was a rest to me. I liked the old ways best, but I was getting so I like the new ones, too, a little bit. The widow said I was coming along slow but sure, and doing very satisfactory. She said she warn't ashamed of me. (18)

Of course this training will be undone by pap's prison regime ("I didn't see how I'd ever got to like it so well at the widow's"). And though Huck becomes innured to this way of life, its outcome is foreseeable: "But by-and-by pap got too handy with his hick'ry" (24).

Finally, the use of "by-and-by" would seem to support our argument that in *Huckleberry Finn* reality is process. This might involve coming to a decision or a resolution: "By-and-by I says to myself, I can't live this way; I'm agoing to find out who it is that's here on the island with me; I'll find it out or bust. Well, I felt better, right off" (37). Or it might be the culmination of a learning or warming-up process: Huck's practicing in the calico gown and the sun-bonnet: "by-and-by I could do pretty well in them" (48); or the duke's calling

Shakespeare back "from recollection's vaults": "By-and-by he got it" (110). Or it might be the outcome of a natural process: the gradual coming into focus of landmarks on the river at dawn ("by-and-by you could see a streak on the water, "96), or the wake of a steamboat finally reaching the raft on a still river ("and by-and-by her waves would get to us, a long time after she was gone, and joggle the raft a bit," 98), or the passing of a storm ("and by-and-by the storm let up for good and all," 104).

History according to Huck Finn

> "You read about them once—you'll see. Look at Henry the Eight; this'n 's a Sunday-School Superintendent to *him*. And look at Charles Second, and Louis Fourteen, and Louis Fifteen, and James Second, and Edward Second, and Richard Third, and forty more; besides all them Saxon heptarchies that used to rip around so in old times and raise Cain. My, you ought to seen old Henry the Eight when he was in bloom. He *was* a blossom. He used to marry a new wife every day, and chop off her head next morning. And he would do it just as indifferent as if he was ordering up eggs. 'Fetch up Nell Gwynn,' he says. They fetch her up. Next morning, 'Chop off her head'—and they chop it off. 'Fetch up Jane Shore,' he says; and up she comes. Next morning, 'Chop off her head'—and they chop it off. 'Ring up fair Rosamun.' Fair Rosamun answers the bell. Next morning, 'Chop off her head.' And he made every one of them tell him a tale every night; and he kept that up till he had hogged a thousand and one tales that way, and then he put them all in a book, and called it Domesday Book—which was a good name and stated the case. You don't know kings, Jim, but I know them; and this old rip of ourn is one of the cleanest I've struck in history. Well, Henry he takes a notion he wants to get up some trouble with this country. How does he go at it—give notice?—give the country a show? No. All of a sudden he heaves all the tea in Boston Harbor overboard, and whacks out a declaration of independence, and dares them to come on. That was *his* style—he never give anybody a chance." (124)

Huck confounds historical periods and geographical zones. He conflates fact and fiction. He is not alone in this, however; nor is Twain's intention merely to entertain the reader at Huck's expense. The semi-literate boy's mixed-up chronicle of English kings is symptomatic of a broader cultural confusion—namely, the "Sir Walter disease"—under which the South as a whole labours:

> There, the genuine and wholesome civilization of the nineteenth century is curiously confused and commingled with the Walter Scott Middle-Age sham civilization and so you have practical, common-sense, progressive ideas, and progressive works, mixed up with the duel, the inflated speech, and the jejune romanticism of an absurd past that is dead, and out of charity ought to be buried. (LM 327)

In other words, there is a scrambling of time-frames in the southern mind (Twain will take his artistic revenge by reversing the direction of this "transposition of epochs" in his historical romance *A Connecticut Yankee in King Arthur's Court*, by bringing the nineteenth century to the sixth).[74] We should recall that the books that help create this confusion of geography and history[75], fact and fiction in Huck's comical survey of European royalty come from "the truck the gang had stole" off the *Walter Scott*: They are at once the source and the fruit of "adventure"; they are all about "style":

> I read considerable to Jim about kings, and dukes, and earls, and such, and how gaudy they dressed, and how much style they put on, and called each other your majesty, and your grace, and your lordship, and so on, 'stead of mister; and Jim's eyes bugged out, and he was interested. (64)

Furthermore, they make it all the easier for Huck and Jim to

---

74. – As the Yankee time-traveler Hank Morgan confides to the reader: "I had had confidential agents trickling through the country some time, whose office was to undermine the knighthood by imperceptible degrees, and to gnaw a little at this and that and the other superstition, and so prepare the way gradually for a better order of things." Among other subversive stratagems, he transforms selected knights-errant into roving billboards advertising soap and toothcare products (CY 83; 139, 180).

75. – In 1883, Twain hit upon the idea of a history board game to teach children names, dates, battles, and statistics. He secured a patent for the invention (later to be called "Mark Twain's Memory-Builder") in 1885 but eventually shelved the project in 1892 (NJ3 19-24).

be taken in by those frauds, the king and the duke:

> "By rights I am a duke!"
>   Jim's eyes bugged out when he heard that; and I reckon mine did, too. (100)

> "Bilgewater, I am the late Dauphin!"
>   You bet you Jim and me stared, this time. (101).

Finally, they also make it easier, after the tyranny of these humbugs, to come under the dominance of Tom, who has read widely in such literature. Huck's "admiration" for his friend's literacy can be traced back to *Tom Sawyer*; in chapter 10 of that book, Tom teaches Huck how to form his first letters (TS 72). In *Huckleberry Finn* Tom's power over Huck and Jim (as over his gang in chapter 2) derives from the written word. It is by appealing to defunct "authorities" that Tom lords it over Huck and Jim. Tom "superintends" (205). Recall also that the final phase of the escape preparations reinforces this domination. In order to conform to the historical and fictional models culled from Tom's reading (HF-WMT 421n), Huck plays the role of a servant-girl (210); Tom, that of Jim's parent ("I'm his mother," 211). Clearly there is power in literacy, but it becomes tyranny when based on false, retrogressive models such as those upheld by romance.

Culture in *Huckleberry Finn* signifies the reign of authority, closure—and confusion, whether in the king's etymology (135), the duke's Shakespeare soliloquy (111), Huck's historical survey of European kings (124), or Tom's adventure fiction and heraldry. "Style" can coexist harmoniously with ignorance:

> "What's a bar sinister?"
> "Oh, *I* don't know. But he's go to have it. All the nobility does."
> (203)

Rank and tradition would appear to be inseparable from illegitimacy. Is it merely a coincidence that the two river-going homages to European literature in *Huckleberry Finn*—the *Walter Scott* and the *Lally Rook* (175)—are both wrecks?

Chapter 3
Illusion

But at the same time the thought *will* intrude itself upon me, How can they see what is not visible? What would you think of a man who looked at some decayed, blind, toothless, pock-marked Cleopatra and said: "What matchless beauty! What soul! What expression!" What would you think of a man who gazed upon a dingy, foggy sunset, and said: "What sublimity! what feeling! what richness of coloring!" What would you think of a man who stared in ecstasy upon a desert of stumps and said: "Oh, my soul, my beating heart, what a noble forest is here!"

You would think that those men had an astonishing talent for seeing things that had already passed away. It was what I thought when I stood before "The Last Supper" and heard men apostrophizing wonders, and beauties and perfections which had faded out of the picture and gone, a hundred years before they were born. We can imagine the beauty that was once in an aged face; we can imagine the forest if we see the stumps; but we cannot absolutely *see* these things when they are not there. (IA 151-152)

"O, my poor boy, thy foolish reading hath wrought its woful work at last and ta'en thy wit away!" (PP 67).

But there warn't no Spaniards and A-rabs, and there warn't no camel nor no elephants. It warn't anything but a Sunday-school picnic, and only a primer-class at that.... I didn't see no di'monds, and I told Tom Sawyer so. He said there was loads of them there, anyway; and he said there was A-rabs there, too, and elephants and things. I said, why couldn't we see them, then? He said if I warn't so ignorant, but had read a book called "Don Quixote," I would know without asking. He said it was all done by enchantment. (16)

He spoke of me all the time, in the blandest way, as "this prodigious giant," and "this horrible sky-towering monster," and "this tushed and taloned man-devouring ogre;" and everybody took in all this bosh in the naivest way, and never smiled or seemed to notice that there was any discrepancy between these watered statistics and me. (CY 31)

Taking the Romance out of It, Throwing Style into It

In all of his major works, from *The Innocents Abroad* onwards, Twain's writing re-enacts time and again the sobering confrontation of high-flown romantic representation and mundane, unpleasant or even violent reality. It shows the danger of taking it for granted that in books we find faithful depictions of reality and reliable guides to action. "Indeed, Twain devoted a major portion of his writing to the project of helping his reader learn to avoid the sin of literalness" (Fishkin 1993, 61), as a brief survey of his writings leading up to *Huckleberry Finn* will demonstrate.

It is the constantly reiterated vocation of *The Innocents Abroad* (1869) to expose all manner of "romantic frauds," from one end of the Old World to the other: the story of Abelard and Héloïse ("the history that Lamartine has shed such cataracts of tears over" at last "stripped of the nauseous sentimentality" 112-117); various fictional stereotypes such as the *grisette* ("another romantic fraud," 119), the peasant girl ("a glaring fraud," 154), the Turkish bath redolent of the "odors of Araby" ("a poor, miserable imposture," 297), the love of the Arab for his horse ("a fraud," 378), the fierce Bedouin (383; "To glance at the genuine son of the desert is to take the romance out of him forever," 434-435), and finally the sacred grottoes of the Holy Land ("bogus," 421). As the narrator exclaims at one point: "When I think how I have been swindled by books of Oriental travel, I want a tourist for breakfast" (297). The aim, then, is to strip away the overlay of "poetry and nonsense" (392) that has accumulated from bookish representations of reality, to show what "one's actual vision" is, to reveal the "dreary" and the "unpoetical" when truth requires it (403). In *The Innocents Abroad* this general process of correcting distorted or otherwise exaggerated representations has a distinct spatial component that Twain calls "reduction," i.e., restoring the true dimensions to what poetry, romance, and sacred history have magnified beyond all realistic physical proportion, especially for those, like the pilgrims in the book, who are used to the scale of American geography. What is being reduced is the Old World (385).

In *Roughing It* (1872), the narrator's mind is full of illusions big and small. He is the victim of "book-frauds" (RI 211). He discovers, for instance, that the sentimental literature that extols the steadfast loyalty of the horse is a poor guide to reality; his own runs away: "We gave them up without an effort at recovering them, and cursed the lying books that said horses would stay by their master for protection and companionship in a distressful time like ours" (RI 212). More importantly, all of the narrator's dreams, all his get-rich-quick schemes and romantic projects—timber-ranching, silver-mining, speculation—come a cropper. All of his pre-conceived notions of the romance of "roughing it" are belied by events. His naive yearning for adventure in the deserts of the Wild West simply cannot withstand the demystifying force of circumstance:

> This enthusiasm, this stern thirst for adventure, wilted under the sultry August sun and did not last above one hour. One poor little hour—and then we were ashamed that we had "gushed" so. The poetry was all in the anticipation—there is none in the reality. (RI 123)

> ... truly and seriously the romance all faded far away and disappeared, and left the desert trip nothing but a harsh reality—a thirsty, sweltering, longing, hateful reality! (RI 124).

Even the trip to earthly paradise—the Sandwich Islands—is doomed to disappoint expectations:

> When the sun sunk down—the one intruder from other realms and persistent in suggestions of them—it was tranced luxury to sit in the perfumed air and forget that there was any world but these enchanted islands.
> It was such ecstasy to dream, and dream—till you got a bite. A scorpion bite. Then the first duty was to get up out of the grass and kill the scorpion; and the next to bathe the bitten place with alcohol or brandy; and the next to resolve to keep out of the grass in future. (RI 434).

Twain's critique extends to the embellishments of history as well, epitomized by the tragic fate of Captain Cook at the hands of bloodthirsty natives:

> Plain unvarnished history takes the romance out of Capt.

Cook's assassination, and renders a deliberate verdict of justifiable homicide. Wherever he went among the islands he was cordially received and welcomed by the inhabitants, and his ships lavishly supplied with all manner of food. He returned these kindnesses with insult and ill-treatment. (RI 490-491)

Similarly, the historical research Twain did for *The Prince and the Pauper* (1881), though at times "erratic and inaccurate"[76], helps to reveal the lurid underside of Tudor England, with its barbaric laws and widespread poverty and ignorance. Finally, the first two chapters of *Life on the Mississippi* (1883) also claim to set the historical record straight—even if at the cost of a few "stretchers."[77] The aim is to lay a firm foundation for the physical and historical grandeur of the Mississippi River, giving it "a most respectable outside-aspect of rustiness and antiquity" (LM 42). This can only be done by exploding competing European pretensions—with the help of an authentic *American* historian, Francis Parkman. The demolition work is to be done by showing the "colossal ironies" and rank illegitimacy of prior claims on the Mississippi basin made on behalf of "Louis XIV of inflated memory" (LM 45; or "Louis the Putrid," LM 48). In this instance, taking the romance out of it means taking *Europe* out of America's— indeed the world's—greatest river. The French acquisition of the waterway was nothing short of an act of "robbery" ceremonialized, "consecrated" by the priesthood (LM 48). Moreover, if one "groups a few neighbouring historical dates and facts," one realizes that many of the great landmarks of European history and culture of which Americans feel so envious *postdate* De Soto's discovery of the Mississippi in 1542, or are at best roughly contemporaneous with it. For instance, when the white man first laid eyes on the river, the "absurd chivalry business" which was later to plague the South in bastardized form was "in full feather" (LM 42). The plain fact

---

76. – Cf. PP 301. For a full analysis of Twain's use of sources, see the *Works of Mark Twain* edition: Victor Fisher, Lin Salamo, eds. *The Prince and the Pauper* (Berkeley: U of California P, 1979).
77. – Such as the "fact" that the Mississippi drains the state of Delaware. Cf. James M. Cox's Introduction, LM 22-23.

is—so Twain's argument runs—the river was *already there*, making much of America's European heritage mere importation, when it is not out-and-out imposture ("sham civilization," LM 327) leading in one instance to tragedy of epic proportions (see Twain's "wild proposition" that Scott was "in great measure" responsible for the Civil War, LM 328).[78] Thus there is no need to revere the romantic past of Europe. The date 1542 is indeed "quite respectable for age" (LM 41).

Huckleberry Finn continues this task of debunking.[79] The first hint of this is on the title page: "Time: Forty to Fifty Years Ago" (2). The time-frame places the action not only in the "flush times" of steamboating on the Mississippi but squarely within the period when, according to Twain, the Sir Walter Scott disease had reached epidemic proportions in the South (LM 328; Doyno 258), destroying the salutary after-effects of the Enlightenment and the French Revolution—reversing in other words the whole tide of History:

> Then comes Sir Walter Scott with his enchantments, and by his single might checks this wave of progress, and even turns it back; sets the world in love with dreams and phantoms; with decayed and swinish forms of religion; with decayed and degraded systems of government; with the sillinesses and emptinesses, sham grandeurs, sham gauds, and sham chivalries of a brainless and worthless long-vanished society. (LM 327)

Moreover, in the South this baleful influence flourishes "pretty

---

78. – For a discussion of this "wild proposition," see Dekker 272-281.

79. – As will the unfinished sequel *Huck Finn and Tom Sawyer among the Indians,* the main artistic aim of which is to debunk the romanticized depiction of the Indian in James Fenimore Cooper's novels. Tom is once again cast as the purveyor of illusions, Cooper his source, Jim and to a lesser extent Huck his converts. But Tom eventually learns how hard "roughing it" in Indian Territory actually is; and before the manuscript breaks off in chapter 9, Huck notices a decided change in his friend: "You see, he had about got it through is noddle, by this time, that book Injuns and real Injuns is different" (HFTSAI 35-37, 50, 70-71, 79). Cf. also Twain's 1870 piece "The Noble Red Man" (TSSE1 442-446), as well as NJ1 324 and IA 161-162, 423. On Twain's consistently dim view of Indians within the broader context of race, see Shelley Fisher Fishkin's excellent article under this heading " in *The Mark Twain Encyclopedia.*

forcefully still"—i.e., in 1883, which falls within the period of the composition of *Huckleberry Finn*. Twain's title for this particular chapter of *Life on the Mississippi* is, significantly, "Enchantments and Enchanters."

If one of the aims of his literary vocation is to undeceive, Twain is also conscious of the extraordinary tenacity of illusions, the fate of which remains to a large extent uncertain in *Huckleberry Finn*.

True, the "sham chivalry" (LM 327) which still flourishes in the Grangerford family eventuates not in honour and glory but in an unspeakable bloodbath. Then, too, the high seriousness of the "graveyard school" of romantic sentimentality is comically deflated by Huck's naive vision, in particular by the crude comparisons he uses to describe Emmeline Grangerford's "crayons":

> One was a woman in a slim black dress, belted small under the armpits, with bulges like a cabbage in the middle of the sleeves, and a large black scoop-shovel bonnet with a black veil, and white slim ankles crossed about with black tape, and very wee black slippers, like a chisel... (84)[80]

And throughout the narrative, "lying books" are arraigned once again: Huck's first-hand experience with animals during the flooding of Jackson's island—"they got so tame, on account of being hungry, that you could paddle right up and put your hand on them if you wanted to; but not the snakes and turtles—they would slide off into the water" (44)—is opposed to Tom's false notions borne of fiction-reading: "Every animal is grateful for kindness and petting, and they wouldn't *think* of hurting a person that pets them. Any book will tell you that" (205).

In addition, the make-believe of Tom Sawyer's band of robbers (chapters 2 and 3) gives way to Huck's all-too-real encounter with the bandits on board the *Walter Scott* and his narrow escape from the gallows with the duke and the king

---

80. – For another example of comic deflation, see the narrrator's "hair-raising" encounter with the legendary desperado Slade in *Roughing It* (RI 67-68).

(*Tom Sawyer* follows a similar trajectory as the boys move from playing Robin Hood to witnessing the graveside murder of Doctor Robinson by Injun Joe). Pap's purported death is followed by his real one in the floating house. Huck's skepticism, even if motivated by an old wives' tale—"I knowed mightly well that a drownded man don't float on his back, but on his face" (15)—seems indicative of his suspicion of neat, imaginary resolutions to problems.

It is not the least of Jim's qualities that he is perceptive enough to realize how hazardous the delusions of fiction can be when the probable consequences outweigh any thrill the adventure might produce:

> I told him all about what happened inside the wreck, and at the ferry boat; and I said these kinds of things was adventures; but he said he didn't want no more adventures. He said that when I went in the texas and he crawled back to get on the raft and found her gone, he nearly died; because he judged it was all up with *him*, anyway it could be fixed; for if he didn't get saved he would get drownded; and if he did get saved, whoever saved him would send him back home so as to get the reward, and then Miss Watson would sell him South, sure. Well, he was right; he was most always right; he had an uncommon level head, for a nigger. (64)[81]

In the *Walter Scott* episode Huck is once again between Tom and Jim. The former is Huck's model:

> "Do you reckon Tom Sawyer would ever go by this thing? Not for pie, he wouldn't. He'd call it an adventure—that's what he'd call it; and he'd land on that wreck if it was his last act. And wouldn't he throw style into it?" (57)

> I was just a-biling with curiosity; and I says to myself, Tom Sawyer

---

81. – See also the book-crazed travelers to the Holy Land in *The Innocents Abroad*: "Some of us will be shot before we finish this pilgrimage. The pilgrims read 'Nomadic Life' [a highly romanticized account of life in Palestine] and keep themselves in a constant state of quixotic heroism. They have their hands on their pistols all the time, and every now and then, when you least expect it, they snatch them out and take aim at Bedouins who are not visible, and draw their knives and make savage passes at other Bedouins who do not exist." Though the author escapes unscathed, these "romantic frenzies" lead to real trouble as two parties are stoned by Bedouins a few pages later (IA 429-430, 437; brackets added).

> wouldn't back out now, and so I won't either; I'm agoing to see
> what's going on here. (58)

But the moral of the episode suggests that the *narrator*
acknowledges with hindsight the wisdom of Jim's position ("he
was most always right"); as a character, however, Huck shows
that any lucidity accruing from his harrowing experience with
real robbers will be wiped out by the books that are the booty
of the very same adventure (64).

On the plot level, then, illusion does appear to prevail. To
give just a few additional examples: Boggs's killing in chapter 21,
to which we shall return, is followed by an elaborate one-man
re-staging of the event, which the townsfolk find as convincing
as the real thing: "The people that had seen the thing said he
done it perfect; said it was just exactly the way it all happened.
Then as much as a dozen people got out their bottles and
treated him" (117). The scenario is performed once again—but
with a happy ending—by the seemingly drunk rider in the circus.
Jim's true story of his daughter's deafness is followed by the
duke's shamming. Huck's real escape in chapter 7, while not
unaided by an element of fiction, stands in sharp contrast to
Tom's swashbuckling vision of Jim's escape. True, in this last
case fiction seems to be outstripped by reality in the end, as
Tom gets shot and Jim recaptured, put in chains, and placed
under close guard; reality is nonetheless recast as "adventure" in
the closing pages of the book when Tom explains everything to
his aunts (226-227). Thus illusion seems to have the last word.
Indeed, the sequel *Huck Finn and Tom Sawyer among the
Indians* begins with Huck and Jim being taken in once again by
Tom's bookish fantasies about Indians, (HFTSAI 37).

The key to understanding the opposition between Huck
and Tom as regards romance is latter's appeal to the authority
of Cervantes, which we have quoted as an epigraph to this
chapter. This appeal is of course based on a total misreading
of *Don Quixote*. As Twain writes in *Life on the Mississippi*:

> A curious exemplification of the power of a single book for
> good or harm is shown in the effects wrought by Don Quixote and
> those wrought by Ivanhoe. The first swept the world's admiration

for the mediaeval chivalry-silliness out of existence; and the other restored it. As far as the South is concerned, the good work done by Cervantes is pretty nearly a dead letter, so effectually has Scott's pernicious work undermined it. (LM 329)

Tom Sawyer is a representative of the Walter Scott school (the two names unite in a common spirit of adventure in chapters 12 and 13); Huck, the Sancho Panza of the novel, stands for that of Cervantes. The foregoing quotation is, in addition, a rather remarkable acknowledgement of how fragile the whole process of debunking by means of fiction can be, how fiction can "snatch a victory from the jaws of defeat." It is quite possible to argue that *Huckleberry Finn* simply restores romance on a higher level—think of Huck's naive vision of the circus or his boundless admiration for Mary Jane Wilks. If the reader has little difficulty perceiving Huck's blind spots in the first example, it is not altogether certain that the treatment of his infatuation for Mary Jane escapes the charge of pandering to a genteel literary taste. Nor is there any doubt that Twain's ultimate triumph in this novel is the successful illusion of a semi-literate boy as narrator-author—a boy able, in other words, to turn his story into a book shortly after learning to "spell, and read, and write just a little" (18). "Huck's story as novel is impossibility followed by implausibility and linked together by unlikelihood"; but the quality of the illusion is such that most of the time these sorts of questions simply do not arise: "The enchantment, the atmosphere of mind, conveyed by Huck's narrative presence is too pleasing, too hypnotic, to permit skepticism. There is considerable magic in the realism of *Huckleberry Finn*" (Quirk 100).

Perhaps an anecdote from *Life on the Mississippi* will help us put this "magical realism" into perspective. Chapter 52 of that work presents a moving letter penned by a semi-literate ex-prisoner, "Jack Hunt," to a former cell-mate named Williams, who was still serving time. The letter, full of grammar and spelling mistakes, details Hunt's tribulations after his release and his eventual conversion to Christianity thanks to Williams's support and encouragement. This is the narrator's reaction after hearing the letter, "the most remarkable one I had ever encountered" (LM 369):

> Here was true eloquence; irresistible eloquence; and
> without a single grace or ornament to help it out. I have seldom
> been so deeply stirred by any piece of writing. (LM 365)

The letter became a sensation and was read in churches far
and wide: "The marvellous letter did its wonted work; all the
people were moved, all the people wept"; "numbers of people
got copies of the letter"; "copies were sent to the Sandwich
Islands and other far regions." Twain's writer-friend Charles
Dudley Warner was the first person to voice any suspicions
about the authenticity of the letter:

> "... it is too neat, and compact, and fluent, and nicely put
> together for an ignorant person, an unpractised hand. I think it
> was done by an educated man" (LM 366).

Indeed, "The literary artist had detected the literary
machinery." The letter turned out to be

> ... the confoundedest, brazenest, ingeniousest piece of fraud and
> humbuggery that was ever concocted to fool poor confiding
> mortals with!
>   The letter was a pure swindle, and that is the truth. And
> take it by and large, it was without compeer among swindles. It
> was perfect, it was rounded, symetrical, complete, colossal! (*ibid.*)
>
> "Jack Hunt," the professed writer of the letter, was an imaginary
> person. The burglar Williams—Harvard graduate, son of a
> minister—wrote the letter himself, *to* himself: got it smuggled out
> of the prison; got it conveyed to persons who had supported and
> encouraged him in his conversion—where he knew two things
> would happen: the genuineness of the letter would not be doubted
> or inquired into; and the nub of it would be noticed, and would
> have a valuable effect—the effect, indeed, of starting a movement
> to get Mr. Williams pardoned out of prison. (LM369)

In *Huckleberry Finn*, we too may detect the "literary
machinery" but still admire the ingeniousness of the hoax.

Style: The Art of Wasting

Flamboyance, glitter, gaudiness, ostentation, sham,
supererogation, extravagance, profligacy, prodigality, point-

lessness, futility, waste, meaninglessness, delusion, enslavement, death—"style" is all of these things in Twain, and many more besides. Style is the mantle of poetic elegance, the trappings and the suits of romance and "modern" chivalry—the flourish of the swashbuckler, the pomp and regalia of the well-born (87), the finery of the gentleman. In language as in dress, in thought as in action, style is always "high-toned," to use Tom's favorite expression (12; TS 213). Style is education (154). Style loves to quibble, to make "gold-leaf distinctions," to borrow Huck's phrase (191). Style is form bereft of content, high-sounding words shorn of meaning, distorted, or made silly (say, "honor" as used by the Grangerfords, "ransom" by Tom, "orgies" by the king). On a conceptual level, style seems to oscillate between the otiose (words that do not signify, kings who "just set around," 65) and the absurd (like the scheme to "set a nigger free that was already free before," 228). Style is family heirlooms like Uncle Silas's "noble brass warming-pan," which are valuable, as Huck explains, "not on account of being any account because they warn't, but on account of them being relicts, you know" (202). In a word, style is the mark of human vanity. It reminds us that "the trail of the serpent is over us all" (IA 416).

By definition style is what is *de trop.* It is uselessness, mere ornament, like metaphorical language according to Tom Sawyer: "They don't put ruffles on a shirt to help keep a person warm, do they?" (TSA 31). The description of Aunt Polly's glasses in *Tom Sawyer* highlights this purely ornamental aspect:

> The old lady pulled her spectacles down and looked over them, about the room; then she put them up and looked out under them. She seldom or never looked through them for so small a thing as a boy; they were her state pair, the pride of her heart, and were built for "style," not service;—she could have seen through a pair of stove lids as well. (TS 9)

Style, as this quotation reveals, is what one takes pride in ("proud" and "grand" apply well to the high-style Grangerfords and their ilk, 87, 88). Which may of course mean a trinket or a relatively small object, like a pair of glasses; but the word often smacks of the oversized, the monumental, the awe-inspiring (as with the cognate term "gaudy": "gaudy big grindstone," 204; "gaudier chances," 207). In Huck's naïve vision, this may even include a craft that steamboat pilots would look down on—a raft:

> We slept most all day, and started out at night, a little ways behind a monstrous long raft that was as long going by as a procession. She had four long sweeps at each end, so we judged she carried as many as thirty men, likely. She had five big wigwams aboard, wide apart, and an open camp fire in the middle, and a tall flagpole at each end. There was a power of style about her. It *amounted* to something being a raftsman on such a craft as that. (72)

The "flush times" of steamboating on the Mississippi were an epoch of high style; in those days, nothing was too good, money was no object:

> We had a perfect love of a sounding boat—long, trim, graceful, and as fleet as a greyhound; her thwarts were cushioned; she carried twelve oarsmen; one of the mates was always sent in her to transmit orders to her crew, for ours was a steamer where no end of "style" was put on. (LM 111).

Purpose and utility are utterly beside the point where style is concerned. Style is devoid of meaning. When the boys play pirates on a raft in chapter 13 of *Tom Sawyer*, Tom's commands—"Luff, and bring her to the wind!" "Steady, steady-y-y-y!" "Let her go off a point!"—are there for "style," as the narrator points out: "As the boys steadily and monotonously drove the raft towards mid-stream, it was no doubt understood that these orders were given only for 'style,' and were not intended to mean anything in particular" (TS 88). As befits so noble a concept, style is usually decked out in ironic quotation marks in Twain—except in *Huckleberry Finn,* where the irony is located rather on the level of reading. If Huck sees through the veneer of style, it is without realizing it. The reader must supply the quotation marks.

Style makes no sense. It is pure foolishness, as Joanna Wilks—who must surely be counted among the sharpest minds in the novel—concludes:

> "Blame it, do you suppose there ain't but one preacher to a church?"
> "Why, what do they want with more?"
> "What!—why to preach before a king? I never see such a girl as you. They don't have no less than seventeen."
> "Seventeen! My land! Why, I wouldn't set out such a string as that, not if I *never* got to glory. It must take 'em a week."
> "Shucks, they don't *all* of 'em preach the same day—only *one* of 'em."
> "Well, then, what does the rest of 'em do?"
> "Oh, nothing much. Loll around, pass the plate—and one thing or another. But mainly they don't do nothing."
> "Well, then, what are they *for*?"
> "Why, they're for *style*. Don't you know nothing?"
> "Well, I don't want to know no such foolishness as that." (138-139)

Joanna, as we recall, is the one who "gives herself to good works" (129). Which appears to be a waste of time in this case: style is something that cannot be gainsaid. It is gratuitous and therefore proof against logic and reason. In this respect, *Huckleberry Finn* already anticipates the pessimistic turn of Twain's later writings, such as *A Connecticut Yankee*, in which Hank Morgan fondly imagines he can extinguish chivalry and knighthood "by making it grotesque and absurd" (CY 200-201). Nevertheless, there are clear voices of reason in *Huck Finn*. Like Joanna Wilks, Huck and Ben Rogers intuitively grasp that Tom's bookish notions of style are little better than foolishness (192, 13). And in this they all agree with the doctor, who calls the result of Tom's putting into practice his romantic ideas—i.e., his delirium—"wild foolishness" (223; cf. Jim's going "out of his head" because of Huck's Tom-like prank, 46)

   As one critic puts it: "It seems that Twain did link, as in a constellation, the following of hollow, meaningless, or destructive forms in monarchy, religion and literary adventures" (Doyno 161). Style is the missing term here; style is what ties these three pillars of culture together in the common cause of futility and idleness. We have just seen king and church mentioned together in Huck's argument with Joanna. The episode of the *Walter Scott* brings royalty and adventure together. The books taken from that wreck are "about kings, and dukes, and earls, and such, and how gaudy they dressed, and how much style they put on." From them Huck learns that style is doing nothing—what kings and preachers do in common—and being paid handsomely for it!

> "How much do a king git?
>   "Get?" I says; why, they get a thousand dollars a month if they want it; they can have just as much as they want; everything belongs to them."
>   "*Ain'* dat gay. En what dey got to do, Huck?"
>   "They don't do nothing! Why how you talk. They just set around."
>   "No—is dat so?"
>   "Of course it is. They just set around. Except maybe when there's a war; then they go to the war. But other times they just lazy around; or go hawking... " (64-65; cf. also TSC 140)

(In one of the numerous ironic twists Twain gives to the structure of the novel, Jim will become a king—Lear—and a hero of adventure fiction—Dantès[82], et al—before enjoying a life of wealth and idleness, 228). The duke and the king, (who is also a "preacher": "Preachin's my line... and "missionaryin' around," 99) also have an "easy life" (102) aboard the raft, where they are waited on hand and foot by Huck and Jim. As Huck later complains, "Sometimes I wish we could hear of a country that's out of kings" (125). Hank Morgan's diatribe against the nobility in *A Connecticut Yankee* will later echo this satire in *Huckleberry Finn*: "some dregs, some refuse, in the shape of a king, nobility and gentry, idle, unproductive, acquainted mainly with the arts of wasting and destroying, and of no sort of use or value in any rationally constructed world" (CY 109-110).[83]

The king and the duke are artful wasters. Certainly the most poignant expression of disgust at the wanton destruction

---

82. – Note too that Jim, like Edmond Dantès, consummates his revenge against the men responsible for his imprisonment (182).
83. – "The institution‹s› of royalty, in any form, is an insult to the human race" (NJ3 424).

wreaked by those travesties of nobility is to be found in chapter 31:

> After all this long journey, and after all we'd done for them scoundrels, here was it all come to nothing, everything all busted up and ruined, because they could have the heart to serve Jim such a trick as that, and make him a slave again all his life, and amongst strangers, too, for forty dirty dollars. (168)

To add insult to injury, the king apparently squanders part of this on drink, and gambles the rest away in a "doggery" (171). The most tragic example of the artistocratic arts of wasting and destroying can be found in the Grangerford-Shepherdson feud, which spans generations, with entire families butchered until not a man in either clan is left standing (89).

Tom's models have always been those "high up in the nobility—dukes and such" (TS 213). In *Huckleberry Finn*, he relays the king and the duke in chapter 32 as the new representative of extravagance. Accordingly, his scheme for the "evasion" of the "prisoner of style" (211) is a textbook example of sheer wastefulness. It is prodigal of everything, short of human lives. First, household goods (candles, a candlestick, plates, a sheet, a spoon), clothes (a shirt), and food (flour, butter) are stolen, torn up, ground down, ruined, thrown away (202). Then effort and time. The jobs—digging, making the pens and the inscription and the journal, hauling the grindstone—are "distressid-tough," as Huck puts it (202). But given Tom's slavish adherence to his romantic models, there is no alternative. The effort has to be gruelling, heroic, superlative ("They *always* make their pens out of the hardest, toughest, troublesomest piece of old brass candlestick or something like that they can get their hands on," 190).[84] Therein lies the "glory" (206; TSC 136), which is directly proportional to the amount of pointless effort expended (Fetterley, BSC 446). That is what makes the entreprise "gaudy" (189). Even actions not directly connected with the "evasion," such as when the boys

---

84. – One of the most telling contrasts between the two boys lies in their use of superlatives. Huck's are nearly always based on experience and often convey a naive sense of wonder; Tom's are consistently bookish and delusional.

turn in for the night, have to be romanticized by an inordinate amount of effort, and fraught with real danger:

> Then we started for the house, and I went in the back door—you only have to pull a buckskin latch-string, they don't fasten the doors—but that warn't romantical enough for Tom Sawyer: no way would do him but he must climb up the lightning-rod. But after he got up half-way about three times, and missed fire and fell every time, and the last time most busted his brains out, he thought he'd got to give it up; but after he was rested, he allowed he would give her one more turn for luck, and this time he made the trip. (185)

In pursuit of the "romantical," Tom nearly kills himself. Later on, in chapter 41, Huck happens upons a pithy expression for this idea that "bookish delusions have consequences" (Doyno 245) when he lies to the doctor about Tom's gunshot wound: "'He had a dream,' I says, 'and it shot him'" (217). "Singular dream" indeed, as the doctors says!

We should note incidentally that later on in the Phelps farm episode, Tom is compelled to take the stairs to get to his room because his hands "was so sore" (194). "Full of principle," though, he has to "let on" that the stairs are a lightning-rod. Thus in *Huckleberry Finn*, fictions are continuously self-consuming and self-perpetuating artifacts. The consequences of one (sore hands from tunnelling for the "evasion"), rather than militating in favour of realism, simply create the need for yet another, for still more "letting on," in an endless cycle in which fiction always appears to have the last word. Fictions are, as it were, "eternal" in the way natural organisms are loosely considered to be: the individual "lives on" in the successive generations of the species. This may be observed earlier in the same chapter, a half an hour before the boys turn in, when Tom acknowledges that the case-knives they are using are not adequate to the task at hand:

> "If we was to put in another night this way, we'd have to knock off for a week to let our hands get well—couldn't touch a case-knife with them sooner."
> "Well, then, what we going to do, Tom?"
> "I'll tell you. It ain't right, and it ain't moral, and I wouldn't like it to get out—but there ain't only just the one way;

we got to dig him out with the picks, and *let on* it's case-knives."
(193-194)

The same consequence of pretending has thus led to two
further, compensatory acts of make-believe. Characteristically,
Tom's moment of lucidity is short-lived; his reluctant admission
shows how morality ultimately depends on fiction to sustain
itself, to provide at least the semblance of fidelity, the form if
not the content. It is hard to imagine a more radical stance
than Twain's on this score. As was the case in chapter 3, for
Tom ignorance is unawareness of the necessities of fiction.

In contrast, it is Huck's lack of "style," his fundamental
indifference to forms and ficitional codes—"Picks is the thing,
moral or no moral; and as for me, I don't care shucks for the
morality of it, nohow"—or rather his awareness of their lack of
purchase on reality, that will allow him to bring about his
remarkable self transformation in chapter 31, for it is his
recognition of the ultimate futility of "letting *on* to give up sin"
(168) that enables him to "take up wickedness again" (169).
The truly extraordinary thing about that passage, the stamp of
Twain's consummate artistry, is the way in which Huck's
intuitive realism allows him, not to escape fictionality
altogether, but rather to choose the fiction (i.e., that of his own
damnation) most likely in reality, if least likely in appearance,
to lead to right action. Huck can thus hit at truth, but only
within a closed loop of fictionality. His recognition of Jim's
humanity must still be defined within the terms laid down by
the social conventions of the South. Tom's attachment to
"letting on" makes this sort of moral progress impossible for
him. One of the functions of the Phelps Farm episode—perhaps
its ultimate justification in esthetic terms—is to demonstrate
this fundamental difference between the two boys.

To return to the subject of wasted time and effort:
unfortunately for Tom, the chroniclers of these Herculean
labours—those who run what Twain was to call in *A
Connecticut Yankee* the "exaggeration mill" (CY 25)—are not
distinguished men of letters but rather a gaggle of country
gossipers:

"A dozen says you!—*forty* couldn't a done everything

> that's been done. Look at them case-knife saws and things, how
> tedious they've been made; look at that bed-leg sawed off with
> 'em, a week's work for six men..."
>
>   "Why, dog my cats, they must a ben a house-full o' niggers
> in there every night for four weeks, to a done all that work, Sister
> Phelps. Look at that shirt—every last inch of it kivered over with
> secret African writ'n done with blood! Must a ben a raft uv'm at
> it right along, all the time, amost." (219)

Jim is of course the one who has done most of the work ("we
was all pretty much fagged out, too, but mainly Jim," 209). The
doctor can see he is "all tired out" because has been "worked
main hard, lately" (223). (And to think that at one point Tom
dares to say that all their efforts to throw style into the escape
are "just about wasted on him," 207!)

    In our view, then, the end of the novel needs to be read
with an eye to this futility, to the wasted time, effort, material
and—the most precious of all—over 3 weeks freedom for Jim.
Twain's comment on his visit to the dungeons of the Château
d'If in *The Innocents Abroad* is apposite here. Of Abbé Faria's
efforts, he concludes:

> It was a pity that so many weeks of dreary labor should have
> come to naught at last. (IA 84)

Tom's orchestration of Jim's escape is thus the ultimate
expression of the rank folly, of the reckless wastefulness of
style—or its literary analogue, adventure. As such, it stands,
structurally speaking, in sharp opposition to the escapes of
both Huck and Jim, once again justifying the Phelps farm
episode in esthetic terms. Huck's remark as he is finishing up
his preparation of the murder scene in chapter 7 heralds this
key opposition: "I did wish Tom Sawyer was there, I knowed
he would take an interest in this kind of business, and throw
in the fancy touches. Nobody could spread himself like Tom
Sawyer in such a thing as that" (31; cf. also 154, 179). When
Huck stages his own escape, he wastes neither time ("I didn't
lose no time," 32) nor material goods (note how sparing he is
with the corn meal, 31-32). As regards time, the same holds
true for Jim's flight ("I lit out mighty quick, I tell you," 39).
Furthermore, within the Phelps farm episode, both argue in

favor of escaping forthwith: Huck's plans could be carried out "the first dark night that comes" (184); Jim is "for having us hunt up a cold chisel to cut the chain off of his leg with, right away, and clearing out without losing any time " (195). All things considered, Huck's enthusiastic reaction to Tom's escape plan ("it was worth fifteen of mine, for style," 184) is not much of a compliment at all (inadvertently or not, Huck introduces an element of doubt with the qualifying tag "for style," which undercuts the whole effect of the praise, much as in, "he had an uncommon level head, for a nigger," 64).

Cost, trouble, waste—these three considerations guide Huck and Jim's pragmatic criticisms of Tom's escape plans[85]:

> "Now, the way I look at it, a hickry-bark ladder don't cost nothing, and don't waste nothing..." (189)

> "Well, then, what's the sense in wasting the plates?" (190).

> "... I ain't got no us f'r no flower, nohow, en she'd be a pow'ful sight o' trouble."

> "One er dem big cat-tail-lookin' mullen-stalks would grow in heah, Mars Tom, I reck'n, but she wouldn' be wuth half de trouble she'd coss." (207)

Tom and Huck follow the path of least resistance, shy away from trouble, avoid squandering anything. They are endowed with something of which Tom is totally innocent—foresight (both are always concerned about where their food and clothing are going to come from, 36, 45, 77). But as we have seen, arguments against style are to no avail. Style splurges, spends as if there is no tomorrow. Style is quixotic. Tom is not amenable to rational or pragmatic criticism, for he is quite simply elsewhere, in a land of romantic delusion:

> "What do we want of a moat, when we're going to snake him out from under the cabin?"

---

85. – Huck's opposition to Tom's extravagance continues in the planning sessions in *Tom Sawyer's Conspiracy*. Tom lives to regret his folly in the same work, as his mindless pursuit of style for its own sake runs the risk of sending Jim to the gallows: "But he said he'd got his lesson, and warn't going to throw any more chances away for glory's sake; no, let glory go, he was for business, from this out. He was going to save Jim the *quickest* way, never mind about the showiest" (TSC 144,198).

> But he never heard me. He had forgot me and everything else. (189)

> "*Now* I know how to fix it. We'll send you some things by them."
> "I said, 'Don't you do nothing of the kind; it's one of the most jackass ideas I ever struck;' but he never paid no attention to me; went right on. It was his way when he'd got his plans set" (195).

Huck asserts at one point, when the boys are digging the tunnel, that "Letting on don't cost nothing; letting on ain't no trouble"(193). Though he may be right in this specific instance, where it is preferable for the boys to *pretend* they have spent thirty-seven years at it, the statement is clearly false if applied to the novel as a whole. In the end, letting on exacts a high price indeed.

This is not to say that *all* forms of extravagance are stigmatized in *Huckleberry Finn*. As we have already observed, there are no absolutes in Twain's thought.[86] Counter-examples always crop up in the narrative. Two will suffice for our purposes here. The first is the circus in chapter 22, where the theme of wastefulness appears once again at the outset, as Huck sneaks in without paying: "I ain't opposed to spending money on circuses, when there ain't no other way, but there ain't no use in *wasting* it on them" (119). There then follows Huck's naive report of a spectacle of lavish proportions, the ladies "looking just like a gang of real sure-enough queens, and dressed in clothes that cost millions of dollars, and just littered with diamonds." Accordingly, the superlatives come thick and fast ("splendidest," "loveliest," "most astonishing," "funniest," "gaudiest," "prettiest"). The high point of the show is the "drunk" who sheds "seventeen suits," revealing himself to be the most elegant of trick riders (120). In a word, a true extravaganza that would have been—as it turns out—well

---

86. – Clemens, one of whose trademarks was to become his spotless white suits, had rather extravagant taste himself. As Walter Blair writes of the author's mansion, one of the most expensive in Hartford, Connecticut: "There was a side of the writer's nature which gloried in the showy, in the theatrical. Like his character Tom Sawyer, he loved to "throw style" into what he did." Howells, as Blair notes, called it "the stately mansion in which Clemens satisfied his love of magnificence" (Blair 1960, 18, 29).

worth the money had Huck paid it: "Anyways it was plenty good enough for *me*; and wherever I run across it, it can have all of *my* custom, every time" (121). The second example, and surely the most telling proof that some forms of waste can be virtuous, is the way Huck and Jim spend their best moments on the raft, just whiling away the time, "lazying around," going with the flow (97).[87] It is not only in adversity, but during these idle hours too that their relationship is formed. Quite naturally, these are also the times Huck thinks back on during that fateful instant—the *kairos*—in chapter 31: "we a floating along, talking, and singing, and laughing" (169). Clearly, some forms of illusion, folly, and waste are innocuous, even beneficial. The key question for Twain would appear to be, as we shall see in a later section on good and bad shows, whether anybody gets hurt or wronged by them.

These two examples of enjoyment are significant for another reason: they immediately follow examples of bloodletting (the feud and the killing of Boggs). We would submit that Huck's typical response to wanton destruction, both as a character and as a narrrator, is to shift to another mode of experience that we might broadly term poetic. Dawn on the river and the whirling spectacle under the big top afford genuine esthetic pleasure to the spectator, even if the shows are of a different sort, one natural and the other artificial (with this last, the *reader's* pleasure is of course further enhanced by his perception of artifices of which Huck is unaware). But the shift we are referring to may be active as well; it may be poetic in the etymological sense (*poesis*, making). Huck's descriptions of these two experiences provide examples of his creative response to (or escape from) acts of senseless violence or waste. This reflex may also take the form of theatrical staging (of his own murder, *after* pap's attempt to murder him) or, more importantly, writing. The sense of desolation that overwhelms Huck in chapter 31 when he learns of the treachery of the king

---

87. – In one of the unfinished sequels to *Huckleberry Finn*, Tom rebukes the two of them for having a "lazy" attitude towards life ("me and Jim never planned out things to do, which wears out a person's brains and ain't any use anyway, and is much easier and more comfortable to set still and let them happen their own way," TSC 135).

and the duke leads to the letter to Miss Watson. Huck's answer to the utter folly of Tom's management of the "evasion" is the narrative itself. True, the letter is destroyed, but its destruction is preceded by Huck's reminiscence of the trip down river, in other words by the middle section of *Huckleberry Finn*, in a sort of unwitting, metonymic gesture towards the future narrative. This act of making will of course be finished with a feeling of disgust, but fortunately not destroyed.

The Phelps farm episode shows the damage that is done when "style" triumphs. The characters and the novel itself both suffer from Tom's "spreading himself." The former are squeezed out (in comparison with their fully developed selves in the middle section of the novel), the latter becomes distended, suddenly a chore to read (Twain is often accused of padding in this section). Consider again the structural contrast we have been discussing: the escape trick that Huck, in his dual role, performs in a couple of days and later narrates in a few exhilirating pages in chapter 7 now lasts a month and takes up ten chapters, or, as Leo Marx points out in a classic critique of the novel, "almost one-fifth of the text" (BSC 337). Form is an expression of content, in other words: the tedious rhythm of the Phelps farm episode of *Huckleberry Finn* is an accurate reflection of Tom's extravagance, of his romantic conception of time, of the confinement and reduction of other characters as a result of his overweening presence and domineering ways. Lest we be accused of overstating the case, it should be pointed out that this is not the only work in which Twain foregrounds the dialectic of narrative content and form by showing the influence a character's action can have on storytelling procedures. To give one example, the narrator of *Puddn'head Wilson* has no choice but to act as an accomplice to Roxana's act of usurpation: "This history must henceforth accomodate itself to the change which Roxana has consummated, and call the the real heir "Chambers" and the usurping little slave 'Thomas à Becket'..." (PW 17). Wily-nily, his discourse must adapt itself to what happens on the plot level, duly registering changes that a slave has forced on him! Isn't this Twain's tongue-in-cheek way of asserting that, regardless of what quixotic characters like Tom may think, narratives cannot simply remain indifferent to the reality they claim to represent?

The implications of the Phelps Farm episode reach well beyond the scope of *Huckleberry Finn* in another sense as well. Style—or what Twain termed "that old inflated style"—was for him the bane of the American prose tradition. It enervates where it should invigorate. Twain observed this particularly in the South, where the writing was in his view still "filled with wordy, windy, flowery 'eloquence'" (LM 328). [88] *Huck Finn* needs to be read in the context of this sweeping attack on bad writing and as an anticipation of Twain's famous indictment of James Fenimore Cooper's prose style ("Fenimore Cooper's Literary Offenses" and "Fenimore Cooper's Further Literary Offenses," 1895; TSSE2 180-200). His strictures against Cooper's novels—their bad grammar, lack of "word-sense," verbosity, inconsistency in tone and diction, bombast, sentimentality—may easily be applied retrospectively to Tom (as we have noted, the two will be closely associated in the unfinished sequel *Huck Finn and Tom Sawyer Among the Indians*). Admired by Huck for the "sublimity of his language" in *Tom Sawyer* (TS 72), praised by the gang for his "real beautiful oath" in chapter 2 of this novel (12), Tom takes over as a writer-in-chief in the Phelps farm section: the motto (203), the inscriptions (204), and the "nonamous letters (211, 212) are all his ideas, all from his hand.[89] Tom's style is effusive, turgid; it reads like an unintentional burlesque of Cooper's literary sins from the pen of a schoolboy. But in point of fact Tom's models in the closing chapters are not American at all; they are exclusively European.[90] If these were in Twain's view often

88. – "South still in the sophomoric (gush) period. All speech there is flowery & gushy—pulpit, law, literature, it is all so" (NJ2 490).

89. – True, Huck uses the first-person plural to describe the preparation of the last "nonamous" letter ("we got another letter ready," 211), but the formulation does not necessarily suggest that Huck had a hand in the writing itself. On the contrary, a number of details point to Tom as the author: the diction ("helish design"), the moral dimension (the repentant bandit who wishes to do "the right thing"), the paraphernalia of adventure fiction (the false key, the secret signal; cf. TSC 165) and the reference to "Ingean Territory" (it will be Tom's idea to go there at the end of the novel, 228).

90. – Before the International Copyright agreement in 1891, bookstores in the United States were flooded with cheap, pirated editions of European literature printed by American publishing houses. Most of the adventure books Tom reads (188) were available in inexpensive reprints costing from ten to fifty cents, whereas the list price

bad, Tom makes them even worse. His tearful inscriptions—
"Tom's voice trembled, whilst he was reading them, and he
most broke down" (204)—are an oversentimentalized version
of those found on the dungeon walls in the Château d'If in *The
Innocents Abroad*, which are notable for the prisoner's lack of
self-pity ("These spoke not of himself and his hard estate," IA
83).

These writings should be contrasted to the last piece of
writing Huck does as a character, his three-line letter to Miss
Watson, a model of concision, utterly devoid of effusion
though written in a state of great inner turmoil. It illustrates a
number of Twain's "rules governing literary art," among which:
"Eschew surplusage" (TSSE2 182).[91] At its best Huck's
vernacular is *the* anti-style *par excellence*: taut, vigorous,
innovative. Every reader has a set of favorite phrases
unmistakably Huck's. Often cited—appropriately enough for a
character who is defined by movement—are verbs: "to lazy"
(97) and "to meeky along" (179) in particular. We could cite
others that attest to an accuracy of observation so lacking in
Cooper (who saw "nearly all things," as Twain quipped, "as
through a glass eye, darkly," TSSE2 184). Take this example
from the circus scene: "He shed [his clothes] so quick they
kind of clogged up the air" (120; brackets added). Or Huck's
wonderfully precise description of a moment of panic aboard
the *Walter Scott*: "It was dark as pitch in there; but I said in a
kind of a coarse whisper, 'Jim!' and he answered up, right at
my elbow, with a sort of a moan" (59). Paradoxically, in neither
of these cases do the expressions "kind of" or "sort of" detract
from the precision of the writing; quite the reverse: their
contrasting vagueness only highlights it. As we have already
suggested, even Huck's literary failures, whether as character
or narrator, redound to his credit: for example, his inability to
write poetry in the Emmeline Grangerford style (86), or this
oft-quoted description of the river in chapter 7:

for *Huckleberry Finn* ranged from \$2.75 to \$4.25 (Doyno 184-198). To Twain and his
contemporaries this trend jeopardized the very existence of an independent American
literature.

91. – The year before the Cooper articles, "Puddn'head Wilson's Calendar " was
arguing for the same principle of good style: "As to the Adjective: when in doubt,
strike it out" (PW 47).

Everything was dead quiet, and it looked late, and *smelt* late. You know what I mean—I don't know the words to put it in. (32; on the "late smell" cf. TSA 14)

As a full-scale enactment of Tom's romantic fantasies, the Phelps farm episode is, as we have argued, a comprehensive object-lesson on the wages of folly. However, the double disclosure in the closing chapters complicates the picture somewhat, for Huck and Jim's downriver trip also turns out to have been in vain, since pap was murdered shortly after Huck's escape and Jim has been free for two months. In other words, all the attempted escapes have been for naught. Even so, it seems that Twain is pointing here to exercises in futility that differ not in degree but in kind. Tom's "evasion" scheme stands as a prodigious waste and as Twain's necessarily laborious attempt to rid American literature of European romance (at the end of *A Connecticut Yankee* the cost of trying to kill the latter off at its historical roots, so to speak, will be the wholesale slaughter of 25,000 knights). Huck and Jim's downriver adventures, on the other hand, though ultimately pointless as well, are in the end redeemed by the very relationship they made possible, as Huck's reminiscences in chapter 31 show.

What saves the Phelps Farm section, then, is what it teaches us about waste. And in many ways it is a hard lesson indeed.

Clothes

"Thou hast the same hair, the same eyes, the same voice and manner, the same form and stature, the same face and countenance, that I bear. Fared we forth naked, there is none could say which was you and which the Prince of Wales" (PP 18).

Clothes make the man. Naked people have little or no influence in society. (TSSE2 942)

"But if Juliet's such a young gal, Duke, my peeled head and my white whiskers is goin' to look oncommon odd on her, maybe."
"No, don't you worry—these country jakes won't ever think of that. Besides, you know, you'll be in costume, and that makes all

the difference in the world" (105).

As with all other signifiers in *Huckleberry Finn*, the meaning and the value of clothing shift constantly. Which is not to say that all generalisations in this regard are false; rather, in typical Twainian fashion they undergo constant revision and qualification as the narrative unfolds—a phenomenon we have already observed with the land-river opposition. As one commentator describes this "mental habit" of Twain's: "At some fairly deep level of consciousness, Clemens/Twain perceived or constructed reality in this paradoxical fashion, seldom letting one view of reality stand uncorrected or unmodified by a contrasting vision" (Doyno 30). At this point we may safely assert, though, that clothes, like style (of which they are one manifestation among others), show us at one and the same time the power and the limits of surface, show, and appearances.

On the most obvious level they are symbolic of the constraints of civilization, of society's most intimate means of hemming in the body, preventing its freest expression and movement. It is significant that in *Tom Sawyer* the narrator says, immediately following a description of Huck's rags: "Huckleberry came and went, at his own free will" (TS 45). Huck's return to the strait-laced world of the Widow Douglas in the third paragraph of the novel is naturally signaled by a change in wardrobe—a change for the worse, it seems: "She put me in them new clothes again, and I couldn't do nothing but sweat and sweat, and feel all cramped up" (7; cf. also TS 212). For Huck clothes bring trouble, both from respectable society ("Well, I got a good going-over, from old Miss Watson, on account of my clothes," 14) and from its polar opposite ("Looky here," Pap warns him, "you stop that putting on frills. I won't have it," 22). The absence of clothing, by contrast, typifies a carefree existence, especially life on the raft: "The waves most washed me off the raft, sometimes, but I hadn't any clothes on, and didn't mind" (104). When Huck dresses up (47-48, 170), it is for a deliberate end; on the raft, however, there is none:

> Soon as it was night, out we shoved; when we got her out to about

the middle, we let her alone, and let her float wherever the current wanted her to; then we lit the pipes, and dangled our legs in the water and talked about all kinds of things—we was always naked, day and night, whenever the mosquitoes would let us—the new clothes Buck's folks made for me was too good to be comfortable, and besides I didn't go much on clothes, nohow. (97).

Note the revaluation of values implicit in the phrase "too good to be comfortable." The bad is comfortable. One could argue that as with the soul in chapter 31, so with the body in this passage. Huck chooses a Hell, the *terminus ad quem* of the path of wickedness, which looks very like paradise. Consistent with the interracial equality that obtains on the raft until the appearance of the duke and the king, Twain writes in one of his notebooks (1897):

> What is civilization? Clothes... Strip the human race absolutely naked, and it would be a real democracy. But the introduction of even a rag of tiger skin or a cowtail would make a badge of distinction and be the beginning of a monarchy.[92]

Clothes are where style and social distinction begin. It is no accident that two of the Southern aristocrats of the novel, Colonels Grangerford and Sherburn, who are both involved in bloodletting, are also the best-dressed men in town (87, 115). Nor that all the loafers are dressed alike ("They generly had on yellow straw hats most as wide as an umbrella, but didn't

---

92. – Quoted in Tanner 158. The same idea had already appeared in *A Connecticut Yankee*: "The newest prisoner's crime was a mere remark which he had made. He said he believed that men were about all alike, and one man as good as another, barring clothes. He said he believed that if you were to strip the nation naked and send a stranger through the crowd, he couldn't tell the king from a quack doctor, nor a duke from a hotel clerk" (CY 166-167). The main character Hank Morgan had also used the monarchy-as-clothing metaphor earlier in the same work: "The country is the real thing, the substantial thing, the eternal thing; it is the thing to watch over, and care for, and be loyal to; institutions are extraneous, they are its mere clothing, and clothing can wear out, become ragged, cease to be comfortable, cease to protect the body from winter, disease, and death. To be loyal to rags, to shout for rags, to worship rags, to die for rags—that is a loyalty of unreason; it is pure animal; it belongs to monarchy, was invented by monarchy; let monarchy keep it" (CY 113). For other images of royalty or nobility stripped naked, cf. NJ3 408, 411.

wear no coats nor waistcoats," 113); nor yet that pap keeps his word and takes the "frills" out of his son ("my clothes got to be all rags and dirt," 24). Pap understands the true, hidden connection between clothes and social oppression:

> "The law takes a man worth six thousand dollars and upards, and jams him into an old trap of a cabin like this, and lets him go round in clothes that ain't fitten for a hog. They all that govment!"

> "Oh, yes, this is a wonderful govment, wonderful. Why, looky here. There was a free nigger there, from Ohio; a mulatter, most as white as a white man. He had the whitest shirt on you ever see, too, and the shiniest hat; and there ain't a man in that town that's got as fine clothes as what he had; and he had a gold watch and chain and a silver-headed cane—the awfulest old gray-headed nabob in the State" (26)

The social order has been turned upside down.

Clothing introduces moral distinctions—or the absence thereof—on the narrative level as well. Let us note two significant examples where Huck accords differential treatment in describing dress. His portrait of the tatterdemalion king goes into great detail—all of it negative ("battered-up," "greasy," "ragged," "slick," 98-99), whereas he says tersely of the duke: "The other fellow was about thirty and dressed about as ornery" (99). This results in a distinction in favor of the duke, who has not borne the brunt of the negative adjectives, a distinction that will be confirmed in the rest of the narrative (125, 126, 163), particularly through language. The second example, describing the appearance of slave and white children on the Phelps farm, reverses the effect of Huck's laconic style:

> And behind the woman comes a little nigger girl and two little nigger boys, without anything on but tow-linen shirts, and they hung onto their mother's gown, and peeped out from behind her at me, bashful, the way they always do. And here comes the white woman running from the house, about forty-five or fifty year old, bare-headed, and her spinning-stick in her hand; and behind her comes her little white children, acting the same way the little niggers was doing. (174)

Paradoxically, the omission stresses not difference but

similarity. The white children's clothing is left out of the description, as it should be; for as the last verbal phrase emphasizes, the important point is not so much what the children are wearing as what they are doing. What is left, in other words, is what truly matters: their resemblance, the common humanity of children, black or white. The paragraph thus gradually erases the effect of false distinctions. Huck's vision corrects itself as it goes along (as it has done with regard to Jim on a larger scale, in the narrative as a whole up to this point).

The way Huck describes clothes does introduce a sharp gender distinction, however. This is perhaps to be expected but should not remain unanalyzed. Simply put, women's clothes are described as everywhere but on women's bodies: they are found either in houses (45, 141), on men (the drowned man in chapter 3, Huck twice, Jim and the king) or in pictures (84). Clothing defines men, in a comic or serious mode—pap, the colonels, the loafers, the king—in a way it does not women. What reader can forget pap's boots?

> He had one ankle resting on 'tother knee; the boot on that foot was busted, and two of his toes stuck through, and he worked them now and then. (20; cf. also 27)

Huck certainly cannot. Along with his black hair and whiskers and "fish-belly white" skin, they are one of pap's identifying traits (as the imprint shows, 18). Probably the sharpest descriptive contrast lies in the way Huck describes the two halves of the Grangerford family: the reader can easily visualize the men (the head of the family in particular); the women, hardly at all (87-88). Huck does not hesitate to draw value distinctions in men's clothes, as we have seen ("a heap the best-dressed man in that town," 115), but seems comically blind to the role of fashion in Emmeline Grangerford's crayon sketches (84). The description of women is mostly limited to the eyes, the hair and vague, flattering qualities like "tall," "beautiful," "proud," "grand," "sweet," "gentle-looking." This is perhaps to be expected from a motherless, fourteen-year-old boy with an aversion to clothes of any sort, not to mention women's. Still, the abstract quality of women in the novel points to the same studious avoidance of female sexuality Twain exhibited in his revisions of the manuscript.[93] (It is worth noting that the ideal society represented by the raft is, in addition to being interracial, *clothesless and male*, cf. Fiedler, BSC 413-420.) With the rare exception of Mary Jane's "silky hand" (149), women in *Huckleberry Finn* are strikingly genteel: idealised, dematerialised, disembodied—in a word spiritual. They are faces (eyes, hair, noses, harelip!) or voices. They are to be admired, worshipped—or run away from. Only in the safe, awe-inspiring, de-sexualised atmosphere of the circus do women truly have bodies (119)!

Clothing partakes of the realm of illusion. Splendid, "gaudy" clothes often dazzle the onlooker in Twain's fiction. Colonel Grangerford's suit is "made out of linen so white it hurt your eyes to look at it" (87). For the Yankee Hank Morgan, the Knights of the Round Table are "dressed in such various and splendid colors that it hurt one's eyes to look at them" (CY 19). Clothes both bind and blind. The supreme irony of the "recognition procession" in *The Prince and the Pauper* is that when the pauper Tom Canty is "tricked out in the gaudy plumage of royalty" he is powerless to fulfill his utmost desire: to be recognized for himself (PP 18, 27-28, 255). Nor is it a coincidence that, as we have just seen, Huck refers to the sun-bonnet he puts on in chapter 10 as a "blinder" (53). Finally, we should note that the Christian simplicity of Uncle Silas is expressed in his indifference to clothing as such, which he appears to be blind to: "you know I don't see them nor have nothing to do with them except when they're on me" (198).

Clothes are not only intrinsically reversible in value; they are what make bodies convertible places. Let us quote Huck's remark on the transformation the newly attired king undergoes:

> We had all bought store clothes where we stopped last; and now the king put his'n on, and he told me to put mine on. I done it of

---

93. – Cf. Doyno 7-10, 82, 148.

course. The king's duds was all black, and he did look real swell
and starchy. I never knowed how clothes could change a body
before. Why, before he looked like the orneriest old rip that ever
was; but now, when he'd take off his new white beaver and make
a bow and a smile, he looked that grand and good and pious that
you'd say he had walked right out of the ark, and maybe was old
Leviticus himself. (127)

This brings to mind the "miracle" that takes place when Tom
Canty and the Prince of Wales trade clothes in chapter 3 of
The Prince and the Pauper (PP 18); in *Puddn'head Wilson*,
Roxana witnesses much the same sort of magical
transformation when she exchanges the clothes of the two
babies, putting Tom Driscoll's on her own son Chambers and
vice versa: "Now who would b'lieve clo'es could do de like o'
dat? Dog my cats if it ain't all I kin do to tell t'other frum
which, let alone his pappy" (PW 14). It should be stressed that
the resemblance becomes obvious only *after the switch*, by
means of clothing, which reveals latent twinhood, unobserved
resemblances. In a variation on the Twainian paradox we saw
with the two groups of children, clothes bring out
resemblances through differentiation, in this case through a
before-and-after contrast. Twain phrases the paradox nicely in
the same passage of *The Prince and the Pauper*: "The two went
and stood side by side before a great mirror, and lo, a miracle:
there did not seem to have been any change made!" (PP 18).
In a two-stage perception process of the sort we are already
familiar with, a change turns out to be no change at all. We
might say that in Twain twinning is simply a more striking
instance of two individuals illustrating the fundamental
sameness of naked humanity. Through clothes, change reveals
sameness. In this respect, corporeal space is ruled by the same
paradoxes as geographical space.

There are nevertheless limits to the "miracles" mere
dress can work. His starchy new suit notwithstanding, the
king's bad grammar reveals that he is not "grand" at all but
rather an "ignorant tramp," as the Doctor Robinson and the
reader perceive with no difficulty. Clothes cannot cover up or
extirpate deeply-ingrained habits, as *A Connecticut Yankee* and
the end of *Puddn'head Wilson* show: in the first, King Arthur

reveals his incapacity to go *incognito*, to adopt a bearing other than regal (CY, chapter 28); in the latter, after twenty-three years of bondage, the real heir's manners are those of a slave, and "clothes could not mend these defects or cover them up" (PW 114)—any more than, say, Huck is able to disguise the fact that he is a boy in front of Judith Loftus, despite Jim's coaching (48).

Huckleberry Finn is a fine illustration of Twain's intuition that clothes are a manifestation of inequality. In this novel, social power broadly understood is the ability to impose the constraints of dress on others. We have seen two extremes of this ("frills" and "rags") with the Widow Douglas and pap. The king, too, requires obedience from Huck in the passage quoted above on the transformation wrought by "store clothes" ("he told me to put mine on. I done it of course"). But in theatricality, play-acting and letting on, clothing, art and literacy combine in a power game of double coercion involving both dress and gender (or race). The most sophisticated form of domination is indeed to force others to cross-dress (males as females). Huck and Jim's cooperation in a *voluntary* act of cross-dressing at the end of chapter 10 stands in marked contrast to the domination of those two natural-born showmen, Tom and the duke.[94] The latter takes advantage of his experience and knowledge of the theater to maneuvre the ignorant king into playing the role of Juliet, with "her night-gown and her ruffled night-cap" (105), and to take over the direction the acting. He later casts Jim in the role of a "sick Arab" in a King Lear costume. This last bit of stage directing suggests that theatre may indeed stand for a more sophisticated form of oppression, since the Lear costume is intended to replace the awkward insignia of slavery, the ropes binding Jim's hands and feet. The power "invested" in Tom is

---

94. – Let us note a few other parallels here: both are associated with theatricality and rule-following; both are admired by Huck and Jim for their intelligence (note Huck's telling phrase: "If I had Tom Sawyer's head, I wouldn't trade it off to be a duke.., " 183). Both withhold information concerning Jim ("A farmer by the name of Silas Ph—"; "What! Why Jim is—, " 172, 178). Finally, Tom is bandaged up with "one of the duke's shirts" (215-216).

prefigured as early as chapter 2, in his manipulation of Jim's hat (11). But it is above all at the Phelps farm that Tom's power as stage director is exercised to the fullest in a festival of cross-dressing, in which Huck dresses up as servant girl ("You'll be her," Tom tells him), Tom plays the role of Jim's mother, Jim's clothes are stuffed with straw (210-21), and Jim puts on Aunt Sally's calico dress, which he will finally suffer the humiliation of being recaptured in (222). We should note that for Tom, as for the duke, the exercise of stage-directing power means the ability to impose a concept of fictional necessity. For the duke, it is dramatic conventions ("we must preserve the unities, as we say on the boards," 109); for Tom, the rules of romantic fiction ("it's usual for the prisoner's mother to change clothes with him"; it is their "*duty*," 210). It should also be observed that this use of disguise is totally gratuitous, unlike Huck's dressing up as a girl for his reconnaissance mission to Judith Loftus's shanty (47). As we have already seen, slavish adherence to the rules of fiction creates the need for new fictions and disguises in a never-ending, closed loop of artifice. In the end, the fate of the duke and the king is nothing other than a spectacular confirmation of the intimate connection between clothing and power relations. Jim's act of revenge-taking eventuates in their being dressed up in tar and feathers (they "just looked like a couple of big soldier-plumes," 182), which is perhaps preferable to their falling victim to that ultimate instance of power as the ability to enforce a dress code—forcing scoundrels to "sleep in cravats" (164).

Like other forms of illusion in Twain, clothes can also be dangerous. Huck's jacket almost costs him his life when pap tries to kill him in a fit of *delirium tremens*: "Once when I turned short and dodged under his arm he made a grab and got me by the jacket between the shoulders, and I thought I was gone; but I slid out of the jacket as quick as lightning, and saved myself" (28). As do Tom's trousers during the escape: "but Tom's britches catched fast on a splinter on the top rail, and then he hear steps coming, so he had to pull loose, which snapped the splinter and made a noise" (215). This snag provides another contrast to the swiftness of Huck's escapes, for example when he and Jim abandon Jackson's Island. In this emergency, Huck knows it is time to relinquish disguises that impede a swift getaway (53).

On the other hand, like all other forms of "extension" in *Huckleberry Finn*, clothes are truly reversible, their value subject to unexpected transfomations, whatever their general meaning may be. Thus the same life-threatening jacket becomes instrumental in Huck's careful staging of the murder, in particular in concealing all traces of artifice: "Then I took up the pig and held him to my breast with my jacket (so he couldn't drip) till I got a good piece below the house and then dumped him into the river" (31). What seemed the very expression of artifice (as opposed to the "natural" nudity aboard the raft) paradoxically serves in its concealment. Pap's distinctive bootprint serves as a warning sign for Huck (18). Similarly, though the calico dress gets him into a trouble with Miss Judith Loftus, Mary Jane's frocks provide a good screen when he eavesdrops on the duke and the king (141). The clothes found in the floating house also yield eight dollars in silver (46).

Clothing would seem to partake in the general triumph of illusion in the novel. In the closing move in Huck's story, Tom transforms the nearly lethal bullet into a piece of jewelry (229): the life-threatening projectile thus becomes an adornment, as appearance subsumes reality once again. Perhaps Twain wants to show us that most of the time we are exchanging one illusion for another, as when pap trades "his new coat for a jug of forty-rod" (23): the pipedream of reform for an alcoholic nightmare at the bottom of a jug of whisky.

Ham and Eggs and Scenery: Huck as Hunger Artist

"I don't ever get enough to eat gen'ally."
(Huck in *The Adventures of Tom Sawyer*, TS 90).

He was ignorant, unwashed, insufficiently fed...
(Twain's description of Tom Blankenship, one of the models for Huck, HF-WMT 374n; BSC 279)

"You tell me whar a man gits his corn-pone, en I'll tell you what his 'pinions is."

> (The black philosopher Jerry in "Corn Pone Opinions,"
> TSSE2 507)

> In the summer the table was set in the middle of that shady,
> breezy floor, and the sumptuous meals—well, it makes me cry to
> think of them.

> (From *Mark Twain's Autobiography*, BSC 280)

In Twain food is often a revealer of illusions. Hunger plays a key role in the process deromanticising (cf. HFTSAI 50-51). *Roughing It,* for example, pokes fun at a jejune romanticism that would make relative pleasures absolute:

> And it was comfort in those succeeding days to sit up and
> contemplate the majestic panorama of mountains and valleys
> spread out below us and eat ham and hard boiled eggs while our
> spiritual natures revelled alternately in rainbows, thunderstorms,
> and peerless sunsets. Nothing helps scenery like ham and eggs.
> Ham and eggs, and after these a pipe—and old, rank, delicious
> pipe—ham and eggs and scenery, a "down grade," a flying coach,
> a fragrant pipe and a contented heart—these make happiness. It
> is what all the ages have struggled for. (RI 120-121; cf. also RI
> 148, 182).

The fact is, as this passage shows, scenery needs to be *helped*. Man cannot live on beauty alone. Beauty cannot keep body and soul together. As an object of enjoyment, the picturesque landscape exhibits a constitutive lack which points to the dependence of higher pleasures on more basic ones. A full stomach is the *sine qua non* of full esthetic enjoyment. In chapter 8 of *Huckleberry Finn* the only thing that Huck finds missing when he watches the steamboat full of people looking for his own corpse is something to eat:

> I was pretty hungry, but it warn't going to do for me to
> start a fire, because they might see the smoke. So I set there and
> watched the cannon-smoke and listened to the boom. The river
> was a mile wide, there, and it always looks pretty on a summer
> morning—so I was having a good enough time seeing them hunt
> for my remainders, if I only had a bite to eat. (34)

A providential loaf of "baker's bread" floats his way; now the spectacle can be enjoyed to the fullest:

> I got a good place amonst the leaves, and set there on a
> log, munching the bread and watching the ferry-boat, and very
> well satisfied. (*ibid*.)

This passage anticipates Huck's mood of contentment at the
beginning of chapter 9, when he revels at one in the same time
in scenery (a spectacular thunderstorm, 43) and a piping hot
meal (44).

Spectacles like the circus are certainly visual feasts for
Huck, opportunities for him to dig into reality with the same
zest he displays when eating; but they prove to be insubstantial
fare when the stomach is empty. The tedium of the inquest into
the rival claims on the Wilks estate, the final settlement of
which Huck had been vaguely imaginaing in circus-like terms
as "fun" (161), is exacerbated by hunger:

> Well, then they sailed in on the general investigation, and
> there we had it, up and down, hour in, hour out, and nobody
> never said a word about supper, nor ever seemed to think about
> it—and so they kept it up and kept it up... (157)

This indifference to food is symptomatic of the mental
confusion of the crowd ("it was the worst mixed-up thing you
ever see," *ibid*.), who are so caught up in the excitement of the
affair and their own illusions about it (Huck calls them
"prejudiced chuckleheads," 158) that they ignore certain basic
priorities such as eating. This recalls Tom Canty of *The Prince
and the Pauper*, whose romantic delusions distract his mind
from his daily lot of hunger and abuse: "Tom got up hungry
and sauntered hungry away but with his thoughts busy with the
shadowy splendours of his night's dreams" (PP 11; 5-6, 9-10).
In Twain, forgetting one's hunger is synonymous with losing
one's grip on reality. It is a sign of gullibility in the people at
the Pokeville camp meeting that they prefer *spiritual*
nourishment of dubious quality:

> There was sheds made out of poles and roofed over with
> branches, where they had lemonade and gingerbread to sell, and
> piles of watermelons and green corn and such-like truck.
>   The preaching was going on under the same kinds of
> sheds, only they was bigger and held crowds of people. (106)

In *Huckleberry Finn* food stands for a sort of bedrock reality, a basic human need as opposed to, say, the realm of false necessity in romance or the purely contemplative pleasures of the picturesque. It is an index to truth, in sharp contrast to verbiage of all sorts. As Huck declares to Tom in chapter 35, he would rather simply "hog a watermelon" than "set down and chaw over a lot of gold-leaf distinctions" beforehand (191; cf. also 194). Food is a reality that words appear powerless to change, for better or worse:

> When you got to the table you couldn't go right to eating, but you had to wait for victuals, though there warn't really anything the matter with them. That is, nothing only everything was cooked by itself. In a barrel of odds and ends it is different; things get mixed up, and the juice kinds of swaps around, and the things go better. (7)[95]

It is proof against the falseness of any language directed at it, as the "big supper" at the Wilkses makes clear:

> Mary Jane she set at the head of the table, with Susan along side of her, and said how bad the biscuits was, and how mean the preserves was, and how ornery and tough the fried chickens was—and all that kind of rot, the way women always do for to force out compliments; and the people all knowed everything was tip-top, and said so—said "How *do* you get biscuits to brown so nice?" and "Where, for the land's sake *did* you get these amaz'n pickles?" and all that kind of humbug talky-talk, just the way people always does at a supper, you know. (137)

It cuts through nonsense—Tom's sophistries, for instance:[96]

---

95. – In place of "barrel of odds and ends" Twain had originally written "swill barrel." As Victor Doyno notes in the most recent edition of the novel, "in Twain's sympathetic imagination his narrator, a desperately poor child, had apparently competed for food with pigs" (HF-CE 366). Huck eats the "leavings" (137).

96. – This is true of smoking, too, in Twain's fiction. After an argument about what the life of a hermit naturally entails—an argument which anticipates the disagreements between the boys at the Phelps farm ("Well," says Tom, "you *would* be a nice old slouch of a hermit. You'd be a disgrace")—the narrator comments that to these strictures Huck "made no response, being better employed. He had finished gouging out a cob, and now he fitted a weed stem to it, loaded it with tobacco, and was pressing a coal to the charge and blowing a cloud of fragrant smoke—he was in the full bloom of luxurious contentment" (TS 91). Let us note finally that another form of pleasure—music—seems to have a similarly salutary effect ("Music *is* a good thing; and after all that soul-butter and hogwash, I never see it freshen up things so, and

"What does the prisoner care whose—"
    He broke off there, because we heard the breakfast-horn
blowing. So we cleared out for the house. (191).

This is one of the most signification interruptions in a novel
where every break is meaningful. It shows how a basic
necessity can from time to time re-establish priorities, even in
a deluded mind like Tom's. When it is time to eat, *everything
else*—books (what the "best authorities" on prisoners say),
social conventions ("humbug talky-talk"), religion (saying
grace)—becomes an interruption, an unnecessary distraction:

> We had dinner out in that broad open passage betwixt the
> house and the kitchen; and there was things enough on that table
> for seven families—and all hot, too; none of your flabby tough
> meat that's laid in a cupboard in a damp cellar all night and tastes
> like a hunk of old cold cannibal in the morning. Uncle Silas he
> asked a pretty long blessing over it, but it was worth it; and it
> didn't cool it a bit, neither, the way I've seen them kind of
> interruptions do, lots of times. (181-182)

Food may be used as a sort of moral yardstick to
evaluate characters in *Huckleberry Finn*. It reveals the
equivocal nature of a family like the Grangerfords. True, Huck
is unstinting in his praise of the meal he is offered at their
home:

> Cold corn-pone, cold corn-beef, butter and butter-milk—that is
> what they had for me down there, and there ain't nothing better
> that ever I've come across yet. (82).

The relish with which Huck devours his food should not
mislead us, though. The repetitions are signficant: the fare is
cold—much like the welcome Huck receives.[97] It also lacks
variety, unlike the hot meal Huck and Jim have on the raft

---

sound so honest and bully," 132; cf. also 86 and 106)—provided that it is *good* music!
Which is not the case at Peter Wilks's funeral: "They had borrowed a melodeum—a
sick one; and when everything was ready, a young woman set down and worked it,
and it was pretty skreeky and colicky, and everybody joined in and sung, and Peter
was the only one that had a good thing, according to my notion" (144).
97. – The Grangerfords' cold fare contrasts also with the author's fond memories of
meals at his Uncle John Quarles's farm: "biscuits, hot batter cakes, hot buckwheat
cakes, hot 'wheat-bread,' hot rolls, hot corn pone" (BSC 280).

after escaping from the Grangerford-Shepherdson shoot-out: "corn-dodgers and buttermilk, and pork and cabbage, and greens—there ain't nothing in the world so good, when it's cooked right" (95). Even more damaging for our opinion of the Grangerfords: on Huck's arrival the colonel even "forgets" to be hospitable. Were it not for Mrs. Grangerford (who is not the "sweetest gray-headed lady" for nothing!), Huck would not even have a cold meal:

> "Why bless you, Saul, the poor thing's as wet as he can be; and don't you reckon may be he's hungry?"
> "True for you, Rachel—I forgot." (81)

Of course, Huck does compliment the family later on: "And warn't the cooking good, and just bushels of it too!" (86). But there he does not enter into the details. The initial impression remains.

True exemplars of Southern hospitality, Mrs. Judith Loftus and Aunt Sally do not need to be reminded to put out a plate for strangers:

> "Hungry, too, I reckon. I'll find you something." (48)

> "Lize, hurry up and get him a hot breakfast, right away..." (174)

If food adds yet another element of ambiguity to the portrait of the Grangerfords, it appears to confirm the kindness of the Phelps family, despite their pro-slavery sentiments. Jim's meals are well-rounded ("bread and meat and things," which includes greens presumably; and watermelon, 183, 186, 224). Nourishment for soul and body are looked after by Uncle Silas and Aunt Sally respectively:

> ... Uncle Silas come in every day or two to pray with him, and Aunt Sally come in to see if he was comfortable and had plenty to eat, and both of them was kind as they could be... (195)

Of course Jim is put on bread and water after his recapture (224); but when Tom reveals that he is free Aunt Sally gives him all he wants to eat "and a good time, and nothing to do" (228).

Jim and Huck both eat with great gusto. Their meals

together, which are all hot, are moments of genuine conviviality (38, 44, 97). Their zest for eating and love of "lazying" will serve to unite them in *Huck Finn and Tom Sawyer among the Indians* as well. When Tom urges them to join him for adventures in Indian Territory, Huck and Jim are reluctant: "But me and Jim kind of hung fire. Plenty to eat and nothing to do. We was very well satisfied" (HFTSAI 34).[98] Given Huck's healthy appetite, it seems appropriate that extreme unpleasantness should call forth a food metaphor: "Then pretty soon Sherburn sort of laughed; not the pleasant kind, but the kind that makes you feel like when you are eating bread that's got sand in it" (118).

Tom, on the other hand, is at war with nature and commonsense where food is concerned. The satisfaction to be derived from food *qua* food seems to be lost on him. His foolishness results in either wasting food, as we have seen, or rendering it inedible or dangerous. The pie with the ladder concealed in it may be "a satisfaction to look at":

> But the person that et it would want to fetch a couple of kags of toothpicks along, for if that rope-ladder wouldn't cramp him down to business, I don't know nothing what I'm talking about, and lay him in enough stomach ache to last him till next time too. (202)

The recipe comes not from a cook-book but from the more authoritative source of romantic fiction ("And we can send it to him in a pie; it's mostly done that way," 189). Eating staple food like corn-pone becomes risky business when Tom meddles with the cooking ("when Jim bit into it it most mashed all his teeth out," 196). Finally, where Tom's schemes do not end up ruining food, they require the adventurers to eat

---

98. – In Huck's "beggar's banquets" with the slave Uncle Jake in*Tom Sawyer*, Twain prefigures this fraternity in a characteristically backhanded manner. Huck says to Tom at the end of chapter 28: "I tote water for Uncle Jake whenever he wants me to, and any time I ask him he gives me a little something to eat if he can spare it. That's a mighty good nigger, Tom. He likes me, becuz I don't ever act as if I was above him. Sometimes I've set right down and eat *with* him. But you needn't tell that. A body's got to do things when he's awful hungry he wouldn't want to do as a steady thing" (TS 170). Here we can already see the "sound heart" and "deformed conscience" in tension (cf. also Lynn 197).

things unfit for human consumption—sawdust, for example:

> ... the bed-leg was sawed in two, and we had et up the sawdust, and it give us a most amazing stomach-ache. We reckoned we was all going to die, but didn't. It was the most undigestible sawdust I ever see; and Tom said the same. (209)

The causal relation between Tom's love for adventure stories and his perverse attitude towards food is already hinted at in chapter 2. His oath for the gang members stipulates that

> ... if anybody done anything to any boy in the band, whichever boy was ordered to kill that persona and his family must do it, and he mustn't eat and he mustn't sleep till he had killed them and hacked a cross in their breasts, which was the sign of the band. (12)

It is hardly a coincidence that Jim and Huck, two characters squarely on the side of nature and common-sense (however relative these terms may be), are also the ones most often seen doing two things one might expect of characters in realistic fiction—eating and sleeping.

Food is seldom referred to except in summary terms in the episodes featuring the king and the duke (110, 113, 122). Even at the "big supper" at the Wilks home they are described not as eating but as being *served*. On the other hand the king, as his partner in crime observes, is always "wanting to swallow *everything*," (155, 165), in particular other people's money and property. His voracious appetite (which he suddenly loses when on the lam: "I didn't wait for no breakfast—I warn't hungry," 99) needs to be contrasted to Aunt Sally's, which appears to be more an expression of love than greed. As she says to Huck (Tom):

> "Dear, dear, it does seem like I could eat you up!"

> "Now I can have a *good* look at you; and laws-a-me, I've hungry for it a many and a many a time, all these long years, and it's come at last!" (174)

Eating is only briefly mentioned in connection with pap (26, 30). Meals with him, unlike those with Jim, are presumably far from convivial. Like Tom—even though the sources of their deliria differ, pap seems also to be at war with a reality symbolised by food:

> Pap was agoing on so, he never noticed where his old
> limber legs as taking him to, so he went head over heels over the
> tub of salt pork, and barked both shins... (27).

The three square meals he eats at the new judge's house appear not to agree with him when they are topped off with a jug of forty-rod, as the judge's spare room attests: "they had to take soundings before they could navigate it" (23).

It seems clear, then, that food is a rather reliable indicator of sanity and uprightness in *Huckleberry Finn*. Like smoking, eating is a source of pleasure and "good times" (96, 196). But as we have tirelessly repeated, things are never simple in Twain. Food is not an absolutely unequivocal signifier. It can lead to trouble: It is while Huck is looking for berries that he happens upon the duke and the king (98). Food is also used to practice deception. Huck conceals the canoe from pap while he is supposed to be getting fish for breakfast (29-30). He uses a chicken bone as a ploy in his conversation with Joanna (137, 138). He also pretends he is starving in order to trick the duke as well (171).

Under the Big Top: Good Shows and Bad

No discussion of romance and illusion in *Huckleberry Finn* would be complete without some mention of the role of theatre. Twain was fascinated by the theatre himself though his literary efforts in that domain were for the most part failures (Goldman 108-131). He was quite aware of the powerful attraction exerted by the theatre on the educated and the uneducated alike.[99] In *Huck Finn* it proves to be a virtually

---

99. – In *Life on the Mississippi* he recounts the sad fate of the apprentice-blacksmith of his village, who gives up his trade to become an actor condemned to cameo roles but full of delusions of grandeur: "a couple of young Englishmen came to the town and sojourned a while; and one day they got themselves up in cheap royal finery and did the Richard III. sword-fight with maniac energy and prodigious powwow, in the presence of the village boys. This blacksmith cub was there, and the histrionic poison entered his bones. This vast, lumbering, ignorant, dull-witted lout was stage-struck, and irrecoverably" (LM 356). Happening upon him some thirty years later, the narrator is unable to "get him down out of the clouds" (LM 357). Some of this boy's sense of wonder is reincarnated in Huck, who pronounces the same scene, re-enacted by the duke and the king, "grand to see" (110).

inexhaustible resource. The King Lear costume enables the gang to run by day without having to tie Jim up (126). The take from the Bricksville performances of the Tragedy of the Burning Shame gives the duke and the king the financial wherewithal for the trick-to-end-all-tricks, the "boss dodge" (i.e., their *replacement* of the money missing from Peter Wilks's bag of gold): "Blest if the old Nonesuch ain't a heppin' us out agin," says the king (134). Though the king's stage antics are far from Shakespeare, the Royal Nonesuch does indeed turn out to be a gold mine ("there was so much money in it," 127). What is more, it appears to be endlessly repeatable ("[The duke] was sticking up a bill for the Royal Nonesuch—three night performance—like that other time. They had the cheek, them frauds!" 170; brackets added); only Jim's revelations about the "scandalous show" (182) put a stop to the theatrical scam. The confidence-man knows how to gauge the relative worth of con games; true to his calling, the duke knows where the real money is:

> The duke went down into his carpet-bag and fetched up a lot of little printed bills, and read them out loud. One bill said "The celebrated Dr. Armand de Montalban of Paris," would "lecture on the Science of Phrenology" at such and such a place, on the blank day of blank, at ten cents admission, and "furnish charts of character at twenty-five cents apiece." The duke said that was *him*. In another bill he was the "world renowned Shaksperean tragedian, Garrick the Younger, of Drury Lane, London." In other bills he had a lot of other names and done other wonderful things, like finding water and gold with a "divining rod," "dissipating witch-spells," and so on. By-and-by, he says—
> "But the histrionic muse is the darling." (105)

When Huck manages to outwit this consummate actor-trickster by shifting the blame for the theft of Wilks's gold on the slaves, the success of his ruse depends on the assumption of the universality of letting-on (cf. also Doyno 53), as the duke's reaction makes clear:

> They stood there a thinking and scratching their heads, a minute, and then the duke he bust into a kind of a little raspy chuckle, and says:

Lí doublend

"It does beat all, how neat the niggers played their hand. They let on to be *sorry* they was going out of this region! and I believed they *was* sorry. And So did you, and so did everybody. Don't ever tell *me* any more that a nigger ain't got any histrionic talent. Why, the way they played that thing, it would fool *anybody*. In my opinion there's a fortune in 'em. If I had capital and a theater, I wouldn't want a better lay out than that...." (147)

The "histrionic muse" is still "the darling" for the duke, even if he is in this instance victim rather than perpetrator (his ability to laugh at himself is, incidentally, a redeeming quality, one that distinguishes him from the king). Huck tricks the master illusionist by banking on the illusion of an illusion (in other words, reality!)—the slaves are, as we know, not acting at all.

Twain's fiction is full of showmen: Tom Sawyer, Tom Canty in *The Prince and the Pauper*, Huck (in his own way), the king and the duke, the Italian twins and David Wilson in *Puddn'head Wilson*, and Hank Morgan in *A Connecticut Yankee*. Hank Morgan is the most representative of the breed because the most accomplished. He openly acknowledges the "circus side" of his nature. He is always seeking to amaze, to dazzle his audience with "gaudy effects." Like his creator, he has keen sense of the power of advertising (Twain was astute enough to realize that the publicity surrounding the Concord Library ban on *Huckleberry Finn* was a godsend for flagging sales, BSC 285-286). And like the nineteenth-century American showman and circus producer P.T. Barnum (1810-1891)[100], most remembered for the phrase "There's a sucker born every minute," he is aware of the profound gullibility of the human race.

In Twain, death is without a doubt the "greatest show on earth," to use a Barnumesque formula. Hank Morgan's show-to-end-all-shows turns out to be the massacre of twenty-five thousand knights. Death is not theatricalised on this sort of epic scale in *Huckleberry Finn* of course, but it is nevertheless

---

100. – See Twain's spoof of Barnumesque jargon in "Barnum's First Speech in Congress," (TSSE1 210-213), written after the announcement of the showman's candidacy for a Congressional seat in Connecticut in 1867.

a crowd-pleaser. Boggs's death is one example:

> Well, pretty soon the whole town was there, squirming and scrouging and pushing and shoving to get at the window and have a look, but people that had the places wouldn't give them up, and folks behind them was saying all the time, 'Say, now, you've looked enough, you fellows; 'taint right and 'taint fair, for you to stay thar all the time, and never give nobody a chance; other folks has their rights as well as you." (116-117)

Huck's "death" is another, as is clear from Jim's description of the resulting bustle on the river:

> "'Long 'bout six in de mawnin', skifts begin to go by, en 'bout eight er nine every skift dat went 'long wuz talkin' 'bout how yo' pap come oever to de town en say you's killed. Dese las' skifts wuz full o' ladies agoin' over for to see de place... Sometimes dey'd pull up at de sho' en take a res' b'fo' dey started acrost, so by de talk I got to know all 'bout de killin'. (39)

Huck's attitude towards death appears to be one of fascination-repulsion. He is as eager to see the gruesome spectacle of Boggs's death as the rest of the Bricksville mob: "I rushed and got a good place at the window, where I was close to him and could see in" (116). He had also found "a good place" to view the Shepherdson-Grangerford bloodbath, even if it makes him "sick" to tell about it and gives him nightmares (93, 94). He shies away from the "gashly" corpse in the floating house: "I didn't look at him at all. Jim throwed some old rags over him, but he needn't done it; I didn't want to see him." His curiosity ends up getting the better of him, however: "After breakfast I wanted to talk about the dead man and guess out how he come to be killed, but Jim didn't want to... I couldn't keep from studying over it and wishing I knowed who shot the man, and what they done it for" (45-46).

But the supreme form of entertainment would appear to be to attend one's own funeral service. This is Tom's scheme in chapter 17 of *Tom Sawyer* (TS117). The funeral is a triumph; Tom, the envy of the other children. It is "the proudest moment of his life" (TS 115). Huck repeats the experience in chapter 8 of *Huckleberry Finn* (34-35). In both cases the boys have the opportunity to hear and see without being perceived themselves, even if they end up joining the congregation in *Tom Sawyer* (The difference between the two events confirms Huck's status as an outsider: the one takes place in church, the other on the river; Tom returns to the fold, whereas Huck remains alone on the island, for the time being at least.) We would argue that Huck's peeping and eavesdropping, which are part and parcel of the experience of adventure in *Huck Finn*, need also to be considered in light of his shifting identity, of his deaths and reincarnations. The unrecognised or unperceived perceiver has all the privileges of a ghost (Huck is taken for one twice, 38, 177). He is admitted to all shows, privy to all secrets: he watches Jim (chapter 2), the search for his corpse, the raftsmen (RP 233-241), the Shepherdson-Grangerford massacre, the men watching Peter Wilks's corpse (143), Mary Jane, the farmers (214), Aunt Sally (222); he overhears the robbers on the Walter Scott and the duke and king. The disguise Huck puts on to visit Mrs. Judith Loftus is a variation on the same desire to see and hear (about his own death) while remaining to all intents and purposes invisible behind a protective screeen of clothing. The decision Twain made under editorial pressure to exclude the Raftsmen's Passage becomes all the more unfortunate as it deprives the most widely-read version of the novel of a striking illustration of Huck as spectral perceiver. In that episode Huck plays the double role of invisible witness and dead person (Charles William Allbright). Significantly, during the moment of crisis in chapter 31, the tables are turned. Huck realizes that *he* is being watched, his every move recorded by "One that's always on the lookout" (168). This crisis is foreshadowed in chapter 8, where the ghost- spectator of the search for his own corpse sees the hand of Providence seeking him out in the guise of a loaf of bread.

In sum, then, Huck's death-wish can be interpreted as a desire to fulfill the child's double fantasy of omniscience and invisibility (cf. TS 25-26; note that these powers are often imagined as a means to secure vengeance: "when they found out what they had driven him to, perhaps they would be sorry," 86). The best he can realistically hope for, however, is an ultimate reincarnation as the most privileged of all witnesses in

Huckleberry Finn.

The river itself is a natural spectacle of often surpassing splendor, full of visual, but also auditory and olfactory marvels (97, 33, 32). It has the acoustic resonance of a vast echo chamber: "I've been in town two days," pap says, "and I hain't heard nothing but about you bein' rich. I heard about it away down the river, too. That's why I come" (22). Steamboats turn into displays of fireworks (98), or become the stage of high dramatic adventure, with Huck in a ringside seat. Rafts are transformed into floating theaters, with performances that are "grand to see," `"first rate," "perfectly lovely," like the duke's ham acting as seen through Huck's eyes:

> So he went to marching up and down, thinking and frowning horrible every now and then; then he would hoist up his eyebrows, next he would squeeze his hand on his forehead and stagger back and kind of moan; next he would sigh, and next he'd let on to drop a tear. It was beautiful to see him. By-and-by he got it. He told us to give attention. Then he strikes a noble attitude, with one leg shoved forewards, and his arms stretched away up, and his head tilted back, looking up at the sky; and then he begins to rip and rave and grit his teeth; and after that, all through his speech he howled, and spread around, and swelled up his chest, and just knocked the spots out of any acting ever *I* see before. (110-111)

Huck's recurrent use of the superlative "I ever see" is not only an expression of his naivety and his "disposition to stretch" (HFTSAI 46) but also a sign of his status as spectator-in-chief. Swelling up and spreading around—images of the expanding self, of the self as spectacle—are essentially theatrical gestures in *Huckleberry Finn* (the tall tale could be considered their narrative equivalent). These phrasal verbs most frequently appear in descriptions of the characters most closely associated with showmanship, i.e. the duke, the king (155, 134), and Tom (31, 56). But Jim's tale of bewitchment in chapter 2 provides the clearest example of how the narrative and theatrical elements work in combination. Jim stretches the story with each new telling:

Afterwards Jim said the witches bewitched him and put him in a trance, and rode him all over the State, and then set him under the trees again and hung his hat on a limb to show who done it. And next time Jim told it he said they rode him down to New Orleans; and after that, every time he told it he spread it more and more, till by-and-by he said they rode him all over the world, and tired him most to death, and his back was all over saddle boils. (11).

And in the end he becomes a spectacle himself:

Niggers would come miles around to hear Jim tell about it, and he was more looked up to than any nigger in that country. Strange niggers would stand with their mouths open and look him all over, same as if he was a wonder.

Niggers would come from all around there and give Jim anything they had, just for a sight of that five-center piece... (*ibid.*)

Though this passage is often criticised for placing Jim in the demeaning role of comic "minstrel darky" (Fishkin 1993, 81-85), Jim's yarn is compensatory, a slave's dream of ever greater mobility. The phrase "tired him most to death" echoes Jim's "staving dream" of the fog ("En I hain't ever had no dream b'fo' dat's tired me out like dis one," 71) and the description of him at end of the novel ("fagged out," 209; "all tired out," 223). The difference is that Jim's tale relates an experience resulting in physical exhaustion but also in self-aggrandizement; Huck's "mean trick" (72) and Tom's staging of the "evasion," on the other hand, belittle Jim, deprive him of freedom of movement, keep him confined to the same place.

It seems that Twain had always imagined Tom as an embodiment of theatricality. In *Tom Sawyer*, "theatrical gorgeousness" appeals "strongly" to the main character's nature (TS 101). Tom is on the lookout for "fine dramatic effect" (TS 103). This sense of showmanship is respected in *Huckleberry Finn*. (179). His arrival in high style at the Phelps Farm is a spectacle in itself;

Everybody made a rush for the front door, because, of course, a stranger don't come *every* year, and so he lays over the

> yaller fever, for interest, when he does come. Tom was over the stile and starting for the house; the wagon was spinning up the road for the village, and we was all bunched in the front door. Tom had his store clothes on, and an audience—and that was always nuts for Tom Sawyer. In those circumstances it warn't no trouble to him to throw in an amount of style that was suitable. He warn't a boy to meeky along up that yard like a sheep; no, he come ca'm and important, like the ram. (179).[101]

This quotation reveals among other things Twain's keen awareness of the role of framing in adding enchantment, beauty or drama to a scene (cf. IA 414-416). The frame may be taken literally, as with the Phelps's front door, or the window through which Huck gazes at the dying Boggs, or finally the cavern door on the night of the spectacular storm on Jackson's Island (43). It may also be taken in a loose, figurative sense as the setting of certain events, such as the graveyard scene in chapter 29 ("and to make it more scary, the sky was darkening up and the lightning beginning to wink and flitter, and the wind to shiver amongst the leaves," 161); or Huck's nightmare glimpse of a horrifically costumed Jim bathed "in lightning" (162); or his vision of the *Walter Scott*:

> Well, it being away in the night, and stormy, and all so mysterious-like, I felt just the way any other boy would a felt when I see that wreck laying there so mournful and lonesome in the middle of the river. It wanted to get aboard of her and slink around a little, and see what was there. (56-57).

Huck's response is fundamentally esthetic. This "gothic" atmosphere corresponds in every respect to conventional notions of an adventure setting, which is the target of Twain's parody here and in the graveyard scene (what would a

---

101. – *Puddn'head Wilson* provides a parallel to this sensation created by the coming of a stranger. Dawson's Landing, archetype of the "dull country town" with its "colorless history," where travelers are unheard of, is set astir by the arrival of the Italian twins, who rapidly turn into a show (PW 28, 26, chaps. 6-7). Cf. also TS 13. On the other hand, Twain felt that the village provided the best environment for the study of man: "Human nature cannot be studied in cities except at a disadvantage—a village is the place. There you can know your man inside & out—in a city you but know his crust; & his crust is usually a lie" (NJ2 503).

graveyard scene be without darkness, wind, and lightning?).
Tom is obsessed with these sorts of "gaudy" romantic framing
elements (the moat, for example, 189), all empty of purpose.
We should not forget that Tom's sensational staging of the
"evasion" was to be followed by a triumphant homecoming
show. His original plan was "to write word ahead and get out
all the niggers around, and have them waltz him into town with
a torchlight procession and a brass band, and then he would be
a hero" (228).

Tom also illustrates Twain's awareness the spectacular
side of cruelty. Readers of *Tom Sawyer* will recall the wild
acrobatics of the family cat after Tom forces pain-killer down
its throat ("Tom lay on the floor expiring with laughter," TS
83). Tom is an excellent producer of sadistic shows of this sort.
The "evasion" is his most dubious achievement in this domain.
It too involves the use of animals, such as the rats and spiders
and snakes set loose in the Phelps house (208-209) and in the
hut where Jim is kept prisoner, creating a circus-like
atmosphere in both. For Jim the performance is non-stop;
there is never a dull moment:

> Jim didn't like the spiders, and the spiders didn't like Jim; and so
> they'd lay for him and make it might warm for him. And he said
> that between the rats, and the snakes, and the grindstone, there
> warn't no room in bed for him, skasely; and when there was, a
> body couldn't sleep, it was so lively, and it was always lively, he
> said, because *they* never all slept at one time, but took turn about,
> so when the snakes was asleep the rats was on deck, and when the
> rats turned in the snakes come on watch, so he always had one
> gang under him, in his way, and t'other gang having a circus over
> him, and if he got up to hunt a new place the spiders would take
> a chance at him as he crossed over. (209)

As Twain's Mississippi writings reveal, the excitement-
starved, one-horse towns along the river provide the perfect
setting for all manner of shows, literal or figurative: theaters,
camp-meetings, circuses, parades, scandals, trials, funerals,
fights, duels, murders, lynchings. Even in the activities that
appear to be respectable, chicanery and violence are always
lurking beneath the surface. The preaching at the Pokeville
camp-meeting begins with a hymn that is "grand" and

"rousing" but soon degenerates into mass hysteria and pandemonium ("they sung, and shouted, and flung themselves down on the straw, crazy and wild," 107), followed up by the swindle of the king's mission to the Indian Ocean (107-108). The most sensational shows, the ones that whip whole towns into a frenzy, are by far the cruellest: tarring-and-feathering, lynching, the murder in cold blood of a harmless man ("never hurt nobody, drunk nor sober," 115) pleading for his life. As Huck says after seeing the duke and the king tarred and feathered and ridden out of town on a rail—their "scandalous show" suddenly transformed into a counter-performance of punishment, "Human beings *can* be awful cruel to one another" (182). But these sensational events are not so much exceptions to the rule of small town life as part of its very fabric. Everyday entertainment is vicious as well:

> And pretty soon, you'd hear a loafer sing out, "Hi! *so* boy! sick him, Tige!" and away the sow would go, squealing most horrible, with a dog or two singing to each ear, and three or four dozen more a-coming; and then you would see all the loafters get up and watch the thing out of sight, and laugh at the fun and look grateful for the noise. Then they'd settle back again till there was a dog-fight. There couldn't anything wake them up all over, and make them happy all over, like a dog-fight—unless it might be putting turpentine on a stray dog and setting fire to him, or tying a tin pan to his tail and see him run himself to death. (114).

Animals are omnipresent in Twain's circuses of cruelty.[102] They are victims, means of punishment or sources of its symbolic power (tarring and *feathering*). They also provide opportunities for comparisons that are usually unflattering for man. These can cut both ways, emphasising either difference: "There ain't no harm in a hound, nohow," as Huck says (174); or similarity: "The dogs were as still as the humans" (80), as he remarks of his hostile reception by the Grangerfords and their animals, all

---

102. – Animals also produce a burlesque intermixture of high and low, emphasising the artificiality of solemn rituals, as in case of the dog and the rat at Peter Wilks's funeral (144-145; NJ2 58) or, in *Tom Sawyer*, the pinch-bug and the poodle, whose commotion and wild yelps shatter the staid atmosphere of the Sunday church service (TS 40-41).

of them poised to attack at the slightest false move. But difference would appear to be uppermost in Twain's mind. As he wrote in 1896, "Man is the Cruel Animal. He is alone in that distinction" (TSSE2 210). Two years earlier, *Puddn'head Wilson* had already given this observation a fictional embodiment in Tom Driscoll's "native viciousness" (PW 20). Mercy towards animals and people seems indeed to be the exception in Twain's fiction. Like the Bricksville loafers, the Knights of the Round Table in *A Connecticut Yankee* take much delight in dogfights (CY 23, 30). Both pilgrims and natives are cruel to horses in *The Innocents Abroad* (IA 355-356, 378). If Edward VI in *The Prince and the Pauper* refrains from killing animals and confirms Tom Canty's abolition of torture in the realm, his "singularly merciful reign," as the narrator insists, was to last "only a few years" (PP 176, 286, 128, 289).

The problem is, there is an undeniable satisfaction to be derived, as Twain appears to be fully aware, from seeing stern retribution for such acts of cruelty. As this passage in *The Innocents Abroad* shows, the satisfaction in witnessing condign punishment, with its appeal to our sense of symmetry ("an eye for an eye, a tooth for a tooth"), might be considered akin to a form of esthetic enjoyment:

> About this time the fellow who was hanging onto the tail of the horse in front of me and practicing all sorts of unnecessary cruelty upon the animal got kicked some fourteen rods, and this incident, *together with the fairy spectacle of lights far in the distance*, made me serenely happy... (IA 248; italics added)

Poetic justice, truly. Pleasure, whether in inflicting pain or in seeing such wantonness punished, would seem to ensure a virtually endless cycle of violence, given the mean streak in human nature. The deep logic of *Huckleberry Finn* 's theater of violence and cruelty corresponds to Blair's "motifs with variations" (Blair 1960, 347): scenes are rehearsed, re-performed, rewritten, travestied, made to undergo tragic or comic reversals. The Bricksville episode, where the action shifts from dogfights to fistfights to murder to an abortive attempt at lynching and finally to a barely averted *mêlée* at the circus, is a case in point. To focus for a moment on the killing of Boggs and its aftermath, we can observe the following sequence: the event (114-116), the re-enactment (117), the mob reaction (117-118), Colonel Sherburn's counterspectacle (118-119), and finally the comic replay of the whole sequence within the circus. In our view, it would be a mistake to consider this final stage as a happy ending. The comic redemption is deprived of much of its force when we realize that it takes place solely within the realm of illusion and will be followed by the Royal Nonesuch scam and the perspective of more violence (123). Boggs is dead, and punishment awaits the duke and the king farther downriver. As for Sherburn, his counter-spectacle does nothing to remove the impression that violence—or the promise thereof—is the very pre-condition of entertainment, that it is manifest (or latent) in all the shows in the novel, including natural phenomena. Huck's tales of death and misfortune find an eager audience for a similar reason. The thrilling prospect of mayhem may also explain the attraction of Tom's escape scheme, its "bulliness":

> ... I see in a minute it was worth fifteen of mine, for style, and would make Jim just as free as mine would, and maybe get us all killed besides. (184)
>
> "Why, I wanted the *adventure* of it; and I'd a waded neck-deep in blood to—..." (226)

Good wholesome fun, with no risk of humiliating, maiming or killing man or beast, is a surprisingly scarce commodity in Twain. Despite his basically "sound heart," Huck's ideas of amusement end up endangering Jim's life or making a fool of him (46-47, 72), or they nearly get himself hanged (161). In his tirade, Sherburn, another of Twain's consummate showmen and often taken to be his spokesman (Blair 1960, 295), of course denounces the despicable combination of cruelty and cowardice in his fellow citizens (their tarring and feathering "poor friendless cast-out women that come along here," 118)—but all the better to argue for a more decorous and manly style of lynching. In a word, something worthy of the Southern tradition: "If any real lynching's to be done, it will be done in the dark, Southern fashion; and when they come they'll bring their masks, and fetch a *man* along" (119).[103] Sherburn is the

---

103. – The scorn Roxana heaps on the cowardly Tom Driscoll in *Puddn'head Wilson*

very embodiment of the explosive potential inherent in entertaintment. As with the snake Huck finds in chapter 10, the fun backfires once again. Sherburn is a one-man show suddenly staring down the spectators, drawing a bead on *them*. The show is over:

> The crowd washed back sudden, and then broke all apart and went tearing off every which way, and Buck Harkness he heeled it after them, looking tolerable cheap. I could a staid, if I'd a wanted to, but I didn't want to. (119)

A balanced judgement of Huck's character needs to take into account not only the exceptional but also the ordinary. On the one hand, he does indeed display an unusual aversion to cruel shows or simply to the sight of impending harm to others ("It warn't funny to me," he says of the "drunken" circus rider, "I was all of a tremble to see his danger," 120; Fishkin 23-24, 39-40; Tanner 178). Hardheartedness seems foreign to his deepest nature ("I couldn't seem to strike no places to harden me against him", 169; "it seemed like I couldn't ever feel any hardness against them any more in the world," 182). On the other hand, Huck's moral progress—which includes his resolution not to play any more "mean tricks" (72) on Jim—is real but relative; it is not unaccompanied by backsliding in the Phelps farm episode, where he acts as Tom's accomplice, if at times under protest. Ingrained habits die hard. Consistently skeptical about sudden conversions, Twain joked in *Puddn'head Wilson*: "Habit is habit, and not to be flung out of the window by any man, but coaxed down-stairs a step at a time" (PW 27). The fact is, Huck is both attracted and repelled by violence, cruelty, and death. Even if the latter reaction predominates, the former reveals him to be a part of the human average. As Louis Budd points out quite rightly, "Huck's virtues get overstated"; "his much acclaimed kindness can shut off." This is true with Joanna Wilks, whom the narrator consistently refers to as "the hare-lip" (Huck had

---

recalls Sherburn's speech to the Bricksville lynch mob: "Set down, you pup! Does youthink you kin sk'yer me? It ain't in you, nor de likes of you. I reckon you'd shoot me in de back, maybe, if you got a chance, for dat's jis yo' style, *I* knows you, thoo en thoo..." (PW 41).

almost slipped up once in her presence: "Why, Harel—why, Joanna...," 139), as well as Miss Watson: "Ridicule of the inherited face and body, which flickers throughout, is cruel, even in the case of Miss Watson, that tolerable slim old maid, with goggles on... Huck is sometimes more ignorant (including the colloquial sense) than innocent" (Budd 1985, 35)

We should note in addition that Huck's occasional refusal to expatiate upon "bad shows" may leave conflicting impressions on the reader. First, his omissions may stand out as a mark of sincerity, as opposed to, say, the cloying effusions of sentimental culture. Huck's reticence on the Grangerford-Shepherdson massacre ("I don't want to talk much about the next day. I reckon I'll cut it pretty short," 93) is one instance of this: "The emotion is conveyed rather than stated, and even Huck's omission of details about the most horrible happening—Buck's death—helps convey it. The indirection and understatement are particularly poignant here because they contrast with the insincere overstatement of Emmeline Gangerford" (Blair 1960, 239). Second, the lack of narrative commentary can be at times perplexing. We recall the lack of any sort of transition between Sherburn's showdown with the crowd and the circus episode, or between the last two paragraphs of the novel. Huck's silence on hearing the news of pap's death is quite simply deafening, in clear contrast to his curiosity about the same dead man at the beginning of chapter 10. Finally, some omissions may be Twain's efforts to preserve his narrator's pre-sexual innocence (Doyno 7-10, 82, 148). In his description of the floating house (45), Huck does not explain what the "ignorantest kind of words and pictures" are exactly, though they are presumably lewd (Twain had first written "vulgarest" in the manuscript, HF-CE 376); the house is in all probability a brothel. As Victor Doyno observes, "Twain's original audience would have had great difficulty dealing with a child's unmistakable description of a brothel" (HF-CE 376-377). Nor does Huck furnish all the details concerning the king's cavortings in the Royal Nonesuch:

> ... and at last when he'd got everybody's expectations up high enough, he rolled up the curtain, and the next minute the king

> come a prancing out on all fours, naked; and he was painted all
> over, ring-streaked-and-striped, all sorts of colors, as splendid as a
> rainbow. And—but never mind the rest of his outfit, it was just
> wild, but it was awful funny. The people almost kiiled themselves
> laughing; and when the king got done capering, and capered off
> behind the scenes, they roared and clapped and stormed and haw-
> hawed till he come back and done it all over again; and after that,
> they made him do it another time. Well, it would a made a cow
> laugh to see the shines that old idiot cut. (122)

As the note to the standard edition of the novel explains, Huck's "pale" version leaves out the key detail; "the rest of his outfit" is a lighted candle protruding from the king's rectum (HF-WMT 414; NJ1 70). This refusal to disclose all the particulars lends a certain teasing quality to the narrative, which always stops short of the nitty-gritty. In this, Huck resembles two other showmen: Tom, who learns the "great law of human action" in the previous book, i.e. "in order to make a man or a boy covet a thing, it is only necessary to make the thing difficult to attain" (TS 20); and the duke, who adds this clincher to the handbills for the Royal Nonesuch:

> Then at the bottom was the biggest line of all—which said:
>
> LADIES AND CHILDREN NOT ADMITTED.
>
> "There," says he, "if that line don't fetch them, I dont know
> Arkansaw!" (121)

Death Disguised

> "And he told me how else they had served the bodies, which was
> horrible, but it would not do to put it in a book." (HFTSAI 48)

Rather than the moment of truth and revelation, death seems inseparable from dissimulation in *Huckleberry Finn*. Consider the following list:

> A drowned woman "dressed up in a man's clothes" (15);
>
> Huck's staged murder (30-32);
>
> Jim's throwing "some old rags" over the dead man (pap) in the
> floating house (45);

Huck's dissimulation of the Grangerford boys' faces (95);

The Bible placed over Boggs's gunshot wounds (116);

The hiding of the gold in Peter Wilks's coffin (143);

The "wet cloth" and shroud covering his face and body (*ibid.*);

The concealment of the two deaths, Miss Watons's and pap's (178, 226, 229).

It is likely that at least one of Twain's targets here is the nineteenth-century sentimental cult of death, finely exemplified by the Grangerfords' transformation of Emmeline's deathbed into a shrine (84-85). As Ann Douglas observes in her discussion of rural cemeteries in the United States, the picturesque style in vogue in that period was akin to a form of camouflaging (Douglas 208-213). In chapter 42 of *Life on the Mississippi* (entitled "Hygiene and Sentiment"), Twain had already poured scorn on this fashion:

> I will gradually drop this subject of graveyards. I have been trying all I could to get down to the sentimental part of it, but I cannot accomplish it. I think there is no genuinely sentimental part to it. It is all grotesque, ghastly, horrible. (LM 306)

One of Twain's efforts to correct his culture's distorted vision of death is to be found in *The Innocents Abroad*, where he provides a glimpse of the sarcophagus of the Bishop of Milan. The discerning eye can see the vanity, the meretriciousness in any attempt to adorn this ultimate reality (note however that Twain's prose ironically assumes the very decorative qualities it is denouncing):

> The decaying head was black with age, the dry skin was drawn tight to the bones, the eyes were gone, there was a hole in the temple and another in the cheek, and the skinny lips were parted as in a ghastly smile! Over this dreadful face, its dust and decay and its mocking grin, hung a crown sown thick with flashing brilliants; and upon the breast lay crosses and crosiers of solid gold that were splendid with emeralds and diamonds.
>
> How poor and cheap and trivial these gewgaws seemed in persence of the solemnity, the grandeur, the awful majesty of death! (IA 140).

In his 1870 essay "Post-Mortem Poetry," Twain conducts a satirical analysis of another fashion of the time, obituary notices that disguise death "in the sweet drapery of verse"— very much in the Emmeline Grangerford spirit (TSSE1 399-402; cf. also NJ3 111).[104] Roxana's gaudy "death-toilet" in *Puddn'head Wilson* is yet another example of picturesque camouflaging:

> She took off her handkerchief-turban and dressed her glossy wealth of hair "like white folks;" she added some odds and ends of rather lurid ribbon and a spray of atrocious artificial flowers; finally she threw over her shoulders a fluffy thing called a "cloud" in that day, which was often of a blazing red complexion. Then she was ready for the tomb. (PW13)

Two interesting counter-examples to this cultural tendency should be noted, however—both of which involve Huck facing death *alone.* The first is a minor but nonetheless significant incident in the Wilks episode. At one point Huck comes into direct, unmediated contact with death when he touches Peter Wilks's corpse (the hands make Huck "creep, they was so cold," 143). The second appears in *Huck Finn and Tom Sawyer among the Indians*, where a flash of lightning (which recalls the night of Peter Wilks's exhumation, 161) reveals to Huck that he has been sleeping next to a dead man:

> And just then comes one of them blind-white glares of lightning that turns midnight to daytime, and there he laid grinning up at me, stone dead.
>
> ... I had been sleeping along perfectly comfortable with his relics I don't know how long, and him the gashliest slight I ever struck. (HFTSAI 68)

It is worth remarking, though, that in the same unfinished sequel, Huck shies away from any detailing of the Indian

---

104. – In Emmeline's "crayons" Twain is parodying stock elements in the mourning prints and engravings that appeared in popular publications of the period such as *Godey's Lady's Book* or *Friendship's Offering*, a copy of which is found in the Grangerford parlor. For examples, see HF-WMT 400-401n.

mutilation of white captives, as witnessed by Tom (see the epigraph to this section).[105] A strong undercurrent of sentimentalism in *Huckleberry Finn*, which does *not* take place "amongst the Injuns," imposes even stricter limits on Twain's realism, especially where sexuality and death are concerned. On these topics Twain was forced into concessions to genteel fastidiousness. The built-in double-bind of the sequel, intended to be an antidote to Cooper's romanticized portrait of Indians and revolving around the unavoidable yet unutterable topic of rape (referred to simply as "it," HFTSAI 54, 59), probably doomed the work from the start, as the editors note: "Unable to write frankly about rape, yet convinced that realism demanded he do so, Mark Twain abandoned the story around the middle of August 1884" (HFTSAI 272n).

It is not childhood as such, but rather the choice of a fourteen-year-old boy as narrator that acts as an additional constraint on authorial freedom. The greater latitude in a work like *The Innocents Abroad*, on the other hand, may be explained by the adoption of an adult's point of view. At one point in that work, the sight of a hideous, excruciatingly accurate sculpture of a man with no skin reminds the adult narrator of his first close encounter with a corpse:

> It is hard to forget repulsive things. I remember yet how I ran off from school once, when I was a boy, and then, pretty late at night, concluded to climb into the window of my father's office and sleep on a lounge, because I had a delicacy about going home and getting thrashed. As I lay on the lounge and my eyes grew accustomed to the darkness, I fancied I could see a long, dusky, shapeless thing stretched upon the floor. A cold shiver went through me. I turned my face to the wall. That did not answer. I was afraid that that thing would creep over and seize me in the dark. I turned back and stared at it for minutes and minutes—they seemed hours. It appeared to me that the lagging moonlight never, never would get to it. I turned to the wall and counted twenty, to pass the feverish time away. I looked—the pale square was nearer. I turned again and counted fifty—it was almost

---

105. – The posthumously published "Letters from the Earth" relates a story of Indian atrocities committed in Minnesota, including a number of lurid details; but even there Twain stops short: "They also—but I will not go into that. There is a limit. There are indignities so atrocious that the pen cannot write them" (TSSE2 927).

touching it. With desperate will I turned again and counted one
hundred, and faced about, all in a tremble. A white human hand
lay in the moonlight! Such an awful sinking at the heart—such a
sudden gasp for breath! I felt—I can not tell *what* I felt. When I
recovered strength enough, I faced the wall again. But no boy
could have remained so with that mysterious hand behind him. I
counted again and looked—the most of a naked arm was exposed.
I put my hands over my eyes and counted till I could stand it no
longer, and then—the pallid face of a man was there, with the
corners of the mouth drawn down, and the eyes fixed and glassy
in death! I raised to a sitting posture and glowered on that corpse
till the light crept down the bare breast,—line by line—inch by
inch—past the nipple,—and then it disclosed a ghastly stab! (IA
139)

The opening sentence will later be echoed in Huck's nightmare
visions of the Shepherdson-Grangerford massacre ("I ain't
ever going to get shut of them—lots of times I dream about
them," 94). Similarly, the boy's inability to resist the allure of
mystery anticipates Huck's reaction on seeing the *Walter Scott*.
At the same time there is a decided difference in approach
between this passage and the reflex of concealment that
pervades the action and narration in *Huckleberry Finn*. The
difference is that in *The Innocents abroad*, despite the
excruciating slowness of the disclosure (emphasised by
repetition and counting), despite the boy's being torn between
curiosity and repulsion, we are finally afforded a reasonably
full view of violent death, in the flesh, grisly details and all.

By "cutting it pretty short" (93), by drawing a curtain
over grim spectacles, Huck participates in this cultural practice
of dissimulating death. The novel studiously avoids the
macabre—or, to borrow Jim's phrase, what is "too gashly"
(45). The reader's eyes are never allowed to see all, to grow
"accustomed to the darkness." Instead, the narrative retains its
teasing quality, constantly playing on a logic of concealment
and partial revelation. The silences and abrupt changes of
subject we noted in the last section need to be read in this
light.

It is important to note that the published text of
Huckleberry Finn is shorn of two interesting passages where
corpses play a key role: the Raftsmen's Passage, which includes

the inset narrative of the haunted barrel containing the naked corpse of a baby, Charles William Allbright (RP 239); and the so-called "cadaver episode" brought to light (so to speak) with the recent discovery of the first half of the manuscript (HF-CE 62-65, 372-376n). This episode was to take place in the cave on Jackson's Island during the storm (in chapter 9, between Jim's line "Chickens know when its gwyne to rain, en so do birds, chile" and the beginning of the following paragraph, "The river went on raising and raising," 44). In this gothic set-piece Jim recalls his adventures on a dark and stormy night in the dissecting room of a medical school, where he had been sent to warm up a cadaver! There can be no doubt that the inclusion of these two passages would have given the novel a decidedly darker cast. Death and sexuality, we might say, are two of those dark Others whose presence the text seeks desperately to deny.

Religion, Superstition

> These that have turned the world upside down are come hither also. (Acts 17: 6)

Twain draws an obvious parallel in the opening chapters of the book between Tom's romantic illusions on the one hand and the religious belief of the Widow Douglas and Miss Watson on the other. Huck puts both to the test in chapter 3 and finds them wanting (14, 17). "Praying and playing actually involve similar fantasizing, both based upon unrealistic bookish authorities" (Doyno 139). In the Phelps Farm episode the parallel is re-established by Huck's sarcastic reaction to Tom's quixotic schemes ("if it ain't unregular and irreligious to sejest it ...," 193; Doyno 164). To return to the beginning for a moment: Huck's critical distance from both camps might bring him closer to pap, who has no use for books or religion (21). But pap's backwoods iconoclasm—recall that he tears up the picture Huck received as a prize for "learning my lessons good"—turns out to be as imprisoning for himself and his son as the bookish authorities he opposes. Though free of formal doctrine, he is a slave to prejudice and alcoholic delusions.

Huck is a "storehouse of superstitious lore" (Blair 1960,105) in this novel and the previous one (9; TS 46-48). As the editors of the standard edition of *Huck Finn* note:

> Huck frequently alludes to folk beliefs and superstitions that, as Mark Twain said, were 'prevalent among children and slaves' in the old Southwest during his own childhood... The author drew upon his recollections—especially of informal instruction he received as a boy from the slaves on his uncle John Quarles farm [Twain's model for the Phelps farm] near Florida, Missouri—for Huck's descriptions of various omens, magical rituals, and methods of prophecy. (HF-WMT 371; brackets added).

A number of these recorded superstitions—among which the slaves' practice of tying up their hair to keep off witches (9, 187)—may be found in Twain's notebooks and journals (NJ1 160, NJ2 103). Two of *Huckleberry Finn*'s greatest ironies concern folk beliefs and Christianity. First, though the unlikeliest candidate for the title, Huck reveals himself in many ways to be *the* exemplar of Christian values in the novel, especially forgiveness. Second, the novel stands the high culture of romance and religion on its head and confirms the truth of popular superstition (18, 43). Despite his initial skepticism about some of Jim's superstitious beliefs (41-42, 43, 46), events compel Huck to admit his error:

> Jim was laid up for four days and nights. Then the swelling was all gone and he was around again. I made up my mind I wouldn't ever take aholt of a snake-skin again with my hands, now that I see what had come of it. Jim said he reckoned I would believe him next time. And he said that handling a snake-skin was such awful bad luck that maybe we hadn't got to the end of it yet. He said he druther see the new moon over his left shoulder as much as a thousand times than take up a snake-skin in his hand. Well, I was beginning to feel that way myself, though I've always reckoned that looking at the new moon over your left shoulder is one of the carelessest and foolishest things a body can do. Old Hank Bunker done it once, and bragged about it; and in less than two years he got drunk and fell of the shot tower and spread himself out so that he was just a kind of layer, as you may say; and they slid him edgeways between two barn doors for a coffin, and buried him so, so they say, but I didn't see it. Pap told me.

> But anyway, it all come of looking at the moon that way, like a fool. (47)

Not only is the snake-skin the cause of their going by Cairo in the fog ("I awluz 'spected dat rattle-snake skin warn't done wid it's work," 77), it is responsible for their collision with the steamboat. As Huck says gravely in chapter 16:

> Anybody that don't believe yet, that it's foolishness to handle a snake-skin, after all that that snake-skin done for us, will believe it now, if they read on and see what more it done for us.

Huck's narrative is "scriptural" proof of the wisdom of a slave superstitions. The "warning" Jim interprets in his "dream" in chapter 15 turns out to apply rather well to their adventures in the following chapters: "The lot of tow-heads was troubles we was going to get into with quarrelsome people and all kinds of mean folks..." (71). Nor is the hair-ball prophecy (20) very wide of the mark when Jim says "it's down in de bills dat you's gwyne to get hung": Huck nearly does at the end of the Wilks episode (161; cf. Oehlschlaeger 125-127, but also Hoffmann 334). And, as Jim delights in pointing out at the end, his prophecy concerning himself comes true:

> "*Dah*, now, Huck, what I tell you?—what I tell you up dah on Jackson islan'? I *tole* you I got a hairy breas', en what's de sign un it; en I *tole* you I ben rich wunst, en gwineter to be rich *agin*; en it's come true; en heah she *is*! *Dah*, now! doan' talk to *me*— signs is *signs*, mine I tell you; en I knowed jis' 's well 'at I 'uz gwineter be rich agin as I's stannin' heah dis minute!" (228)

Unlike prayer, which appears to work "for only just the right kind" (35), superstition holds out the promise of empowerment for all, child and man, bond and free, "mudcat" and "quality." Therein lies one of the sources of its appeal. Another is the concreteness of omens (birds in flight, chest-hair, a burning spider) and of charms for warding off bad luck (a dead cat, a cross on a boot heel, a lock of hair tied with thread). As Jim says, "signs is *signs*" They have all the self-evidence of perceptible objects. They speak for themselves. *Res ipsa loquitur.* Prayer, on the other hand, appears powerless to produce something as simple as fishhook (14)—or to save a "poor lost lamb" (7) like Huck: "Pray for me! I reckoned if she knowed me she'd take a job that was more nearer her size," (152). Its efficacy is repeatedly called into question: "if ever I'd a thought it would do any good for me to pray for *her*, blamed if I wouldn't a done it or bust" (*ibid.*) The most it can procure is "spiritual gifts," as the Widow says (15). Twain often satirised two of the weaknesses of the Christianity of his day: its abstraction and its sentimentalism. Miss Watson's vision of heaven is hardly compelling, as Huck's reaction to it shows: "She said all a body would have to do there was to go around all day long with a harp and sing, forever and ever. So I didn't think much of it" (8).[106] Materiality provides the key to Huck's conversion to "wickedness" in chapter 31. As Huck says after his failure to say a prayer ("But the words wouldn't come," 168), "At last I had an idea; and I says, I'll go and write the letter—and *then* see if I can pray." Huck's "salvation" is not through prayer—he never gets around to trying a second time—but through the act of writing: "I felt good and all washed clean of sin for the first time I had ever felt so in my life." The letter, in all its tangibility, is the true agent of change; it is what Huck sees, takes up, holds in his hand, and finally tears up (169). Salvation, then, lies in the highly concrete form of the written word as opposed to formal, abstract ritual. The individual, emancipatory act of writing on the part of a semi-literate boy, whether in this letter or in the book as a whole, stands in opposition to the respectable cults of the written word represented by Tom and Miss Watson, whose names appear together at the very beginning of this same episode (168).

---

106. – Cf. HF-WMT 376n. Twain's satire on conventional depictions of heaven like Miss Watson's appears in a story published in 1907-1908, "Extract from Captain Stormfield's Visit to Heaven," which Twain had begun work on in 1869 and returned to periodically in the decade before the publication of *Huckleberry Finn*: "Singing hymns and waving palm branches through all eternity is pretty when you hear about it in the pulpit, but it's as poor a way to put in valuable time as a body could contrive"; "Eternal rest sounds comforting in the pulpit, too. Well, you try it once, and see how heavy time will hang on your hands" (TSSE2 838). See also "Letters from the Earth," TSSE2 887-888.

In *Huckleberry Finn*, "images exposing hypocrisy are drawn from religion, in part because the author was increasingly irritated by the pretenses of Christianity, in part because historically riverside villagers had been religious folk" (Blair 1960, 341). The Grangerfords, whose parlour proudly displays the family Bible and Hymn Book (83), who tote their guns to church and then admire the sermon "all about brotherly love, and such-like tiresomeness" (90), are obvious targets for Twain's satire. Here again, animals come in handy for unflattering comparisons: "If you notice, most folks don't go to church only when they've got to; but a hog is different." Hogs put so-called Christians to shame. And as Huck says of Sophia Grangerford's peculiar behavior, "it ain't natural for a girl to be in such a sweat about a Testament" (91). The Bible itself proves to be a vehicle of death rather than salvation: the note hidden in Sophia's Testament sparks off the bloodbath (91) and the "large Bible" placed on Boggs's chest "hastens his death" (Blair 1960, 341).

Religion is the ideal scam for a con-man plying the river—the king, for example, who plays the preacher twice (as Elexander Blodgett and Harvey Wilks): "Preachin's my line, too; and workin' camp-meetin's; and missionaryin' around" (99). It is arguably an even slicker con-game than the theater. When the king decides to "work that camp-meeting for all it was worth" (106) in Pokeville, the take is indeed quite handsome: the "missionarying line" yields him $87.75, the equivalent of "well over $1,200" by today's standards (108; Doyno 144) and nearly ten times what the duke makes for a day's (dishonest) labor (109). But all things considered, this is simply a rehearsal for the most lucrative of all religious performances, the Wilks funeral, where as Huck notes upon their arrival, the king "worked the crowd like you never see anything like it" (131).[107]

---

107. – "Significantly, Twain did not give the genuine minister an active role in detecting the frauds" (Doyno 145). The Reverend Hobson is, with the doctor, absent on the gang's arrival (132), and it is the doctor who will finally help to expose the king and the duke as impostors. The doctor in the Phelps farm episode, "a very nice, kind-looking old man" (216), seems also to be the most clear-sighted man in the village ("The physician's is the highest & the worthiest of all occupations—or would be, if human nature did not make superstitions and priests necessary," NJ2 500; cf. also IA

The Phelpses are also the objects of Twain's satire on religion. They too have a "sound hearts" but "deformed consciences," and Huck acts accordingly when first talking to Aunt Sally. Her oft-quoted reaction to news of a fatal accident on the steamboat is characteristic:

> "We blowed out a cylinder-head."
> "Good gracious! Anybody hurt?"
> "No'm. Killed a nigger."
> "Well, it's lucky; because sometimes people do get hurt." (175)

The main focus of Twain's attention is on Uncle Silas, however. On the one hand, he is, like his wife, fundamentally kind and decent ("mighty nice," as Huck insists, 200):

> He was the innocentest, best old soul I ever see. But it warn't surprising; because he warn't only just a farmer, he was a preacher, too, and had a little one-horse log church down back of the plantation, which he built it himself at his own expense, for a church and a school-house, and never charged nothing for his preaching, and it was worth it. There was plenty other farmer-preachers like that, and done the same way, down South. (179)

In a novel where preaching is shown to be a very lucrative line, this indifference to money is already remarkable in itself. On the other hand, Uncle Silas's mind has been corrupted by slavery. The most glaring proof of his failure to practice what he preaches is his reading of the Bible. As he tells Aunt Sally in chapter 37, "I was a-studying over my text in Acts Seventeen" (199). In that chapter, he would have read in verse 26 that God "hath made of one blood all nations of men for to dwell on all the face of the earth." The preceding books of Acts, with which Uncle Silas is certainly familiar, are echoed in the novel as well:

> Among many relevant parallels between Acts and *Huck* are several references to imprisonment and escapes; in Acts 12, after two angels get Peter out of prison, Herod threatens to kill

---

376). The "good turn" he does Jim (224) stands in clear opposition to Uncle Silas's blindness and bumbling ways (note that in chapter 42, Silas fades into the background as the other farmers—"the men"—take charge of Jim and impose harsh conditions on him, 222-223).

the ineffective jailors. Later in Acts 16... the apostles Paul and Silas pray for release and God shakes the prison so that all may go free, but the worried jailor considers suicide. Paul and Silas, however, are considerate and do not flee and accordingly the grateful jailor is converted. In Acts 16:36-39, the unjustly imprisoned will not agree to go quietly free out of jail but instead—in Tom Sawyer fashion—insist upon a prison release ceremony. (Doyno 160)

It seems that Twain's final intention was to leave Silas purblind, to deprive him of any ability to project the experience of his imprisoned namesake onto the slave he is holding captive. Twain's working notes for *Huckleberry Finn* reveal that at one point that he had contemplated making Silas a far more complex character (presumably by adding a monologue for Huck to overhear): "Uncle S wishes he would escape—if it warn't wrong, he'd set him free—but its a too... gushy generosity with another man's property" (HF-WMT 746, 756). The effect of this would have been to burden him with a moral dilemma similar to Huck's in chapters 16 and 31. As the novel stands, Silas exemplifies the narrow-mindedness of institutional religion, even in its humble, grass-roots form. Religion, it seems, is a tool of deception and self-deception. It can be used for wrong but is useless for right.

Appendix 1: Dialect

The man who attempts to wield a dialect which he has not been actually bred to is a muggins. Neither Bret Harte nor Dickens nor anybody else can write a dialect not acquainted with. I never undertook to produce an [early] cockney [lest] I should not succeed. Unless I had heard him say it. But when Mr. Dickens tries to produce Yankee dialect, he [showed for once mistake]. He made his Yankee talk as no Yankee. Bret Harte ‹ was the › is not acquainted with Pike County dialect. And been called the great master of dialect. Defy him to write 3 sentences. [*one word*] Christmas ([one of] his sketches) he mixes about 7 dialects, put them all in the one unhappy Missouri mouth.

(Twain in an 1873 notebook entry, NJ1 552-553.

Cf. also NJ3 467n208).

I amend this dialect stuff by talking & talking & *talking* it till it sounds right—& I had difficulty with this negro talk because a negro sometimes (rarely) says "goin' " & sometimes "gwyne," & they make just such discrepancies in other words—& when you come to reproduce them on paper they look as if the variation resulted from the writer's carelessness. But I want to work at the proofs & get the dialect as nearly right as possible.

(Twain in a 1874 letter to in William Dean Howells)[108]

A landmark essay by David Carkeet on Twain's use of dialect, the first analysis to give serious consideration to the claims made in the "Explanatory" note, showed that the author had taken great pains to distinguish among the different forms of dialect and non-standard English in *Huckleberry Finn*. The editors of the Iowa-California edition of *Huck Finn* acknowledge that their subsequent work on the novel has confirmed the findings of Carkeet's essay. With a few slight modifications, we have reproduced below the note of the standard edition of the novel (HF-WMT 373n), which

---

108. – Quoted in Fishkin 1993, 97. Twain is describing his method for transcribing the speech of "Aunt Rachel" (based on the Clemenses' servant Mary Ann Cord) for an *Atlantic Monthly* piece entitled "A True Story" (TSSE1 578-582).

identifies the speakers of the seven different dialects mentioned in Twain's Notice:

1. The "Missouri negro dialect":

> Jim,
> Jack (91),
> Lize (199),
> Nat (186-187, 196-197),
> Young "wench" at Phelps farm (199);

2. The "extremest form of the backwoods South-Western dialect":

> Mrs. Hotchkiss and the other Arkansas gossips (218-220);

3. The "ordinary 'Pike-County' dialect":

> Huck,
> Tom,
> Aunt Polly (226-228),
> Ben Rogers (12-14),
> Pap Finn,
> Judith Loftus,
> The duke,
> Buck Grangerford,
> The Wilks girls,
> The watchman in the *Walter Scott* episode (61-63);

4-7. "[F]our modified varieties of this last":

> a) The thieves on the Walter Scott (57-60);
> b) The king, Tim Collins (127-129);
> c) the Bricksville loafers (113-115);
> d) Aunt Sally and Uncle Silas Phelps, the Pikesville boy (167).

In the "Textual Introduction" to the standard edition, the editors note that Twain applied his dialectal shadings four major ways:

⌀   *Word choice or idiom:* for the word "steal" Huck says "smouch";
the king says "hook."
Word form (often affecting tense or agreement): Huck says "I
know"; Jim says "I knows."
Pronunciation: Huck says "been"; Jim says "ben."
Eye dialect (notstandard spelling for standard pronunciation):
Huck says "was"; Jim says "wuz." (HF-WMT 503)

At the same time, Twain was aware that a compromise had to be struck, one that would yield "accuracy as well as readability" (Fishkin 1993, 103). As Bridgman observes of Twain's orthography, "In *Huckleberry Finn* Mark Twain did not simply assemble a mechanical system of misspellings in order to approximate dialect. Rather, he sketched in just enough of the vagaries of human speech to sustain his illusion." Unlike earlier attempts at transcribing dialect, Twain's produces more than just "the laughter of incongruity"; "As Mark Twain well knew, such selectivity [in the use of incongruous spellings] generates more power than does an overwhelming reproduction of verbal effects" (Bridgman 87, 115, 116; brackets added).

Jim provides a good illustration here: "Jim's speech represented Twain's 'pains-taking' efforts to accurately record, to the best of his ability, 'Missouri Negro Dialect.' But unlike virtually all other white writers of African-American dialect before him (and many who came after him), Twain refused to allow the dialect to break the flow of the speaker's words. His use of eye dialect (like 'wuz') is minimal. His primary concern [in the story of Elizabeth, 125-126] is communicating Jim's very human pain." In a word, "a key gift Twain gave to American literature would be a standard for translating spoken speech into print without robbing it of its energy and power" (Fishkin 1983, 101, 97; brackets added).[109]

---

109. – On eye dialect, see also McKay 1985, 74-75 and Fishkin 1993, 157n. For the characteristics of Huck's diction and syntax and tense, and on *Huck Finn* as opposed to earlier examples of dialect, see Fishkin 1993, 28, 39-40,45-49,156n. Castex provides an extremely useful overview of the vocabulary, syntax, and pronunciation of Black dialect in Twain, along with the relevant technical terminology.

Appendix 2: Maps

(from Mark Twain, *The Adventures of Huckleberry Finn*, éd. Walter Blair, Victor Fisher, *et al.*, *The Works of Mark Twain*, vol. 8, Berkeley: U. of California P., 1988)

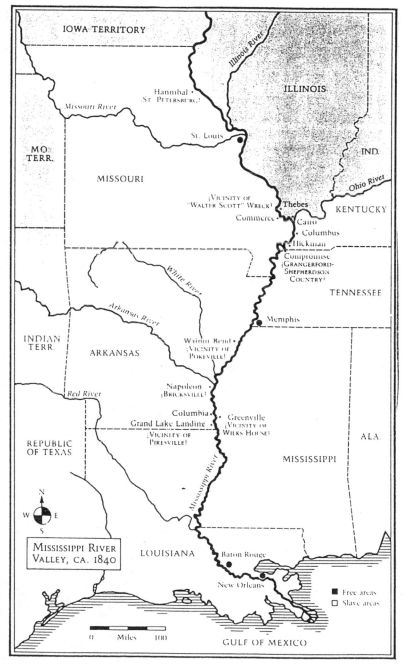

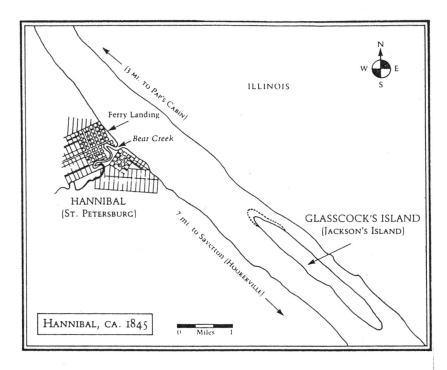

ILLINOIS

(3 MI. TO PAP'S CABIN)

Ferry Landing

Bear Creek

HANNIBAL
(ST. PETERSBURG)

7 mi. to Saverton (Hookerville)

GLASSCOCK'S ISLAND
(JACKSON'S ISLAND)

HANNIBAL, CA. 1845

0   Miles   1

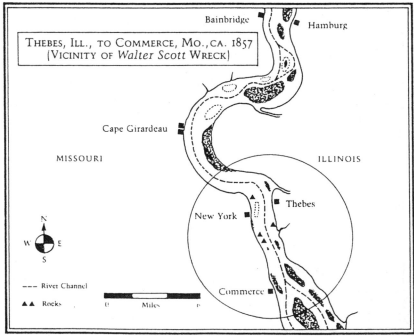

Bainbridge   Hamburg

THEBES, ILL., TO COMMERCE, MO., CA. 1857
(VICINITY OF *Walter Scott* WRECK)

Cape Girardeau

MISSOURI   ILLINOIS

Thebes

New York

Commerce

– – – River Channel

▲ ▲ Rocks   0   Miles   6

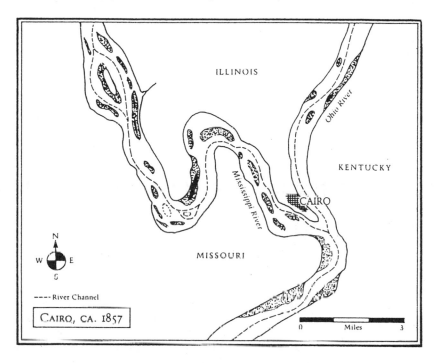

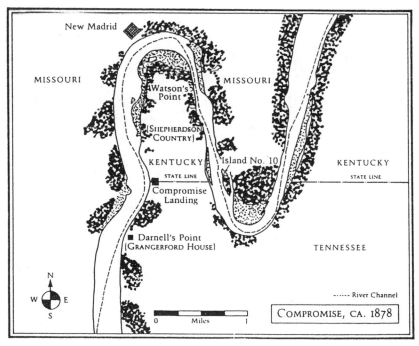

Editions and Abbreviations

All page references are to the second Norton Critical Edition of *Adventures of Huckleberry Finn* and will appear between parentheses in the text, as will all references to the Raftsmen's Passage (RP) or to the background, source material and criticism (BSC) provided in the same edition. References to other editions of Mark Twain's writings will be abbreviated as follows:

I. Editions of Adventures of Huckleberry Finn

HF-CE: *Adventures of Huckleberry Finn*. Introd. Justin Kaplan. Ed. Victor Doyno. London: Bloomsbury, 1996. ("Comprehensive edition" including recently discovered portions of the manuscript).

HF-WMT: *Adventures of Huckleberry Finn*. Ed. Walter Blair, Victor Fischer, et al. *The Works of Mark Twain*, vol. 8. Berkeley: U. of California P, 1988.

II. Published Sequels

TSA, TSD: *Tom Sawyer Abroad, Tom Sawyer, Detective*. Ed. John C. Gerber and Terry Firkins. *The Mark Twain Library*. Berkeley: U of California P, 1982.

III. Unfinished Sequels:
Huck Finn and Tom Sawyer among the Indians
and Tom Sawyer's Conspiracy

HFTSAI, TSC: *Huck Finn and Tom Sawyer among the*

Indians, and Other Unfinished Stories. Ed. Dahlia Armon, Walter Blair, et al. *The Mark Twain Library.* Berkeley: U of California P, 1989.

IV. Other Writings by Twain

IA: *The Innocents Abroad* and *Roughing it.* Ed. Guy Cardwell. New York: Library of America, 1987.

RI: *Roughing It.* Ed. Harriet Elinor Smith, Edgar Marquess Branch et al. *The Works of Mark Twain,* vol. 2. Berkeley: U of California P, 1993.

TS: *Mississippi Writings: The Adventures of Tom Sawyer, Life on the Mississippi, Huckleberry Finn, Puddn'head Wilson.* Ed. Guy Cardwell. New York: Library of America, 1982.

PP: *The Prince and the Pauper.* Ed. Victor Fischer. *The Mark Twain Library.* Berkeley: U of California P, 1983.

LM: *Life on the Mississippi.* Ed. James M. Cox. New York: Penguin, 1984.

CY: *A Connecticut Yankee in King Arthur's Court.* Ed. Bernard L. Stein. *The Mark Twain Library.* Berkeley: U of California P, 1983.

PW: *Puddn'head Wilson* and *Those Extraordinary Twins.* Ed. Sidney E. Berger. New York: Norton, 1980.

TSSE1:   *Collected Tales, Sketches, Speeches, and Essays, 1852-1890.* Ed. Louis J. Budd. New York: Library of America, 1992.

TSSE2:   *Collected Tales, Sketches, Speeches, and Essays, 1891-1910.* Ed. Louis J. Budd. New York: Library of America, 1992.

NJ1:   *Mark Twain's Notebooks and Journals, vol. 1 (1855-1873)*. Ed. Frederick Anderson, Michael B. Frank, Kenneth M. Sanderson. *The Mark Twain Papers*. Berkeley: U of California P, 1975.

NJ2:   *Mark Twain's Notebooks and Journals, vol. 2 (1877-1883)*. Ed. Frederick Anderson, Lin Salamo, Bernard L. Stein. *The Mark Twain Papers*. Berkeley: U of California P, 1975.

NJ3:   *Mark Twain's Notebooks and Journals, vol. 3 (1883-1891)*. Ed. Robert Pack Browning, Michael B. Frank, Lin Salamo. *The Mark Twain Papers*. Berkeley: U of California P, 1979.

N.B. All italics, brackets, and carets appear in the originals unless otherwise indicated. Following the general practice of the standard editions, we have converted all chapter references to arabic.

The most authoritative scholarly editions of Twain's works are those published by The Mark Twain Project, with its headquarters in The Bancroft Library (University of California, Berkeley). Mark Twain Project publications are divided into three series:

1. *The Works of Mark Twain*, in cooperation with the University of Iowa (sometimes referred to as the Iowa-California edition), provides the standard scholarly editions of novels, sketches and other writings published in Twain's lifetime.

2. *The Mark Twain Papers* publishes scholarly editions of the notebooks, correspondence, and previously unpublished works.

3. *The Mark Twain Library*. Inexpensive yet reliable CEAA (Center for Editions of American Authors)-approved editions, using the same texts as in the Works and Papers collections but without the critical apparatus.

Mark Twain Project publications do not offer as of yet a

complete edition of all of Twain's writings (for details, see the
entry "Editions" in Lemaster).

Selected Bibliography

Additional references to publications on Twain may be found in the MLA International Listings under CLEMENS, Samuel. Annual supplements to Tenney's standard bibliography appeared from 1977 to 1983 in *American Literary Realism* and have since1984 been included in the *Mark Twain Circular* (published by the Mark Twain Circle of America). *American Literary Scholarship: An Annual* (Duke UP) publishes a yearly overview of Twain scholarship. *American Literature* and the *Mississippi Quarterly* ("Checklist of Scholarship on Southern Literature") also contain regular listings of current publications on Twain. *The Mark Twain Encyclopedia* provides an excellent starting point for research; see especially the headings "Bibliographies," "Editions," and "Trends in Mark Twain Scholarship."

Other Editions of *Huckleberry Finn*
TWAIN, Mark [Samuel Clemens]. *Adventures of Huckleberry Finn*. Ed. Walter Blair and Victor Fischer. *The Mark Twain Library*. Berkeley: U of California P, 1985.

—. *Adventures of Huckleberry Finn: A Facsimile of the Manuscript*. Introduction Louis J. Budd. 2 vols. Detroit: Bruccoli Clark, Gale, 1983.

—. *Les aventures de Huckleberry Finn*. Trans. André Bay. Ed. Claude Grimal. Paris: GF-Flammarion, 1994.

Correspondence
Mark Twain's Letters. 2 vols. Ed. Albert Bigelow Paine. New York: Harper, 1917.

Mark Twain-Howells Letters: The Correspondence of Samuel L. Clemens and William Dean Howells, 1872-1910. Ed. Henry Nash Smith and William Gibson. 2 vols. Cambridge (Ma.): Harvard UP, 1960.

In the Mark Twain Papers edition:
Mark Twain's Letters to His Publishers, 1867-1894. Ed. Hamlin Hill. Berkeley: U of California P, 1967.

Mark Twain's Letters. Vol. 1 (1853-1866). Ed. Edgar Marquess Branch, et al. Berkeley: U of California P, 1988; —Vol. 2 (1867-1868). Ed. Harrriet Elinor Smith and Richard Bucci. Berkeley: U of California P, 1990;—Vol. 3 (1869). Ed. Victor Fischer and Michael B. Frank. Berkeley: U of California P, 1992;— Vol. 4 (1870-1871). Ed. Victor Fischer and Michael B. Frank. Berkeley: U of California P, 1995.

Books on Twain and *Huckleberry Finn:* Criticism, Reference Works, Anthologies

ANDERSON, Frederick, ed. *Mark Twain: The Critical Heritage.* London: RKP, 1971.

ASSELINEAU, Roger. *The Literary Reptutaion of Mark Twain, from 1910 to 1950*. 1954. Rpt. Westport (Ct.): Greenwood P, 1971.

BEAVER, Harold. *Huckleberry Finn*. London: Unwin Hyman, 1987.

BLAIR, Walter. *Mark Twain and Huck Finn*. Berkeley: U of California P, 1960.

BLOOM, Harold, ed. *Mark Twain: Modern Critical Views*. New York: Chelsea House, 1986.

BOOTH, Wayne. *The Company We Keep: An Ethics of Fiction*. Berkeley: U of California P, 1988.

BRANCH, Edgar Marquess. *The Literary Apprenticeship of Mark Twain*. Urbana (Ill.): U of Illinois P, 1950.

BRIDGMAN, Richard. *The Colloquial Style in America*. New York: Oxford UP, 1966.

BUDD, Louis J. *Mark Twain: Social Philosopher*. Bloomington: Indiana UP, 1962.

—, ed. *Critical Essays on Mark Twain, 1910-1980*. Boston: G.K Hall, 1983.

—, ed. *New Essays on* Huckleberry Finn. New York: Cambridge UP, 1985.

CARDWELL, Guy. *The Man Who Was Mark Twain: Images and Ideologies*. New Haven (Ct.): Yale UP, 1991.

CARRINGTON, George C., Jr. *The Dramatic Unity of* Huckleberry Finn. Columbia (Oh.): Ohio State UP, 1976.

CHAMPION, Laurie, ed. *The Critical Response to Mark Twain's* Huckleberry Finn. Westport (Ct.): Greenwood P, 1991.

COVICI, Pascal, Jr. *Mark Twain's Humor: The Image of a World.* Dallas: Southern Methodist UP, 1962.

COX, James M. *Mark Twain: The Fate of Humor.* Princeton: Princeton UP, 1966.

DEKKER, George. *The American Historical Romance.* Cambridge: Cambridge UP, 1987.

DE SAUSSURE DAVIS, Sara, and Philip D. Beidler, eds. *The Mythologizing of Mark Twain.* Alabama UP, 1984.

DE VOTO, Bernard. *Mark Twain at Work.* Cambridge (Ma.): Harvard UP, 1942.

DOYNO, Victor A. *Writing* Huckleberry Finn: *Mark Twain's Creative Process.* Philadelphia: U of Pennsylvania P, 1991.

DOUGLAS, Ann.*The Feminization of American Culture.* New York: Knopf, 1978.

ELLISON, Ralph. *The Collected Essays of Ralph Ellison.* Ed. John F. Callahan. New York: Modern Library, 1995.

EMERSON, Everett. *The Authentic Mark Twain: A Literary Biography of Samuel L. Clemens.* Philadelphia: U of Pennsylvania P, 1984.

FIEDLER, Leslie A. *Love and Death in the American Novel.* New York: Criterion Books, 1960.

FISHER FISHKIN, Shelley. *Was Huck Black? Mark Twain and African American Voices.* New York: Oxford UP, 1993.

FONER, Philip S. *Mark Twain, Social Critic.* New York: International Publishers, 1958.

GABLER-HOVER, Janet. *Truth in American Fiction: The Legacy of Rhetorical Idealism.* Athens (Ga.): U of Georgia P, 1990.

GIBBEN, Alan. *Mark Twain's Library: A Reconstruction.* 2 vols. Boston: G.K. Hall, 1980.

GIBSON, William M. *The Art of Mark Twain.* New York: Oxford UP, 1976.

GILLMAN, Susan. *Dark Twins: Imposture and Identity in Mark Twain's America.* Chicago: U of Chicago P, 1989.

GITTINGS, Robert, ed. *Mark Twain: A Sumptuous Variety.* London/Totowa (N.J.): Vision/Barnes and Noble, 1985.

GOAD, Mary Ellen. *The Image of the Woman in the Life and Writings of Mark Twain.* Emporia (Ks.): Kansas State College, 1971.

HARRIS, Susan K. *Mark Twain's Escape from Time: A Study of Patterns and Images*. Columbia (Mo.): U of Missouri P, 1982.

HEMINGWAY, Ernest. *The Green Hills of Africa*. New York: Scribner's, 1935.

HILL, Hamlin. *Mark Twain: God's Fool*. New York: Harper, 1973.

HOFFMANN, Daniel G. *Form and Fable in American Fiction*. New York: Oxford UP, 1961.

HOWELLS, William Dean. *My Mark Twain*. New York: Harper, 1910.

KAPLAN, Justin. *Mr. Clemens and Mark Twain*. New York: Simon and Schuster, 1966.

LAUBER, John. *The Making of Mark Twain*. New York: Houghton and Mifflin, 1985.

LEMASTER, J.R., and James D. Wilson. *The Mark Twain Encyclopedia*. N.Y: Garland P, 1993.

LEONARD, James S. et al., ed. *Satire or Evasion? Black Perspectives on* Huckleberry Finn. Durham (N.C.): Duke UP, 1992.

LONG, E. Hudson, and J. R. Le Master. *The New Mark Twain Handbook*. New York: Garland, 1985.

LYNN, Kenneth S. *Mark Twain and Southwestern Humor*. 1959. Repr. Westport (Ct.): Greenwood P, 1972.

MICHELSON, Bruce. *Mark Twain on the Loose: A Comic Writer and the American Self*. Amherst: U of Massachussetts P, 1995.

NEIDER, Charles, ed. *The Autobiography of Mark Twain*. New York: Harper and Row, 1966.

PAINE, Thomas Bigelow. *Mark Twain: A Biography*. 1912. Rpt. New York: Chelsea House, 1980.

POLI, Bernard. *Mark Twain, écrivain de l'Ouest: régionalisme et humour*. Paris: PUF, 1965.

QUIRK, Tom. *Coming to Grips with* Huckleberry Finn: *Essays on a Book, a Boy, and a Man*. Columbia (Mo.): U of Missouri P, 1993.

RASMUSSEN, R. Kent. *Mark Twain A to Z: The Essential Reference to his Life and Writings*. New York: Facts on File, 1995.

REGAN, Robert. *Unpromising Heroes: Mark Twain and his*

Characters. Berkeley: U of California P, 1966.

REISING, Russell. *The Unusable Past: Theory and the Study of American Literature*. London: Methuen, 1986.

ROBINSON, Forrest G. *In Bad Faith: The Dynamics of Deception in Mark Twain's America*. Cambridge (Ma.): Harvard UP, 1986.

—, ed. *Cambridge Companion to Mark Twain*. London: Cambridge UP, 1993.

SALOMON, Roger B. *Twain and the Image of History*. New Haven (Ct.): Yale UP, 1961.

SATTLEMEYER, Robert, and J. Donald Crowley, eds. *One Hundred Years of* Huckleberry Finn: *The Boy, His Book and American Culture*. Columbia (Mo.): U of Missouri P, 1985.

SCOTT, Arthur L., ed. *Mark Twain: Selected Criticism*. Dallas: Southern Methodist UP, 1955.

SEWELL, David R. *Mark Twain's Languages: Discourse, Dialogue, and Linguistic Variety*. Berkeley: U of California P, 1987.

SIMPSON, Claude M., ed. *Twentieth Century Views:* Adventures of Huckleberry Finn. Englewood Cliffs (N.J.): Prentice Hall, 1968.

SKANDERA-TROMBLEY, Laura E. *Mark Twain in the Company of Women*. Philadelphia: U of Pennsylvania P, 1995.

SLOANE, David E.E. *"Adventures of Huckleberry Finn": American Comic Vision*. Boston: Twayne, 1988.

—, *Mark Twain as a Literary Comedian*. Baton Rouge: Lousiana State UP, 1979.

SMITH, Henry Nash. *Mark Twain: The Development of a Writer*. Cambridge (Ma.): Harvard UP, 1962.

SPENGEMANN, William C. *Mark Twain and the Backwoods Angel: The Matter of Innocence in the Works of Samuel L. Clemens*. Kent (Oh.): Kent State UP, 1966.

STEINBRICK, Jeffrey. *Getting to be Mark Twain*. Berkeley: U of California P, 1991.

STONE, Albert E., Jr. *The Innocent Eye: Childhood in Mark Twain's Imagination*. New Haven (Ct.): Yale UP, 1962.

STONELEY, Peter. *Mark Twain and the Feminine Aesthetic*. Cambridge: Cambridge UP, 1992.

SUNDQUIST, Eric J., ed. *Mark Twain: A Collection of Critical Essays*. New York: Prentice-Hall, 1994.

TANNER, Tony. *The Reign of Wonder: Naivety and Reality in American Literature*. Cambridge: Cambridge UP, 1965.

TENNEY, Thomas Asa. *Mark Twain: A Reference Guide*. Boston: G. K.Hall, 1977.

WADLINGTON, Warwick. *The Confidence Game in American Literature*. Princeton (N.J.): Princeton UP, 1975.

WARREN, Joyce W. *The American Narcissus: Individualism and Women in Nineteenth-Century America*. New Brunswick (N.J.): Rutgers UP, 1984.

WECTER, Dixon. *Sam Clemens of Hannibal*. Boston: Houghton Mifflin, 1952.

WILDING, Michael. *Political Fictions*. London: RKP, 1980.

WONHAM, Henry B. *Mark Twain and the Art of the Tall Tale*. New York: Oxford UP., 1993.

Articles

ADAMS, Richard P. "The Unity and Coherence of *Huckleberry Finn*." *Twentieth- Century Interpretations of* Adventures of Huckleberry Finn. Ed. Claude M. Simpson. Englewood Cliffs (N.J.): Prentice-Hall, 1968. 41-53.

ARAC, Jonathan. "Nationalism, Hypercanonization, and *Huckleberry Finn*." *Boundary 2* (1992). 14-33.

BEAVER, Harold. "Run, Nigger, Run." *The Critical Response to Mark Twain's* Huckleberry Finn. Ed. Laurie Champion. Westport (Ct.): Greenwood P, 1991. 187-194.

BELL, Michael Davitt. "Mark Twain, 'Realism,' and *Huckleberry Finn. New Essays on* Huckleberry Finn. Ed. Louis J. Budd. Cambridge: Cambridge UP, 1985. 35-59.

BELL, Millicent. "*Huckleberry Finn* and the Sleights of the Imagination." *One Hundred Years of* Huckleberry Finn: The Boy, His Book, and American Culture. Ed. Robert Sattelmeyer and J. Donald Crowley. Columbia (Mo.): U of Missouri P, 1985. 128-145.

BLAIR, Walter. "Was *Huckleberry Finn* Written?" *The Critical Response to Mark Twain's* Huckleberry Finn. Ed. Laurie Champion. Westport (Ct.): Greenwood P, 1991. 108-112.

BONNET, Michèle. "*Huckleberry Finn:* Le langage en question." *Voix et langages aux Etats-Unis, II.* Ed. Serge Ricard. Aix-en-Provence: U de Aix-en-Provence, 1993. 33-60.

BUDD, Louis J. "'A Nobler Roman Aspect' of *Adventures of Huckleberry Finn.*" *One Hundred Years of* Huckleberry Finn: *The Boy, His Book, and American Culture.* Ed. Robert Sattelmeyer and J. Donald Crowley. Columbia (Mo.): U of Missouri P, 1985. 26-40.

—, "The Recomposition of *Adventures of Huckleberry Finn.*" *The Critical Response to Mark Twain's* Huckleberry Finn. Ed. Laurie Champion. Westport (Ct.): Greenwood P, 1991. 195-206.

CARKEET, David. "The Dialects in *Huckleberry Finn.*" *The Critical Response to Mark Twain's* Huckleberry Finn. Ed. Laurie Champion. Westport (Ct.): Greenwood P, 1991. 113-125.

CASTEX, Peggy. "Negro Dialect in Mark Twain's Puddn'head Wilson." *Americana* 1 (January 1988): 23-42.

COX, James M. "A Hard Book to Take." *One Hundred Years of* Huckleberry Finn: *The Boy, His Book, and American Culture.* Ed. Robert Sattelmeyer and J. Donald Crowley. Columbia (Mo.): U of Missouri P, 1985. 386-402.

FETTERLEY, Judith. "Mark Twain and the Anxiety of Entertainment." *Critical Essays on Mark Twain, 1910-1980.* Ed. Louis J. Budd. Boston: G.K. Hall, 1983. 216- 224.

FISHKIN, Shelley Fisher. "Mark Twain and Women." *The Cambridge Companion to Mark Twain.* Ed. Forrest G. Robinson. Cambridge: Cambridge UP, 1995. 52-73.

GERBER, John C. Introduction. *One Hundred Years of* Huckleberry Finn: *The Boy, His Book, and American Culture.* Ed. Robert Sattelmeyer and J. Donald Crowley. Columbia (Mo.): U of Missouri P, 1985. 1-12.

GOLDMAN, Robert. "Mark Twain as Playwright." *Mark Twain: A Sumptuous Variety.* Ed. Robert Giddings. London/Totowa (N.J.): Vision/Barnes and Noble, 1985. 108-131.

GRAYBILL, Robert. "*Don Quixote* and *Huckleberry Finn*: Points of Contact." *Romance Languages Annual* (1990): 442-444.

GRIBBEN, Alan. "'I Did Wish Tom Sawyer Was There': Boy-Book Elements in *Tom Sawyer* and *Huckleberry Finn*." *One Hundred Years of* Huckleberry Finn: *The Boy, His Book, and American Culture.* Ed. Robert Sattelmeyer and J. Donald Crowley. Columbia (Mo.): U of Missouri P, 1985. 149-170.

HOLLAND, Laurence B. "A 'Raft of Trouble': Word and Deed in *Huckleberry Finn*." *Mark Twain: A Collection of Critical Essays*. Ed. Eric J. Sundquist. Englewood Cliffs (N.J.): Prentice-Hall, 1994. 75-89.

JEHLEN, Myra. "Banned in Concord: *Adventures of Huckleberry Finn* and Classic American Literature." *The Cambridge Companion to Mark Twain*. Ed. Forrest G. Robinson. Cambridge: Cambridge UP, 1995. 93-115.

KAUFMANN, William. "The Comedic Stance: Sam Clemens, His Masquerade." *Mark Twain: A Sumptuous Variety*. Ed. Robert Giddings. London/Totowa (N.J.): Vision/Barnes and Noble, 1985. 77-107.

KEARNS, Cleo McNelly. "The Limits of Semiotics in *Huckleberry Finn*." *Modern Critical Views: Mark Twain*. Ed. Harold Bloom. New York: Chelsea House, 1986. 207-222.

LEE, A. Robert. "'Sivilization', and the Civilization of the Heart." *Mark Twain: A Sumptuous Variety*. Ed. Robert Giddings. London/Totowa (N.J.): Vision/Barnes and Noble, 1985. 132-154.

LENZ, William E. "Confidence and Convention in *Huckleberry Finn*." *One Hundred Years of* Huckleberry Finn: *The Boy, His Book, and American Culture*. Ed. Robert Sattelmeyer and J. Donald Crowley. Columbia (Mo.): U of Missouri P, 1985. 186-200.

MAILLOUX, Steven. "Reading *Huckleberry Finn*: The Rhetoric of Performed Ideology." *New Essays on* Huckleberry Finn. Ed. Louis J. Budd. Cambridge: Cambridge UP, 1985. 107-133.

MARKS, Barry A. "The Making of a Humorist: The Narrative Strategy of *Huckleberry Finn*." *The Critical Response to Mark Twain's* Huckleberry Finn. Ed. Laurie Champion.

Westport (Ct.): Greenwood P, 1991. 136-140.

McKAY, Janet Holmgren. "'And Art So High': Style in *Adventures of Huckleberry Finn.*" *New Essays on* Huckleberry Finn. Ed. Louis J. Budd. Cambridge: Cambridge UP, 1985. 61-81.

—, "'Tears and Flapdoodle': Point of View and Style in *Adventures of Huckleberry Finn.*" *Critical Essays on Mark Twain, 1910-1980*. Ed. Louis J. Budd. Boston: G. K. Hall, 1983. 194-201.

MELLING, Philip. "Sport on the River and the Science of Play." *Mark Twain: A Sumptuous Variety*. Ed. Robert Giddings. London/Totowa (N.J.): Vision/Barnes and Noble, 1985. 27-56.

MILLER, J. Hillis. "First-Person Narration in *David Copperfield* and *Huckleberry Finn.*" *Modern Critical Views: Mark Twain*. Ed. Harold Bloom. New York: Chelsea House, 1986. 45-54.

MITCHELL, Lee Clark. "'Nobody but Our Gang Warn't Around': The Authority of Language in *Huckleberry Finn. New Essays on* Huckleberry Finn." Ed. Louis J. Budd. Cambridge: Cambridge UP, 1985. 83-106.

NADEAU, Robert. "*Huckleberry Finn* Is a Moral Story." *The Critical Response to Mark Twain's* Huckleberry Finn. Ed. Laurie Champion. Westport (Ct.): Greenwood P, 1991. 141-144.

OEHLSCHLAEGER, Fritz. "'Gwyne to Git Hung': The Conclusion of *Huckleberry Finn. One Hundred Years of* Huckleberry Finn: *The Boy, His Book, and American Culture*. Ed. Robert Sattelmeyer and J. Donald Crowley. Columbia (Mo.): U of Missouri P, 1985. 117-127.

OLIVER, Robert T. "Mark Twain's Views on Education." *Critical Essays on Mark Twain, 1910-1980*. Ed. Louis J. Budd. Boston: G. K. Hall, 1983. 112-115.

POIRIER, Richard. "Huck Finn and the Metaphors of Society." *Twentieth-Century Interpretations of* Adventures of Huckleberry Finn. Ed. Claude M. Simpson. Englewood Cliffs (N.J.): Prentice-Hall, 1968. 95-101.

POWERS, Lyall. "Mark Twain and the Future of the Picaresque." *Mark Twain: A Sumptuous Variety*. Ed. Robert Giddings.

London/Totowa (N.J.): Vision/Barnes and Noble, 1985. 155-175.

ROBINSON, Forrest G. "The Characterization of Jim in *Huckleberry Finn.*" *The Critical Response to Mark Twain's* Huckleberry Finn. Ed. Laurie Champion. Westport (Ct.): Greenwood P, 1991. 207-225.

—, "The Lie of Silent Assertion: Late Twain." *Mark Twain: A Collection of Critical Essays.* Ed. Eric J. Sundquist. Englewood Cliffs (N.J.): Prentice-Hall, 1994. 184-196.

SATTELMEYER, Robert. "'Interesting, but Tough': *Huckleberry Finn* and the Problem of Tradition." *One Hundred Years of* Huckleberry Finn: *The Boy, His Book, and American Culture.* Ed. Robert Sattelmeyer and J. Donald Crowley. Columbia (Mo.): U of Missouri P, 1985. 354-370.

SCHMITZ, Neil. "The Paradox of Liberation in *Huckleberry Finn.*" *The Critical Response to Mark Twain's* Huckleberry Finn. Ed. Laurie Champion. Westport (Ct.): Greenwood P, 1991. 99-107.

SMITH, David Lionel. "Black Critics and Mark Twain." *The Cambridge Companion to Mark Twain.* Ed. Forrest G. Robinson. Cambridge: Cambridge UP, 1995. 116-128.

TRACHTENBERG, Alan. "The Form of Freedom in *Adventures of Huckleberry Finn.*" *The Critical Response to Mark Twain's* Huckleberry Finn. Ed. Laurie Champion. Westport (Ct.): Greenwood P, 1991. 87-98.

WALKER, Nancy. "Reformers and Young Maidens: Women and Virtue in *Adventures of Huckleberry Finn.*" *One Hundred Years of* Huckleberry Finn: *The Boy, His Book, and American Culture.* Ed. Robert Sattelmeyer and J. Donald Crowley. Columbia (Mo.): U of Missouri P, 1985. 171-185.

WHITLEY, John S. "Kids' Stuff: Mark Twain's Boys." *Mark Twain: A Sumptuous Variety.* Ed. Robert Giddings. London/Totowa (N.J.): Vision/Barnes and Noble, 1985. 57-76.